Managing International Financial Instability

To Luciana,
who once again allowed me,
lovingly,
to devote more time to
foreign affairs
than to domestic cares.

Managing International Financial Instability

National Tamers versus Global Tigers

Fabrizio Saccomanni

Director General, Banca d'Italia

Edward Elgar

Cheltenham, UK • Northampton, MA, USA

Published by
Edward Elgar Publishing Limited
The Lypiatts
15 Lansdown Road
Cheltenham
Glos GL50 2JA
UK

Edward Elgar Publishing, Inc.
William Pratt House
9 Dewey Court
Northampton
Massachusetts 01060
USA

Reprinted 2008

A catalogue record for this book
is available from the British Library

Library of Congress Control Number: 2008926578

This is an expanded version of a book titled *Tigri globali, domatori nazionali. Il difficile rapporto tra finanza globale e autorità monetarie nazionali*, published by Il Mulino, Bologna, in 2002. Translation from Italian by Alice Chambers.

The illustration on the cover is by Domenico Rosa and appeared first in the Italian business newspaper *Il Sole 24 Ore* on 23 June 2002. Reprinted by permission.

ISBN 978 1 84542 142 7 (cased)

Printed in the UK by the MPG Books Group

Contents

Figures

Tables

Abbreviations

ABS	asset-backed securities
ACU	Asian Currency Unit
ADB	Asian Development Bank
APEC	Asian Pacific Economic Cooperation
ASEAN	Association of South-East Asian Nations
BBC	Basket peg with a wide fluctuation Band and a Crawling parity
BCBS	Basel Committee on Banking Supervision
BIS	Bank for International Settlements
CAC	collective action clause
CalPERS	California Public Employees' Retirement System
CCL	contingent credit lines
CDO	collateralized debt obligations
CDS	credit default swaps
CEPR	Centre for Economic Policy Research
CFF	compensatory financing facility
CGFS	Committee on the Global Financial System
CPI	consumer price index
CPSS	Committee on Payment and Settlement Systems
CSFI	Centre for the Study of Financial Innovation
DM	Deutsche mark
ECB	European Central Bank
ECU	European Currency Unit
EFF	extended fund facilities
EFM	emergency financing mechanism
EMS	European Monetary System
EMU	Economic and Monetary Union
ERM	Exchange Rate Mechanism
FDI	foreign direct investment
Fed	Federal Reserve System (USA)
FSA	Financial Services Authority (UK)
FSAP	Financial Sector Assessment Program
FSF	Financial Stability Forum
G3	Group of Three
G5	Group of Five

G7	Group of Seven
G8	Group of Eight
G10	Group of Ten
G20	Group of Twenty
GDP	gross domestic product
GFSR	*Global Financial Stability Report*
HKMA	Hong Kong Monetary Authority
HLI	highly leveraged institution
IAIS	International Association of Insurance Supervisors
ICT	information and communication technologies
IEO	Independent Evaluation Office (IMF)
IFA	international financial architecture
IIF	International Institute of Finance
IMF	International Monetary Fund
IMFC	International Monetary and Financial Committee
IOSCO	International Organization of Securities Commissions
IT	information technology
LCFI	large and complex financial institution
LIA	lending into arrears
LTCM	long term capital management
NAB	new arrangements to borrow
NAFTA	North American Free Trade Agreement
NASDAQ	National Association of Securities Dealers Automated Quotations
NATO	North Atlantic Treaty Organization
NBER	National Bureau of Economic Research (US)
NPL	non-performing loans
OAU	Organization for African Unity
OECD	Organisation for Economic Co-operation and Development
OFC	offshore financial centre
OPEC	Organization of Petroleum Exporting Countries
PIMCo	Pacific Investment Management Company
PPP	purchasing power parity
PRGF	poverty reduction and growth facility
PSI	private sector involvement
ROSC	Report on Observance of Standards and Codes
SAR	Special Administrative Region (China)
SBA	stand-by arrangements
SDP	Social-Democratic Party (Germany)
SDR	special drawing rights
SDRM	Sovereign Debt Reconstruction Mechanism
SEC	Securities and Exchange Commission

SRF	supplemental reserve facility
VaR	value at risk
WEO	*World Economic Outlook*
WTO	World Trade Organization
$	US dollar (unless specified)

Foreword

In presenting this book I have to acknowledge a personal involvement with the genesis of the underlying research project. In 1994, Fred Bergsten invited me to take part in a seminar organized by his Institute for International Economics to celebrate the 50th anniversary of the Bretton Woods Conference. I accepted on condition that I could associate in the endeavour Fabrizio Saccomanni, friend and colleague of many decades. At the time, Fabrizio was head of the Bank of Italy's Foreign Department and Chairman of the Exchange Rate Policy Committee of the European Monetary Institute, the precursor of the European Central Bank; he combined a solid background in international economics – based on his earlier experience at the IMF – with a rare insight into the operation of foreign exchange and capital markets. We had been discussing international monetary problems for many years and had become convinced, particularly after the EMS crisis of 1992–93, that all was not well with the working of what used to be called the international monetary system. We thought that the IIE seminar provided a good opportunity for us to express our misgivings about current international monetary arrangements. We quickly agreed that in our paper we should avoid following the path of those who regarded the combination of freely floating exchange rates and full capital mobility as a 'non system'; we also agreed to refrain from advocating a 'new Bretton Woods'. In the paper we prepared, which is quoted in this book, we asked ourselves what kind of institutional underpinnings were needed to ensure the smooth functioning of the 'market-led international monetary system' that had emerged from the demise of the old 'government-led international monetary system' created in 1944 at Bretton Woods. We argued that under the new system, global financial markets would determine the creation and the distribution of international liquidity and the level of exchange rates. We urged monetary authorities to improve their understanding of the unwritten rules and conventions of the market-led system and of their implications for the world economy. Indeed, we feared that, in the likely context of further expansion and increased globalization of financial markets, there was a risk of 'disturbances that may have an impact on the stability of the financial system'. As our paper was delivered in the summer of 1994, the Mexican crisis was just months away and it would usher in one of the most difficult periods in the recent history of the world's monetary system.

Although plenty has been written on the financial turbulence of the late 1990s, particularly on the debt crises of emerging countries, the hint we gave about the need to investigate the systemic causes of financial instability and the role that global financial markets could play in the process did not find many followers. Fabrizio's book, when it was first published in Italy in 2002, provided an important contribution to filling that gap. I found then the book to be very rich in analytical, technical and historical insights and only regretted that it had been written in Italian, a language not widely read internationally on matters other than religion, art, gastronomy, and fashion. I think it is very good that the book appears now in English, in an updated and expanded version covering the new episodes of financial instability that have marked the early years of the third millennium.

The main theme of the book is the relationship between policy-makers and global financial markets. It makes for fascinating reading to follow the author's detailed yet concise description of the actions and reactions that have generated, amplified and propagated situations of financial instability. Although the book strives to project an objective analysis of the underlying economic and political determinants of instability, the conclusion the reader is led to draw is that the blame for the many crises of the era of financial globalization rests more with the policy-makers than with the market. Monetary and financial authorities are constrained by political and institutional considerations to formulate and implement policies in a national context; but in the case of systemically important countries, policies have significant international repercussions via global financial markets. Of course, policy-makers are fully aware of the existence of the markets, but they tend to believe that these will reconcile the inconsistency of their national approaches, correct the inadequacy of their measures, or can be convinced through appropriate communication strategies that there are no inconsistencies or inadequacies to worry about. The book provides ample evidence that none of these assumptions is correct. Markets are willing to listen to policy-makers and to analyse carefully their strategies and statements but when, sooner or later, they detect any inconsistency or inadequacy they react with speed and severity. The book also clearly describes the situations in which markets may overreact, leading to unsustainable trends in financial flows and asset prices. The correction of any such overshooting is generally abrupt and painful.

The author does not believe that dealing with international financial instability would require a major institutional reform or innovative policy strategies, a belief I am not sure I share in full. He is convinced that the international community already possesses the analytical tools and the policy instruments to deal with the problem; but he is adamant in suggesting that policy-makers have the duty to guide the markets towards achieving monetary and financial stability. He fears, correctly in my view, that recurrent episodes of turbulence in asset markets – if left unchecked – may eventually lead to protectionist pressures that could be detrimental to the growth of output, trade and employment worldwide. In suggesting a more pre-emptive and active policy approach he departs from conventional wisdom. At times, he seems openly 'interventionist' and goes so far as to advocate 'interference' by the IMF in the operation of the international monetary system. It is clear, however, that in the pragmatic framework of multilateral cooperation that he advocates, he would easily settle for any realistic, 'golden mean', policy strategy provided it delivered the required results.

All in all, this is a book well worth reading by any person interested in understanding how the global financial system works and in having a critical appraisal of its performance. It also contains a number of suggestions that could be part of the 'research agenda' of monetary and financial authorities, both national and international, as well as of academic and business economists. The book flows smoothly and the narration is pleasantly supported by personal recollections of events that the author witnessed. There are also many clever economic and literary quotations, evidence of the author's broad cultural interests and sharp wit. I found particularly appropriate, in the turbulent liquidity conditions currently prevailing in global financial markets, the quote in Chapter 14 from Shakespeare's *Julius Caesar*, where the Bard reminds us that 'on such a full sea are we now afloat;/and we must take the current when it serves,/or lose our ventures'.

Tommaso Padoa-Schioppa
Minister for Economy and Finance, Italy
Chairman, IMFC
Rome, September 2007

Preface

This book has had a long gestation. It was first published in Italy in 2002 and reflected my own professional experience in dealing with international financial instability at the International Monetary Fund and the Bank of Italy over a period running from the collapse of the Bretton Woods system in 1971 to the creation of the euro and the debt crises of emerging markets in the 1990s. When I moved to London at the beginning of 2003 to work for the European Bank for Reconstruction and Development as Vice President for Risk Management, Edward Elgar offered me the opportunity to publish an English version of the book. I realized then that a major revision of my earlier work was required. I had to expand the analysis to cover new important developments in the third millennium, such as the 'peaceful rising' of China on the world economic and financial stage, the bursting of asset price bubbles in equity and real estate markets worldwide, and the widening of global payments imbalances. More importantly, I had to assess how these new factors would affect my own interpretation of international financial instability. The review took quite some time and was nearing completion at the end of 2006 when I was appointed Director General of the Bank of Italy. Although my return to Rome meant further delay, testing again the immense patience of my publisher, it has given me the opportunity to catch up with the latest developments in international monetary cooperation in early 2007 as I resumed participating in meetings of the European Central Bank, the Bank for International Settlements and the International Monetary Fund.

In short, this book is the expression of my recurrent dismay, over the last 35 years, at the seemingly incurable nature of international financial instability, which has manifested itself lately with increased frequency. Dismay at the pointless toing and froing of recriminations, after each episode of tension, between those who firmly believe that crises are the result of the excessive power of free market forces and those who believe, equally firmly, that crises occur because of government interference in the operation of markets. And, finally, dismay at the inability of economics, in this case a truly dismal science, not only to help forecast and prevent financial crises, but also to assist in providing a consensus view of their causes and remedies. To ease my dismay I have reviewed the vicissitudes of the international monetary and financial system since the dawn of globalization, focusing on the relationship between monetary authorities and the global financial market. I have tried to understand the objectives and the strategies of both actors and to identify in what conditions situations of crisis have materialized or have been avoided. I have reached a few conclusions that I hope readers might share.

The global financial market is an institution that plays a fundamental role for the growth of the world economy and it should be free to operate within a regulatory framework that guarantees soundness and transparency without distorting market operations. Monetary and financial authorities, however, must not refrain from guiding the market, through their economic policies, in order to achieve monetary and financial stability, which are the prerequisites for a sustainable growth of output and employment. Economic policies, in a broad sense, do 'matter' and can be all the more effective insofar as they are able to credibly influence the expectations of economic and financial agents and the working of global markets. Monetary and financial authorities should use all the instruments at their disposal in the pursuit of stability, explaining clearly to the market their policy intentions and ensuring consistency between announcements and measures. Central banks should be fully involved in these efforts because of their mandate to ensure price stability and their dual capacity as regulators and market participants. Cooperation among systemically important countries is essential to ensure stability of the global financial system and should be conducted within a multilateral institutional framework.

There is nothing particularly new in these conclusions, but the aim of this book is rather to argue whether old-fashioned ideas may be of help in understanding how the global financial system works and how to cope with its dysfunctions. In writing it, I have become convinced that such a task cannot be accomplished solely with sophisticated mathematical models of financial markets and instruments. What is needed is a political economy approach to globalization, which I see as an interdisciplinary endeavour capable of bringing together not only the main economic and financial determinants, but also the underlying political, social, institutional and legal implications. It is a task that the generation of my nephew Francesco, who is just beginning graduate studies in international economics, will have to undertake.

The ideas expressed in this book are entirely personal but they have been developed and sharpened in endless discussions over the years with colleagues at the Bank of Italy. International monetary issues have been a subject of constant attention by all the governors with whom I have been privileged to work, Guido Carli, Paolo Baffi, Carlo Azeglio Ciampi, Antonio Fazio, Mario Draghi, and under their leadership the Bank has continued to be a unique workshop of empirical analysis and policy debate. I have also learned a lot from, in chronological order, Rinaldo Ossola, Tommaso Padoa-Schioppa, Lamberto Dini, Pierluigi Ciocca, Rainer Masera and Ignazio Visco. With Tommaso, who entered the Bank at about the same time I did, a lifetime friendship and collaboration has developed, the implications of which are visible throughout the book. The Bank has also given me an opportunity to get to know a number of outstanding government officials, central bank governors and international civil servants from other countries, whose ideas and achievements have greatly influenced my own thinking about the power and the limits of international cooperation. Among these, I would like to mention Jacques de Larosière, Toyoo Gyohten, Mervyn King, Jacques Polak, Hans Tietmeyer and Paul Volcker.

I am greatly indebted to a number of people who have assisted me in various ways in the preparation of this book. At the EBRD, Joe Colombano; at the Bank of Italy, Marco Committeri, Giorgio Gomel, Fabio Panetta and especially Aviram Levy, who has read the entire manuscript and provided a number of valuable comments and improvements. Obviously, I am solely responsible for any remaining flaws. Alice Chambers has valiantly translated into English the original text and the subsequent additions, occasionally unmasking hidden flaws in my sometimes convoluted Italian prose. Christine Stone has volunteered some precious last-minute polishing of the final text. But the greatest debt I owe is to my long-time Personal Assistant, Anna Buttarelli, who has miraculously managed over the last two years to coordinate all phases of the production process, making sense of a huge flow of e-mails, handwritten notes and bibliographical references; maintaining contact with me in London and with the translator in Rome; and never losing control or patience. Truly, this book would not have seen the light without her.

Rome, September 2007

PART I

The tigers, the tamers, the circus

1. An uneasy relationship

> The relationship between markets and central banks ... is similar to that
> between tigers and their tamer. The latter can bend the former to his will if
> he uses superior skill, great care, and intelligence. If, instead, the tamer excites
> and irritates the tigers, they will win. The spectacular growth in the size of
> markets of the last ten years has widened the gap between the strength of the
> tigers and that of the tamers, and having more than one tamer in the cage does
> not help.
>
> Tommaso Padoa-Schioppa (1994, p. 19)

The relationship between monetary authorities and financial markets has,
for most of the twentieth century, been difficult, confrontational and at
times openly conflictual. This has reflected the different objectives pursued:
monetary and financial stability by monetary authorities; and the optimum
combination of risk and return on investments by market intermediaries.
The relationship has often been described by the press, but also in economic
literature, as a never-ending contest between allegedly sovereign authorities
and forces that behave unpredictably, even crazily or irrationally, and
are endowed with magic or supernatural powers. These descriptions recall
characters such as the 'gnomes of Zurich' or financial 'wizards' *à la* George
Soros. But there are also references to the 'casino capitalism' and 'mad
money' denounced by Strange (1986 and 1998), the 'manias and panics' dis-
passionately psychoanalysed by Kindleberger (1978) or the 'irrational exuberance' evoked by the then Federal Reserve Chairman Alan Greenspan
(1996). More recently, in 2005, Franz Müntefering, Chairman of what was
then Germany's ruling Social-Democratic Party (SDP) introduced a new
variation on the theme, comparing global financial intermediaries to
'swarms of locusts that fall on companies, stripping them bare before
moving on' (*The Economist* 2005c, p. 65).

These images fail to fully capture the essence of the relationship between
monetary authorities and global finance; moreover, they convey a misleading sense of pessimism as regards the effectiveness of monetary and
financial policies. Padoa-Schioppa's metaphor is more apt because it recognizes that in terms of sheer brute force the tigers are clearly superior, but
implies that their 'animal spirits' can be studied and understood by the
tamers. The tamers can then use this knowledge to pursue their goals, but
in order to tame the tigers they have to enter the cage, show no fear, send

clear signals and appropriately administer threats and rewards. Managing international financial instability is in many ways a similar exercise.

Metaphors aside, for the purposes of this book and in the context of financial globalization, the 'tigers' are the intermediaries who operate simultaneously on the bond, stock, foreign exchange and derivatives markets wherever there are adequate banking and financial structures. The 'tamers' also belong to a broad category, including first and foremost the monetary authorities, namely the treasury or finance ministries and central banks, but also the various supervisory agencies of different specialized markets. The 'circus' is the institutional framework within which authorities and markets operate. The interaction among these characters is complicated by the global nature of the market and the national jurisdiction of the authorities. But what makes the relationship potentially conflictual is the innate tendency for the authorities to 'regulate' markets where participants would prefer to operate free of any impediment or restriction.

Official meddling in the operation of financial markets can take several forms. Most countries acknowledge that it is incumbent on authorities to ensure 'orderly market conditions'. This means allowing intermediaries to engage in financial transactions in ways and according to terms that have been freely agreed on, while supervising – and if necessary taking appropriate steps – to cope with market manipulation, illiquidity or extreme price volatility. If it is in the public interest, the authorities may devise rules of behaviour for market participants or set limits to price variations. This has been the case, for example, for transactions carried out on foreign exchange markets, given the implications that exchange rate fluctuations can have for a currency's purchasing power and a country's balance of payments. The authorities can, moreover, 'intervene in the market' by acting as buyers or sellers of financial assets (government bonds, foreign exchange and sometimes shares) for monetary and exchange rate policy purposes.

The nature of the relationship between monetary authorities and markets naturally varies in line with the evolution of the economic, political and institutional context, both in individual countries and internationally. Especially influential is the pattern of the international monetary system: that is, the set of standards, practices and institutions governing inter-state economic and financial transactions, which may change in line with shifts in the balance of power on the world's stage. Basically, the 'system' comprises the exchange rate regime between the various currencies, mechanisms for the creation and distribution of international liquidity and policies for adjusting balance of payments disequilibria. From around the middle of the nineteenth century, when the gold standard system prevailed, it was thought that the operation of automatic mechanisms based on fixing a parity for currencies in terms of a specified amount of gold, and the use of gold as an official reserve and means of international payment, could reconcile the objectives of market forces and government authorities by ensuring stable monetary conditions on an international scale. In reality, stability to the extent that it was effectively achieved owed more to the hegemony of the British Empire and the discount rate policy of the Bank of England.[1] After the First World War, attempts to re-establish an international monetary order failed and the conflict between markets and governments became increasingly apparent. Despite the widespread destruction of productive capacity, governments attempted to restore the pre-war gold parities, triggering economic recession and eventually the depression of 1929–30. The markets' lack of confidence forced a series of competitive devaluations of exchange rates: first sterling in 1931, followed by the dollar and the other main currencies. Unable to contain market pressures, governments further reacted by introducing restrictions on trade and foreign exchange operations. The international economic and trading system crumbled, paving the way for the Second World War.

It was not until the United Nations conference held in Bretton Woods in 1944 that the problematic relationship between markets and monetary authorities was tackled and managed in a comprehensive and systematic way (James 1996). It was at this time that the rules were drawn up and the institutions established for an international monetary system based on intergovernmental cooperation. The Articles of Agreement of the newly established International Monetary Fund (IMF) obliged member countries to fix a parity for their national currency in terms of gold and dollars, remove restrictions on international trade of goods and services and pursue economic policies compatible with the maintenance of fixed exchange rates. To achieve these objectives, members were allowed to introduce restrictions on capital movements. If, however, a country was unable to maintain the equilibrium of its balance of payments, it could apply to the Fund for credit that would be granted on condition that the applicant take all necessary economic policy measures to correct the imbalance in its foreign accounts. Only in the event of a 'fundamental disequilibrium' could the IMF authorize a change in the par value and the resulting devaluation or revaluation of a national currency. Under the Bretton Woods system, therefore, the market was conditioned by decisions taken by monetary authorities at both a national and international level, and the set of rules and instruments devised to keep it under control seemed to be exhaustive and efficient. Monetary authorities determined not only exchange rates but also the process for the creation and distribution of international liquidity, thereby promoting monetary stability worldwide through the international coordination of economic policies.

The cohesion of the Bretton Woods system was jeopardized by the behaviour of some of its most important members and by the operation of market forces that revealed a fundamental inconsistency in the system's architecture. In the early 1960s it had already become clear that the obligation to pursue economic policies compatible with exchange rate stability constituted a politically intolerable constraint not only for the United States but also for the major European countries and Japan. While theoretically possible, the alternative of changing par values was considered impractical for reasons of national prestige, because this was equated with a declaration of failure to play by the rules of the system. Specifically, the idea of changing the par value of the system's key currency – the dollar – was ruled out for fear this would trigger an international monetary meltdown. At the time of his election in 1960, President John Kennedy had identified the correction of the deficit in America's balance of payments as being among his administration's top priorities. But the need to sustain economic growth and later, under President Lyndon Johnson, the Vietnam War, persuaded the United States to eschew adjustment policies that would have entailed the devaluation of the dollar and a contraction of domestic demand. Instead, the United States financed its balance of payments deficit by increasing liabilities to foreign central banks. Meanwhile, even those countries that were accumulating substantial surpluses in their balances of payments vis-à-vis the United States, such as Germany, France, Italy and Japan, were not willing to revalue their currencies or increase domestic demand, preferring instead to keep a competitive exchange rate and to bolster their dollar reserves. The result of these inconsistent approaches was the creation of international liquidity denominated in dollars that far exceeded demand, fuelling inflationary pressures worldwide. At the same time, trade liberalization, one of the linchpins of the Bretton Woods system, provided strong stimuli for foreign investment, the development of multinational corporations and the international integration of economic and financial systems. In these circumstances, restrictions on capital movements, permitted and indeed recommended by the Bretton Woods system to guarantee exchange rate stability, became an obstacle to the financing of international trade and global growth. This is what prompted intermediaries to lobby governments to liberalize banking and financial transactions while simultaneously trying to circumvent national restrictions by seeking non-regulated foreign havens as operational bases. That is how the Eurodollar financial market was born.

It was against this backdrop that the conditions for the gradual dismantling of the Bretton Woods system were created. The first pillar to tumble was the system of fixed exchange rates, with President Nixon's decision of August 1971 to discontinue the dollar's convertibility into gold. Once the exchange rate of the key currency was allowed to fluctuate, the entire international monetary system effectively moved to a floating exchange rate regime. The second pillar, controls on capital movements, was eroded gradually in the course of the 1970s. Its demise was accelerated by monetary and foreign currency upheavals stemming from the devaluations of the dollar over the period 1971–73, and the subsequent oil crises that enhanced the role of the markets in 'recycling petro-dollars' and in financing balance of payment deficits.

It was not until the beginning of the 1980s, however, with the coming to power of Margaret Thatcher in the United Kingdom and Ronald Reagan in the United States, that financial liberalization would find its full legitimization. Passionate advocates of the superiority of free market mechanisms for the creation and distribution of wealth, the two leaders promoted programmes of rapid and complete deregulation of financial markets, at both a national and international level. The impact of full-scale liberalization proved momentous, given that Reagan represented the greatest economic and military power on earth, and Thatcher the world's most efficient and sophisticated financial market. The Anglo-American leadership drove continental European countries to participate in the deregulation process and the European Community adopted, in the late 1980s, a plan for the gradual liberalization of capital movements that became the prelude to Economic and Monetary Union (EMU). At the end of the decade, the collapse of the Soviet bloc and the reunification of Germany created unprecedented and significant opportunities for international financial integration.

By the early 1990s, the era of financial globalization had effectively dawned, fully adhered to by all the major industrial countries of North America, Asia and Europe, alongside a growing number of countries with economies that were sufficiently advanced in order to access international capital markets. The result was the establishment of an entirely new international monetary system with respect to the one conceived at Bretton Woods. Whereas the latter had been led and influenced by governments and the IMF, the system at the close of the twentieth century was led and influenced by market forces (Padoa-Schioppa and Saccomanni 1994). It is the market that now determines the exchange rates of major currencies and governs the creation and distribution of international liquidity, deciding which businesses, financial institutions and countries are 'creditworthy' and under what conditions. One may well wonder whether a scenario such as this can be defined a system in the general sense of the term, that is as denoting a set of institutions and agreed rules for the achievement of systemic objectives. The current arrangements are certainly not based on any one central institution responsible for general governance, nor on rules sanctioned by an international treaty. The 'market', however, despite its multifaceted nature, is an institution within which the rules of the game and behavioural modes have been established, albeit subject to an ongoing reformulation and reinterpretation in the light of new developments and experiences. Even if the rules of such a system are not written down, they are nonetheless stringently applied and the players must respect them. The role of monetary authorities in a market-led system is clearly a very different one: they can no longer fix prices or authorize individual transactions and must limit themselves to establishing the overall legal framework for the activity of markets and the standards of conduct for market participants. They can, however, try to influence market trends by adopting economic policy measures, acting as counterparties for market intermediaries in financial transactions, and by communicating to the market information, assessments and policy intentions.

Since the establishment of the regime of financial globalization in the early 1990s, episodes of international monetary and financial instability have increased in number and frequency. These episodes have been associated with large one-way movements in the price of assets, such as bonds, shares, currencies and real estate, followed by sharp reversals. This has led to disruptions in the orderly functioning of financial markets, the bankruptcy of intermediaries and corporations or, in some cases, to the suspension of the debt servicing obligations of major sovereign borrowers. Contrary to popular belief, these episodes have not occurred only in emerging or transition countries, but have also involved mature economies, like Japan, or affected efficient markets like the New York Stock Exchange, NASDAQ or the international bond market. Exchange rate misalignments have not been concentrated in Latin America or South East Asia, but have at one time or another affected the three key currencies of the world monetary system: the dollar, the euro and the yen. Instability has generally manifested itself first on exchange markets, but this is not surprising. In a global financial system the exchange market is the channel through which most financial transactions are funnelled, and tensions are transmitted internationally. The ups and downs of the relationship between markets and authorities, therefore, has increasingly been felt at the level of exchange rates, thus drawing the attention of both economic operators and international public opinion to this crucial indicator. The currency market is, in fact, particularly relevant because the exchange rate is the yardstick that determines the external value of a given currency. Its level and performance express a synthetic – but clear and immediate – judgement on the health of a national economy, its ability to compete worldwide, and the confidence it inspires among citizens and the international community. Finally, the exchange rate is the indicator that most rapidly provides an assessment by the market of the adequacy of policy actions taken by monetary authorities and, in particular, by central banks.

Unfortunately, in a scenario of recurrent instability and financial market volatility, public opinion, even among the most informed commentators, has become increasingly convinced of the existence of a cause and effect relationship between globalization and financial crises and of the impossibility of governing global finance. The argument most frequently used in support of this conclusion is the divergence between the 'firepower' of financial markets and the 'ammunition' available to monetary authorities in the form of official reserves. While such arguments do not stand up to scrutiny, as it will be shown throughout this book, they nonetheless raise questions that must be taken seriously if we are to arrive at a full understanding of both the dynamics of the global economic and financial system, and of the wider political implications of globalization.

Commenting on the completion, in March 1990, of the liberalization of foreign exchange restrictions in Italy, the then Italian Treasury Minister Guido Carli (1993, p. 388) wrote: 'I wanted to allow Italian citizens to acquire the right to cast a daily vote of confidence on the government and the country, by exercising the possibility of investing their savings in securities issued by other countries and expressed in other currencies' (this author's translation from the original). This quotation highlights a further vital component of the relationship between monetary authorities and markets, the political aspect *tout court*. The management of financial portfolios, the hedging of risks, the constant reassessment of government economic policies, all play a role in the direct exercise of democracy by market participants whereby the concepts of citizenship, sovereignty and representation are continually redefined and reinterpreted. Just who are the market participants entitled to 'vote' in this context? Are they the citizens in the narrow sense of the state where the securities they own are bought or sold? Or are they the holders and the asset managers of these securities, irrespective of their nationality? And in this broader context, would those holding securities for saving purposes be the only ones entitled to vote? And what about those who managed them for profit or speculative purposes on behalf of their clients? These questions, that are for political scientists and experts of constitutional law to analyse, are recalled here to underline the fact that the comprehension of financial market behavioural patterns should not be a task reserved solely for financial analysts and economists. Rather, it is in the interest of all those 'entitled to vote' to understand the underlying motivations of market behaviour, the mechanisms and instruments used, and the reaction functions of markets to the economic policy of monetary and financial authorities.

NOTE

1. The gold standard has been the subject of countless studies by economists and historians. Among the former, see de Cecco (1974) and Eichengreen (1985); among the latter, Ferguson puts it in this way: 'The gold standard had become, in effect, the global monetary system. In all but name, it was a sterling standard' (2004a, p. 247).

2. Global financial players

What an extraordinary episode in the economic progress of man that age was which came to an end in August, 1914! . . . The inhabitant of London could order by telephone, sipping his morning tea in bed, the various products of the whole earth, . . . and reasonably expect their early delivery upon his doorstep; he could at the same moment and by the same means adventure his wealth in the natural resources and new enterprises of any quarter of the world, and share, without exertion or even trouble, in their prospective fruits and advantages; . . . and could then proceed abroad to foreign quarters . . . bearing coined wealth upon his person, and would consider himself greatly aggrieved and much surprised at the least interference. But, most important of all, he regarded this state of affairs as normal, certain and permanent, except in the direction of further improvement, and any deviation from it as aberrant, scandalous, and avoidable.

John M. Keynes ([1919] 1971, p. 6)

Despite the general usefulness of the assumption of rationality, markets can on occasions – infrequent occasions, let me emphasize – act in destabilizing ways that are irrational overall, even when each participant in the market is acting rationally.

Charles P. Kindleberger (1978, p. 41)

2.1 THE ORIGINS OF FINANCIAL GLOBALIZATION

The globalization of finance is a recent phenomenon but its roots are ancient.[1] The books that a scholar of international financial history such as Kindleberger (1978 and 1984) has devoted to the subject provide readers with a host of episodes, dating back to the seventeenth and eighteenth centuries, rich in analogy with current developments in globalization. But it was the introduction of the gold standard in the last quarter of the nineteenth century in England and subsequently in other major European countries and in the United States that created the conditions for the internationalization of the economic and financial system described by Keynes above. In all likelihood, had the First World War not broken out, the process would have expanded further, enabling the free trade of goods, financial services and capital on a truly global scale. In the post-war era, any return to that regime proved impossible. This was due to the difficulties of reconstruction and the political turmoil that followed the advent of communism in Russia, Fascism in Italy and Nazism in Germany: regimes that were hostile to the market economy and free trade for ideological reasons or out of necessity. Not even after the Second World War was it possible to re-establish the degree of financial liberalization that characterized the gold standard era. Keynes himself, one of the key architects of the Bretton Woods system, was so shocked by the devastating effects of trade protectionism during the 1920s and 1930s that he believed the absolute priority of the new international economic order to be the free movement of goods and services, even at the expense of the free movement of capital. In any event, the severe economic difficulties in which the countries of continental Europe found themselves made a return to the convertibility of major European currencies impossible until 1958, and it took three more decades to remove foreign exchange controls and restrictions on capital movements.

The process of financial globalization was accordingly frozen until the 1980s.[2] The technical 'de-freezing' factors, in addition to those of a political and economic nature already mentioned in Chapter 1, were the widespread use of new information and communication technologies, and of new financial instruments and techniques. The main components of the process of financial innovation were: (1) securitization: the possibility of transforming any kind of financial fiduciary operation into a securitized instrument that can be traded on the market; (2) the development of derivatives: instruments permitting the pricing and unbundling of risks connected to financial transactions (interest rate risk, exchange rate risk, credit risk); (3) the growing importance of non-banking financial intermediaries, entailing an enhanced role for market indicators in assessing client creditworthiness; (4) the institutionalization of private savings management as financial wealth grew, which implied an expanding role for professional managers in the allocation of savings among the various instruments available; (5) the international consolidation of banking and financial intermediaries, which drastically reduced the number of global players active on the market through mergers and acquisitions, and at the same time augmented structural dimensions and operational potential.

Since the liberalization of foreign exchange restrictions, advances in information technologies have enabled market participants to increase the range of opportunities for investment on an international scale, by dealing in bonds and shares of foreign issuers and using market instruments to manage exchange risk. The development of advanced data processing systems has slashed transaction costs in and across various markets allowing intermediaries to manage an ever higher number of positions and operations. Comprehensive accounting entries can be obtained for each trade, as well as an instantaneous assessment of its impact on the intermediary's overall exposure to specific market instruments, currencies or countries. Computer technology assists traders in the decision-making process by providing models for managing financial positions and for assessing the overall risk to which any single intermediary is exposed. Finally, the development of telecommunications has given market participants access to a continuous flow of real-time information on asset prices across all the major monetary and financial markets worldwide, as well as on the economic situation and financial accounts of companies, banks and countries.

The simultaneous listing on the market of liabilities issued by individual debtors, be they countries or companies, allows the ongoing assessment of the risk rating attributed by the market to each borrower. This is expressed as the difference, or spread, between the yield of any given security under consideration and that of an analogous security associated with a low to nil risk. For example, the spread on ten-year bonds issued in US dollars by the Brazilian or Korean governments is calculated with reference to bonds having the same maturity issued by the US Treasury (T-bond). In Europe, the reference spread is generally that calculated on securities issued by the German federal government (Bund); similar methods are used to calculate the spreads on securities of corporate issuers. The spread gives a measure of the risk premium that each issuer must pay investors to convince them to accept an implicitly higher risk associated with their security compared with other lower-risk securities. Market participants can, therefore, continually assess the degree of risk they intend to take on and monitor its movement over time. With globalization and the growth of markets in financial assets, the practice of calculating the value of assets and liabilities at market prices ('mark to market') has become widespread among debtors, investors and intermediaries and plays a vital role in global finance. This allows each market participant to obtain a rapid, realistic and updated assessment of profits and losses made on various activities.

It is through the generalized application of these financial and technological innovations that the conditions are created for a levelling of prices of financial assets on a global scale and for the harmonization of behavioural models – conditions that constitute the essential traits of financial globalization.

2.2 THE GLOBAL PLAYERS

Globalization has paved the way for an unprecedented expansion of international financial flows and intermediation as well as of the size and turnover of financial markets, both in absolute terms and in relation to gross domestic product (GDP). For instance, between 1990 and 2003 external assets of industrial countries rose from $9.7 trillion to $36 trillion, that is from 75 to over 200 per cent of GDP. External assets of emerging and developing countries rose from $336 billion to $1849 billion, that is from 30 to 70 per cent of GDP (IMF 2005b, pp. 110–12). Similar trends are recorded in the volume of foreign liabilities for both groups of countries. In the period 1990–2005 capitalization of stock exchanges in the G7 countries rose from 59 to 96 per cent of the area's GDP, after a peak of 141 per cent in 2000 (World Bank 2006). The nominal value of exchange-traded derivatives rose between 1990 and 2005 from $2.3 trillion to $58 trillion, that is from 16 to 214 per cent of the group's GDP (*BIS Quarterly Review*, various issues). At the beginning of the third millennium, the *daily* turnover in the major financial markets ranged from $0.2 trillion for equity markets (excluding derivatives) to $2.4 trillion for exchange-traded derivatives (see Borio 2004).

Myriads of intermediaries and investors operate in the various segments of the global financial market. The number of truly global players is, however, relatively small as the widening of financial markets has led to a significant consolidation of intermediaries, most of which now perform 'universal banking' functions covering a broad range of financial services. The activity of large and complex financial institutions (LCFIs) that play an important role as channels for the cross-border transmission of financial market developments has become the focus of increasing attention by supervisors and regulators, among other things because of the high share of business in certain segments of the market, such as that for derivatives, that is concentrated in the hands of a few institutions.[3]

Institutional investors, hedge funds and private equity firms are playing an increasingly important role in global financial markets. Although comparable historical data are not always available for all of these players, a few figures are sufficient to illustrate the magnitude of their operational capabilities. According to the IMF (2007b) at the end of 2005 non-bank institutional investors (insurance companies, pension funds and mutual funds) in industrial countries had total assets under management amounting to $46 trillion, 132 per cent of the area's GDP; compared with 1995, the rate of increase was in the order of 100 per cent in the United States and in Germany, 240 per cent in the United Kingdom and in France; much smaller in Japan. Some of these institutional investors are individually very big: the largest US bond mutual funds' manager, Pacific Investment Management Company (PIMCo), had $668 billion in fixed-income investments at the end of 2006 (www.pimco.com); the largest US pension fund, the California Public Employees' Retirement System (CalPERS) had an investment portfolio valued at $241.7 billion at the end of March 2007 (www.calpers. ca.gov). Hedge funds are among the newest categories of intermediaries to have acquired an important role on the global stage and have attracted considerable media attention for their alleged part in the currency crisis of 1992, which forced sterling and the Italian lira to abandon the Exchange Rate Mechanism (ERM) of the European Monetary System (EMS), and in the 'serial killing' of Asian currencies in 1997. Because of their nature as private partnerships, hedge funds are not subject to the disclosure and regulatory requirements that apply to banks, security houses or institutional investors. This means that little is known about their strategies and the size of their financial activity. On the basis of the information provided voluntarily by hedge funds and collected by private market research companies, the IMF estimates that, at the end of September 2006, about 9000 hedge funds were in operation worldwide, with total assets under management of about $1.34 trillion (see IMF 2007a), although the figures may underestimate the actual size of the phenomenon. A growing role in the global financial system, albeit on a smaller scale, is being played by private firms that invest mostly in buyouts of companies and in venture capital. Again, information on the activities of these firms is limited because of their nature, but it is estimated that there are currently about 2700 private equity firms operating worldwide and in 2006 the value of private equity buyouts was $440 billion in the United States and Europe combined, up from roughly $70 billion in 2000. The size of individual firms dealing in private equity has also increased considerably over time and the ten largest firms in 2006 all raised between $8 and $16 billion each.[4] Despite their relatively small size, private equity firms have attracted considerable attention from the media because of their role in aggressive corporate takeovers, through 'leveraged buyouts', sometimes followed by a breakup and resale of the various components of the original company. The Carlyle Group has been the target of special attention because of its alleged influential political connections in the United States and in other major countries.[5] The distinction between the various categories of global players mentioned above is by no means clear-cut. In fact, commercial banks, security houses and investment banks have created their own hedge fund and private equity firms to broaden the range of financial services provided to their clients and to attract investors with a higher propensity to risk.

2.3 OBJECTIVES AND STRATEGIES OF GLOBAL FINANCIAL PLAYERS

Financial globalization is much more than a purely geographical phenomenon. The global player is, by definition, present all over the globe. But this is nothing new. As early as the 1960s, large banks in industrial countries had

branches in all the major financial centres, mostly to assist domestic customers in their foreign trade transactions. What is new is the fact that global
players are now simultaneously present in all countries but also in all
markets, using the full spectrum of instruments at their disposal (bonds,
shares, currencies, derivatives and so on), and carrying out a multiplicity of
functions. In addition to borrowing and lending, they manage assets on
behalf of clients, invest their own resources, hedge risks, and engage in
speculation. The global vocation of these intermediaries has affected their
internal organization. Activity is no longer divided between departments
dealing with 'domestic' and 'foreign' markets, but has been broken down
into specialized functions carried out on a global scale. For example, one
department will look after global equity markets, another global fixed
income or global foreign exchange. Within each sector there are further
specializations but always in a global perspective. For example, within the
global equity department there will be a separate division to deal with
telecom sectors worldwide and monitor the stock market performance of,
say, AT&T, Deutsche Telekom and British Telecom in order to make appropriate reallocations of investments based on the relative profitability of
each. Integrated control structures determine what the maximum limit of
exposure towards any given country or sector should be. This assessment
will include all transactions concluded with counterparts in the country or
sector with reference to the totality of instruments used. At the top of the
organization there will be a committee to determine the intermediary's
global strategy, identify potential growth areas and set profit objectives,
fixing the maximum amount of risk that can be borne by the institution in
respect of its capital or net worth.

Like every other economic agent, global players attempt to maximize the
profit of their overall investment position, while containing risk within
acceptable limits. Given that competition tends to reduce yields on less
risky investments, up to the point that the intermediation margin is almost
completely annulled, the pursuit of higher yields and spreads necessarily
involves the financing of clients carrying a higher risk or having limited
access to the market, and therefore, willing to pay higher interest rates. This
often implies the decision to include new countries in the list of those with
access to the global market. The process is a complex one, involving not
only the global players themselves, but also the authorities of the country
in question, international financial institutions such as the IMF and the
World Bank, as well as the authorities of countries that host the world's
main financial markets. The admission to the market of a country with
strong potential for economic growth creates major opportunities for the
development of a substantial volume of business for all parties including
global intermediaries. The issue of foreign currency denominated bonds

and shares, the involvement of foreign investors in mergers, acquisitions and privatizations, the diversification of the currency composition of private portfolios: these are just some examples of the vast range of opportunities that access to the global market makes possible at competitive costs and in a short time.

Risks can, of course, increase or decrease over time, because of factors affecting the creditworthiness of debtors (credit risk) or due to changes in interest and exchange rates (market risk) that can affect the market value of the financial instrument utilized (bonds, shares, derivatives). In a floating exchange rate regime, the risk that exchange rates will undergo significant fluctuations has grown enormously and has important implications for the work of global intermediaries. In assessing, for instance, the attractiveness of an investment in Brazilian sovereign bonds, American banks must take into account the risk of devaluation of the real with respect to the dollar. Even if this risk is theoretically covered by the higher rate of interest obtainable on Brazilian securities compared with that paid by the US government, in practice it is possible for exchange rate fluctuations to be so abrupt and large as to annul or exceed the yield of the securities. Instruments and techniques for currency risk hedging are available, but are often quite costly, even to the point of offsetting the greater yield of the foreign investment. In any event, global players tend to take on exchange rate risks that are not fully covered, believing the vast amount of available market liquidity will allow them to withdraw without losses from an investment for which the exchange rate risk has unexpectedly risen. However, this exit route, which is viable under normal conditions, can be abruptly closed off in crisis situations (see section 2.6, below). Intermediaries must, therefore, constantly monitor developments in the exchange market in order to intercept any signals that could require a timely and radical review of investment and portfolio management strategies.

2.4 SPECULATION

Operations of a speculative nature occupy an especially important place in global finance, even though this activity has been an integral part of commodity and capital markets since time immemorial. The concept of speculation is often misunderstood and unfairly censured. To speculate, in the original Latin, means to observe from a height affording a broader view of the horizon than that which is visible at sea level. In this sense all global market intermediaries are speculators, since they reassess risks on an ongoing basis, taking into account all available data and information that enables them to foresee the development of positions subject to risk.

Naturally, given that forecasting is an activity with a rather uncertain outcome, the speculator par excellence is often seen as a gambler, who has no valid reason for supposing the ball on the roulette wheel will come to rest on a black number rather than on a red one. But this is not the case of a player operating on the global market today, who can – without incurring excessive costs and with great ease – make use of all the information available on the market. In the same way, young Nathan Rothschild, who is said to have made his fortune in England from successfully arranging to be informed of the outcome of the Battle of Waterloo – and Napoleon's defeat – before other London bankers, was no gambler. He was just smarter and more efficient than his peers.[6]

What makes speculators unpopular probably has to do with the fact that they often tend to operate 'short', selling, that is, with delivery at a given time and at a pre-fixed price, goods, currencies or securities they do not actually possess. In this case it is said speculators 'short the market' because they will only make a profit if the price of the goods or securities they must deliver drops in the interval between the forward sale and the date of consignment. But operations like these make a vital contribution to the correct functioning of the market as they allow dealers to quote buying and selling prices continuously. In fact, the most serious dysfunction of a financial market is illiquidity, when sellers no longer find buyers or vice versa. In normal conditions, a downward price movement attracts buyers to the market and a rise attracts sellers. But anomalous conditions can occur, for example, when all market participants want to sell shares because they fear a stock market collapse; in this case falling share prices only have the effect of increasing the number of sellers and driving prices further down. In this illiquid or one-way market profit opportunities may open up for speculators. If they believe that the general panic and pressure to sell is overstated, they will 'lean against the wind' and will purchase securities speculating that the tendency will invert. If, instead, they believe the downward trend will continue, they will sell short, but in order to honour the contract will nonetheless have to buy the securities on the due date. In both cases, the speculator brings liquidity to the market by becoming a buyer among sellers. Naturally, speculators can get their sums wrong and incur a loss, and, if they have used credit to finance their speculations, can even be declared insolvent. But this is a risk any market always runs, irrespective of the presence of speculators.

When seeking the optimum combination of return and risk on investments, global players pay particular attention to opportunities afforded by temporary glitches in the working of market mechanisms whereby the same commodity or currency is quoted at different prices on different markets. Arbitrage is the technique used to make a profit from diverging market quotations: it consists in buying the commodity or currency on the market quoting the lower price and reselling it on the market quoting the higher price. If the transactions can be carried out simultaneously and operational costs can be contained, the risk is very low or even nil. The risk is greater for what are called 'relative-value arbitrage' transactions. In a perfect market, the yield of two financial assets with the same risk profile should be identical. However, it can happen that two securities issued by the same debtor with identical financial characteristics have different market quotations for reasons of an entirely fortuitous nature. Then an alert dealer can sell the overvalued security short, using the proceeds to buy the undervalued security and speculating that the latter will soon be quoted at a higher price than the former. Many operations like the one described are called convergence trades as they are based on the likely convergence of market quotations to what are seen as normal or equilibrium levels: these trades imply making a wager where the result, however reasonable convergence may seem in theory, is highly uncertain. Of course, when it becomes apparent the bet cannot be won, intermediaries are forced to unwind the transaction rapidly, either taking whatever profit may have materialized or adopting stop loss strategies.

Hedge funds have developed a full range of speculative investment strategies, involving to varying degrees active trading, short selling and relative-value arbitrage; some funds specialize in investments based on the anticipation of movements in interest rates, exchange rates, stock or commodities prices (known as 'macro' strategies), while some invest in other hedge funds ('fund of funds') (IMF 2004a, pp. 45–58). Speculative strategies are by no means the exclusive preserve of hedge funds as all categories of global players may be pursuing speculative objectives in any of their lines of activity. A recent example is provided by the notorious episode involving the large transactions carried out by Citigroup, a major global player, on the electronic trading platform for EU government bonds managed by Euro-MTS, where participants commit themselves to providing quotations at narrow bid–ask spreads for at least five hours a day. As reported by the *Financial Times*, on 2 August 2004, Citigroup London-based bond traders bought bond futures at the Eurex derivatives exchange in Germany to drive up bond prices; then, in two minutes of trading, sold on the Euro-MTS various bonds worth €11 billion. As prices fell on Euro-MTS, Citigroup was able to repurchase bonds for €4 billion with a profit of €17.5 million (see Van Duyn and Munter 2004). Citigroup top management, while maintaining no regulation had been violated, disapproved of the trading strategy which it termed 'knuckleheaded'. Some observers, however, have regarded the strategy as a legitimate attempt to increase competition in the European bond market by exposing the limitation of the market-making agreement (see Gapper 2005). In the end, the strategy became the subject of an investigation by regulatory agencies in the United Kingdom, Germany and Italy (from where the Euro-MTS originates) for alleged market manipulation: eventually the UK's Financial Services Authority (FSA) fined Citigroup £13.9 million for 'failing to conduct its business with due skill, care and diligence and failing to control its business effectively' (FSA 2005b).

2.5   RISK MANAGEMENT

In today's global financial system, risk management is vitally important and must cover risks arising from a whole range of counterparts (other intermediaries, companies, sovereign states) and financial instruments (bonds, shares, currencies, derivatives).[7] Global operators have responded to this challenge, in part following the recommendations of financial regulators, by investing large amounts of human and financial resources in risk analysis and in techniques and instruments for risk management. Risk management in highly integrated and volatile markets is a non-stop process incorporating all the price variations of assets and liabilities as they occur over time.

Normally, risk managers make use of statistical and mathematical models enabling the degree of risk to which a portfolio of assets and liabilities is exposed to be assessed in relation to variations in market interest rates and exchange rates or in default probabilities. The aim is to quantify the maximum potential loss that can be incurred on a given financial position over a fixed time period and at a certain level of probability.[8] On the basis of these models, intermediaries determine the maximum amount of losses they are willing to accept given their capital base (net worth). Within this limit, individual traders in currency, bonds or derivatives are free to choose the risk–return combination. The drawback of these models is that since they are based on the analysis of past performance of prices they are not able to factor in any 'unprecedented' variations in quotations, as happened during the international financial crises of 1998 (more on this in Chapter 5, section 5.2.2).[9] Moreover, the widespread use of VaR models tends to generate a certain uniformity of behaviour among intermediaries, helping to amplify the intensity of the expansion and contraction of investment in specific categories of assets (or risks). Avinash Persaud (2004), an expert in risk management, puts it this way:

> The common current practice amongst risk managers is to take some data on returns, their volatility and correlation and to optimise and draw risk–return

frontiers. Our risk–return frontiers are similar if not identical because today investors use the same information, the same statistical techniques and the same investment universe. Seventy per cent of international equity and bond investors have near identical benchmarks. The problem is that we assume that we react to seeing the optimal portfolio but nobody else does. (p. 2)

The global financial market offers a broad range of instruments, mostly derivatives, to mitigate or manage unwanted risks. Interest rate risk can be hedged through interest rate swaps or by operating in the futures market. Forward exchange rate transactions or foreign exchange options can be used to deal with exchange rate risk. Credit risk can be transferred to other market participants or investors via securitization, including the use of structured financial products such as asset-backed securities (ABS), collateralized debt obligations (CDO) or through the purchase of credit default swaps (CDS).[10]

For global players, risk analysis implies not only the correct assessment of quantifiable available data, but also an estimate of the future evolution of qualitative variables liable to influence the degree of risk. This quest for indicators of future behaviour and performance induces global players to venture into uncharted territory, where they may find themselves treading on thin ice. When it comes to assessing the degree of risk of a company or a bank, account will be taken not only of its capital base and profitability, but also of the validity and consistency of its business strategies and the quality of corporate governance, involving an analysis of factors that are difficult to calculate, such as the level of protection afforded to shareholding minorities, the efficiency of internal controls, and management's commitment to creating value for shareholders. If the risk assessment involves an investment in securities issued by a sovereign state or in its currency, then macroeconomic data, such as GDP, the rate of inflation, and the balance of payments, will all be factored in. But account will also be taken of political and social indicators. An attempt will be made to assess the consistency of monetary, fiscal and wage policies to determine whether there is a risk of 'policy dilemmas' liable to compromise the sustainability of a government's action. Other less easily quantifiable factors will also be considered, such as the credibility of a government's strategies and of its communication practices, the 'staying power' of a cabinet in Parliament or the popularity of its leader. While elements of subjective judgement and arbitrariness will inevitably be present, these will nonetheless be subject to immediate examination by the market to verify, if not the reliability of the assessment, at least its consistency with the prevailing consensus of other market participants. If, for example, an institutional investor believes the fiscal policy of the Italian government involves an unacceptable risk of inflation in the medium term, it will liquidate its portfolio of Italian

Treasury bonds on the market; if this risk assessment is shared by the market, there will be further offers of Italian bonds and a drop in their price, widening the spread between the yield of the Italian securities and those of other industrial countries. If, instead, the market does not share this assessment, liquidation by an individual investor will have no lasting implications for the security's quotation. The drop in the price owing to the initial sale will, in fact, make the security more attractive to other dealers, whose purchases will bring the quotation back to its original level.

When assessing the degree of risk associated with financing a sovereign state, operators attach considerable importance to constitutional and institutional factors as these can influence the nature of a country's economic policies and its ability to honour its international obligations. A democracy is less risky than an authoritarian state because the government's action is subject to parliamentary control, ensuring greater transparency and accountability, even if this can imply greater uncertainty as to the timing and content of government strategies. When it comes to managing economic and monetary policies, the market tends to react positively to regulations distinguishing clearly between the functions of the government and those of the central bank, or where the autonomy of the central bank to pursue price stability is guaranteed under explicit rules, because this reduces the risk that the country will fall prey to inflation.

The global market also takes into account a country's membership in institutions and international bodies that can provide support in times of difficulty, both from a financial point of view, and in terms of cooperation on strategies for economic recovery and the correction of disequilibria. Membership of the IMF, the World Bank or the World Trade Organization (WTO) is certainly a positive factor when assessing a country's risk, but perhaps even more important is its participation in international bodies with a more political mandate such as NATO, the European Union or the G7. A country's admission to one of these bodies has strong implications for its credit rating and risk premium and is seen as a fundamental step in the 'graduation process' that will eventually involve access to the global market. This was true of Mexico and Korea's accession to the Organization for Economic Cooperation and Development (OECD), generally regarded as an elite club of industrial countries. Mexico's standing significantly improved when it joined the North American Free Trade Agreement (NAFTA), alongside the United States and Canada. Similar positive effects on Russia's risk rating were seen in 1997, following its participation in some of the G7 meetings. Naturally, the importance attributed to these factors is subjective and debatable. Often they are seen as indicators that a country has the same credit rating as other members of the organization or group, or that they would benefit from a bail-out operation in the event of a financial crisis. These assumptions were proved partially valid in the case of Mexico, which received substantial financial assistance from the United States and the other G7 countries following the financial crisis of end-1994, but turned out to be completely unfounded in the debt crises of Korea in 1997 and of Russia in 1998.

The assessment of risk for issuers of securities traded on the market is also carried out by specialized agencies which, on their own initiative or following a request by the issuer, provide a risk rating that is then made public. In this way, all potential investors are aware of the degree of risk assigned to each market instrument and can determine the risk–return combination for their own portfolio. Globalization has led to a rise in the demand for ratings of sovereign risks, that is risks on securities issued by a state or associated with state guarantees. Nowadays, there are around 90 countries with a rating assigned by one of the three major agencies operating worldwide: Standard & Poor's, Moody's Investor Services and Fitch Ratings. Many institutional investors, such as pension funds and insurance companies, choose the riskiness of their own portfolio by identifying a rating level under which they believe it is unwise to invest (the 'investment grade'). If the rating of an issuer falls below the investment grade, its securities will immediately be sold by institutional investors that are guided by an agency's rating. Widespread recourse to rating agencies is another factor that leads to uniformity of behaviour among intermediaries and investors with respect to decisions to extend or curtail credit, accentuating financial market cycles. It has also frequently happened that rating agencies have been unable to foresee the increasing riskiness of countries (as in the Asian crisis of 1997) or companies (as in the case of Enron and Parmalat), while they tend to react with hasty reductions in a rating when financial turbulence has already occurred (*The Economist* 2005a). Italy in the 1980s is a further example I can cite from personal experience: despite a deteriorating economic performance, its rating was maintained at the highest level of triple A until the eve of the currency crisis of 1992; yet over the next three years, when the process of adjustment of the structural imbalances of the Italian economy was already underway, its rating was repeatedly downgraded.

2.6 GLOBAL MARKET CONVENTIONS

Aside from economic and financial indicators, global market players also rely on pre-established guidelines or reference models when assessing the significance (in terms of risk) of particular events and data concerning countries, companies or intermediaries to which they are exposed. These models vary depending on the set of principles around which there appears to be a prevailing market consensus, accepted by all participants. Given its informal nature, this general consensus among intermediaries can be defined as a convention that nonetheless has the power to influence market behaviour. It is not important whether the content of the convention is true or false: what matters is whether market consensus tends towards believing it to be true. The concept of a convention, in the sense used here, was introduced by Keynes (1936) in his *General Theory* as one of the fundamental traits underpinning the operation of financial markets in a monetary economy. This definition was taken up by Ciocca and Nardozzi (1996) to explain the persistence in industrial countries of high real interest rates during the 1980s. The role played by conventions in global finance is analysed by Eatwell and Taylor (2000). As conventions evolve over time, it is important, both for monetary authorities and for market participants, to detect rapidly signs of any changes to a convention triggered by new events.

The convention that currently influences the behaviour of global financial players is based on the emergence in the 1980s of an international consensus strongly advocating monetary and fiscal discipline and the deregulation of economic and financial activity. The collapse of the Soviet bloc and the failure of the theories of economic planning cleared the way for the global dissemination of new principles for the conduct of economic policies in countries willing to participate in the global economic and financial system. This set of principles became known in the 1990s as the 'Washington Consensus', after the definition coined by John Williamson (1990), since it enjoyed the strong support of both the US Treasury and of the IMF. In operational terms the current convention attaches great importance, for example, to the efficient management and protection of private savings. This means asset managers will take a positive view of factors contributing to an enhanced return on savings and give a more negative assessment of any factors tending to reduce current and future returns, making it harder to liquidate investments, or to benefit from them. These assessments are translated into strategies for portfolio management (that is, into decisions to buy or sell) which have the effect of varying the risk premium managers believe is acceptable in order to carry out the investment itself. Through the choices of single asset managers, the market 'rewards' or 'penalizes' the conduct of issuers of securities depending on whether they behave either in a manner that is consistent with or in contrast to the convention. Given the aim of protecting the present and future value of savings, the convention will reward – in the case of investments made in securities issued by a sovereign state – economic policies that pursue monetary stability and budgetary equilibrium, the deregulation of markets and of entrepreneurial activities, the privatization of public companies and so forth. The convention will penalize, by contrast, inflationary economic policies, growing imbalances in public finances, restrictions on the movement of capital and currency transactions, and the nationalization of private enterprise. Similarly, in respect of private stock companies, the convention rewards corporate strategies that create value for shareholders, transparent corporate accounts and actions, and effective internal controls. Again it will penalize the opposite behaviour and any conduct likely to translate into stocks performing below the sector average. These rewards and penalties are likely to result in, respectively, the purchase or sale of the security, currency or share and, therefore, a rise or fall in the instrument's price and value.

Because of their informal nature, conventions may be changed over time in ways that are also informal. For example, a major pillar of the Washington Consensus, the prescription to remove restrictions on capital movements, was severely criticized by academics and officials following the debt crises of emerging countries (see Eichengreen et al. 1998; Stiglitz 2002). In particular, the case of Russia's default provided evidence of the problems created by a premature capital account liberalization in the absence of adequate financial market structures and of regulatory and supervisory institutions. Thus a proposal to make capital account liberalization mandatory for members of the IMF has now been shelved indefinitely.[11]

One might well ask at this point whether it is possible for a country to escape the judgement of the global market altogether, but the question is not well put. The market does not oblige any country to borrow from it; Romania under the dictatorship of Nicolae Ceauşescu is an extreme example of a regime that survived until the 1980s without incurring any form of foreign debt, thus eluding any direct judgement by the market. The nature of the problem changes if a country needs financial resources but wants to avoid being conditioned by foreign creditors or the international market. This can be costly, and not necessarily successful: a country can issue state securities on the domestic market and request credit from domestic banks. Businesses can do the same: small and medium enterprises in Germany or Italy are known to prefer to turn to banks or self-financing rather than obtain a stock exchange listing. The possibility of resorting to such alternatives, however, is increasingly ineffective: the distinction between domestic and foreign financial markets is becoming blurred in today's globalized economy, except for those countries where strict controls on the economic and financial activities of residents are in force. In the absence of such a regime, which can work only in countries where no true political and economic freedom exists, it is highly probable that international intermediaries will invest in securities issued by domestic borrowers (and meant for domestic investors) and apply their own rules for managing them. As regards credit lines from banks too, the possibility of securitizing credits and selling them on the international market makes it difficult for debtors to evade the market's judgement.

If one concludes it is not possible to escape the market's verdict, the next question is whether the 'trial' will be a fair one, or whether there is something fundamentally unacceptable about the way in which market conventions are arrived at and how the market assesses deviant behaviour. Ultimately, the only truly discriminating factor the market stubbornly applies is the assurance it will recover invested capital and enjoy the fruit of its investments. If this assurance is compromised, or merely called into question, the market reacts negatively by liquidating the investment. Contrary to appearance, markets are not guided by any particular political ideology. Prior to the fall of the Berlin Wall, countries such as the Soviet Union and Poland used to obtain substantial credit from international markets. There were times in the 1970s when the market preferred to give credit to a Communist country – where order reigned and where there were no doubts as to the government's commitment to honouring its international debts – rather than to a Western capitalist country like Italy, bogged down in grave political uncertainties, the terrorism of the Red Brigades and an economic crisis of dubious outcome. Certainly the market is not willing to support economic policies that deliberately march in the opposite direction to the one mapped out by the prevailing convention. But this premise rests less on ideology than on the conviction that such policies can compromise a country's ability to repay its foreign debts. If, for example, a country decides to nationalize a private company, there is the risk that residents will react by exporting capital, thereby reducing the foreign exchange reserves of the state and its creditworthiness. On the contrary, the market will welcome strategies of convergence towards the 'conventional model' and accept that this process will occur gradually and over the long term or might entail the use of instruments that curb market forces, such as restrictions on capital movement or a regime of fixed exchange rates. This is the case, for example, of the People's Republic of China, which has gained access to substantial credit on the international market despite its 'unconventional' policies; in such instances the cost and conditions for obtaining finance are determined by the market on a case-by-case basis and depend on its assessment of the risk involved, although credit will in any event be granted.

Markets also take a negative view of any inconsistency of behaviour, either between stated objectives and measures taken to achieve them, or over time. When debtors, be they a sovereign state or private company, obtain financing from the market, they are also lent additional creditworthiness over and above their own personal and subjective standing.

Whoever is 'admitted to the market' can carry out a series of operations at costs and in ways that are inaccessible to outsiders: credibility has a value and a market price. Like a financial loan, a 'credibility loan' must be honoured and duly 'serviced'. Exploiting the trust of the market by acting inconsistently is not tolerated (no free riders allowed). The market regards signs of inconsistency as strong indicators that its trust has been abused, and was therefore misplaced. The market may be slow initially to detect an inconsistent behaviour, due to a lack of transparency on the part of governments (or companies) or because of a deliberate ploy of misinformation. Incidents of this kind occurred in the Asian crisis of 1997, when Thailand and Korea provided incomplete and misleading information to the market as to the real size of their official currency reserves. Similarly, companies like Enron or Parmalat went bankrupt in the early 2000s after using various fraudulent techniques to conceal the real state of their financial accounts from the market. However, the potential for analysing and assessing data and information at the market's disposal is such that sooner or later inconsistencies are unmasked. In general, the market's reaction to these belated discoveries is fierce: in fact the logic of the market does not permit it to stand by while a crisis evolves in the hope that the debtor's actions will become consistent again. The logic is that of 'closing the position', taking the profit made or the loss incurred and thereby concluding an operation where the riskiness turned out to be higher than originally foreseen. Naturally, this does not stop the market from setting terms for subsequent dealings with the same debtor, but subject to new conditions that are a better reflection of the change in his economic and financial circumstances as well as creditworthiness. This will lead to a wider spread and in all likelihood, given the market's proverbial 'long memory', the situation will remain unchanged until further developments justify a reduction in the risk premium.

The growing sophistication of information technologies that has accompanied financial globalization has highlighted some of the drawbacks of decision-making mechanisms based on conventions even though they may have their own rationale. The need to react promptly to the avalanche of new data continuously flooding the computer screens of dealers in securities, shares and currencies has given rise to a proliferation of conventions. Aside from the basic Washington Consensus, mentioned above, that is applied principally to emerging and developing countries, other conventions focusing on specific aspects of the economic systems of the most advanced countries have now emerged and are used to assess the impact of specific measures on the economy's cyclical evolution. Complex economic situations are analysed with reference to rough data conventionally held to be meaningful. The examples abound: data on industrial production in Germany is seen as a valid indicator of the economic shape of the euro area, able to influence the exchange rate of the euro even if Germany 'weighs' less than 33 per cent of the area total; data on America's balance of payments do not generally have an impact on the dollar's performance (although they should), while the data on productivity in the US manufacturing industry can influence share, bond and currency markets across the globe; data once considered to be of vital importance, such as the growth of the money supply M2 in the United States, are now ignored by traders.

Ahead of the release of indicators that are considered significant, dealers require from analysts a range of estimates of likely outcomes and elaborate possible alternative responses for immediate adoption depending on whether the new information is in line or not with forecasts. Some intermediaries will have an economist in the dealing room to provide an instant assessment of the economic significance of the data or news which they then translate into suggestions for transactions. TV channels specialized in financial reporting like Bloomberg and Reuters also provide instant analysis and the possible market implications of new data and policy developments. In any event, when waiting for the data to be announced, dealers will take a position based on the prevailing opinion of the market. But they will remain ready to close it and open another based on the new information. In general, the risk is that the operational strategies triggered by the publication of a single item of information turn out to be short-lived and later have to be radically re-worked, thereby increasing market volatility.

In a scenario where new conventions are frequently introduced to the market, replacing and at times contradicting conventions previously held to be sound and durable, the dissemination by monetary authorities of information and interpretations able to support the investment choices of operators becomes crucial. As the market is continually on the lookout for an optimal operational model, and therefore willing to review conventions, monetary authorities can contribute to the review process by providing appropriate analytical and statistical support. This issue will be addressed in detail in Chapter 3 and in the concluding chapter of this book. Here, it is enough to recall, as an especially important example, the interpretation provided by the Chairman of the Fed, Alan Greenspan, of such a complex phenomenon as the development of the 'new economy' in the United States. Paul Krugman (2003) used these words to describe the attitude of the Fed Chairman:

in early 1997 Mr Greenspan discovered that his tentative efforts to deflate the emerging bubble made investors furious, and lost his nerve. Worse, he then began giving ever more euphoric speeches about the wonders of the new economy.

Surely he must have known that these speeches were interpreted by investors as a retraction of his own previous warning, as a signal that soaring stock prices were justified after all. (p. 86)

The positive assessment by the Fed of the implications of new information technologies for the productivity of the American economy and for its long-term growth and non-inflationary prospects significantly influenced the behaviour of stock and foreign exchange markets in the closing years of the last century, orienting financial flows on a global scale (see Chapter 5, page 128 below).

2.7 GLOBAL MARKET FAILURES

Structural defects in the working of the global market were revealed during the financial crises of the 1990s. The single biggest dysfunction was the tendency of intermediaries to underestimate the credit risk and overvalue the degree of liquidity of the market. The causes of these anomalies are manifold.[12] However efficient the market is in collecting and assessing data, it is inevitable that asymmetries in information persist, as do situations of insufficient transparency preventing an accurate assessment of risk. In a highly competitive market, opportunities for profit depend on the ability of investors to detect at an early stage a tendency of a debtor or issuer towards 'virtuous' behaviour, as revealed, for example, by measures that bring about a significant and lasting improvement in the market price of securities, shares, or a currency. The substantial similarity of risk assessment models and of the operational conduct of portfolio managers ensures the market's reaction to a new profit opportunity will most often be uniform. It follows that if the market believes a potential borrower, based on the information available, is on the point of becoming fully creditworthy, then the competition among intermediaries will be such that the borrower will be offered financing well beyond its effective requirements and, perhaps, its ability to honour the debt. In this instance, market participants are said to behave as a herd since they follow, for no other reason than their trust in the judgement of the leader, a course whose motives and final destination are unknown to them. This is known to happen in particular in the case of investment decisions involving complex financial strategies and instruments where only a few major players have full knowledge of the underlying risks and of the appropriate techniques to deal with them. Naturally, cases of herd behaviour can also occur on stock markets and be intensified by the practice of online trading by non-professional investors, easily swayed by the indications of analysts at the main financial companies posted on the Internet. It is in this competitive climate that phenomena of adverse selection materialize whereby the market ends up being exposed to the most risky clients. Persaud (2004) describes this perverse development as follows:

> What happens is that as I adopt the optimal portfolio of high returns and low volatility and correlation so does everybody else, a process that changes the portfolio's characteristics as there is now an over-concentration of investors, lowering future returns and raising risks. Here is another juicy paradox that has been flatteringly called the Persaud Paradox: the result of the widespread adoption of common market sensitive risk management systems is that the observation of a safe area of the financial markets makes it riskier – as the herd flows there – and the observation of a risky area of financial markets, makes it safer as investors depart, leaving little firewood for a future contagion. (p. 2)

More importantly, these dysfunctions may lead to situations of excessive credit expansion followed by an abrupt contraction, generating conditions of illiquidity or of crisis (boom and bust cycles). When situations such as these involve a wide spectrum of debtors, private investors or sovereign states, they can generate instability across the entire international monetary and financial system.

A second dysfunction of the market consists in the possibility – during a phase of rapid disinvestment triggering illiquidity – that countries and debtors, which in normal circumstances would be fully able to meet their international debts, see their credit lines abruptly withdrawn due to a perverse 'contagion' effect.[13] The very existence of contagion and the way it spreads are among the most controversial issues of global finance. The victims of contagion claim it derives from arbitrary categorizations used by intermediaries to classify debtors and issuers. The 'emerging markets' category, for example, includes a wide range of countries with very different economic and financial systems, such as Brazil, Argentina, Mexico, China, Korea and Russia. The accusation is that if a country in this group registers a deterioration in its economic situation serious enough to warrant a review of the risk premium paid to the market, the same review will be applied to all the other countries regardless, even if their economic situation has remained unchanged. The crisis of 1997 involving Asian countries, which was sparked off by Thailand, ended up affecting countries such as Singapore, Hong Kong and even China, whose financial situations were markedly stronger. The contagion was made worse by the intervention of speculators who, anticipating an upward movement in the risk premium for all the countries in the group, began shorting the currencies, securities and shares even in those countries whose economy was 'healthy', thereby 'infecting' the whole group. A second school of thought, often championed by creditor countries and their major financial institutions, claims truly healthy debtors are immune to such contagion, and that it would affect only those organisms already weakened by structural deficiencies and therefore predisposed to infection.

Mechanisms of contagion certainly play a role in the workings of global finance, but their operation is not as irrational or perverse as it is sometimes claimed. There are, in fact, economic linkages capable of justifying pre-cautionary behaviour by market participants. If, for instance, as actually happened in 1999, Brazil devalues its currency, it is not entirely irrational to assume its principal trading partners in Latin America will feel the impact of this on their own balance of trade or on the exchange rate and, therefore, on economic activity and inflation. In a situation of this kind, the market must assess how a country such as Argentina is likely to react to the devaluation of the Brazilian real: one possibility is that it might imitate Brazil and devalue the peso, but this might be unlikely given that Argentina has adopted a fixed exchange rate regime with the dollar as the foundation of its anti-inflation strategy. Market participants, therefore, conclude that Argentina will maintain its exchange rate, that its trade balance will deteri-orate, that its authorities will be forced to adopt a restrictive fiscal policy, and before this bears fruit, will be forced to turn to the international market to finance the trade deficit. Following this line of reasoning, financial insti-tutions will conclude, given the new developments, that the risk premium paid by Argentina is insufficient, and will therefore ensure, through selling transactions, that listed Argentinean securities reflect the higher risk.[14] This complex sequence of analytical forecasting and operational decisions occurs very rapidly since it is part of the reaction model implicit in the current convention. Indeed, one may be under the impression that the market's reaction has been hasty or irrational, with the spread of contagion as its sole objective – just as people in the Dark Ages believed the spread-ing of a plague was the result of deliberate action by malignant plague carriers.

A contagion mechanism with some degree of arbitrariness occurs when a global financial institution, which faces a loss due to the devaluation of the exchange rate in, say, Korea, decides to liquidate a position on which it is making a profit (Greek state bonds, for example). In this instance, Greece can rightly claim to have fallen foul of Korean contagion, but the investor's behaviour is entirely rational since it aims not to damage Greece but rather rebalance its profit and loss account. If the situation in Greece does not give rise to concern, the impact on the quotation of the securities will be entirely temporary and the market will replace the original investor with another one. Contagion spreads in a less rational manner when the crisis situation in one emerging country functions as an alarm bell for global players, leading to a drastic and sweeping reduction in their propensity to take on risk with respect to any emerging country irrespective of their creditworthiness. Here the risk of contagion toppling a whole array of 'healthy' debtors is quite high, because excessive caution on the part of financial institutions translates into an indiscriminate upward adjustment of the risk premium across a wide range of market securities. This hampers the risk diversification strategies normally adopted by investors, obliging them to modify the composition of their portfolio to achieve a more acceptable combination of risks.

Market failures, or dysfunctions, would not merit special attention if they remained limited to the sphere of bilateral relations between intermediaries and clients. They become significant for national and international monetary authorities because in a globalized financial regime they have an impact on the world's monetary and financial system, often generating conditions of systemic crisis. Because of these failures, the market loses its ability to discipline debtors, as it becomes unable to induce them to behave 'virtuously' through constant and meticulous scrutiny. In reality, the market frequently falls prey to the 'too much too late' syndrome (Willett 2000), being overly clement in boom periods and applying disciplinary measures with delay and in a draconian manner.

The establishment of a global financial market at the close of the twentieth century marked an extraordinary development in international economic and financial relations. In the 1990s, the market channelled net flows of private capital of over a thousand billion dollars to emerging countries alone, providing a fundamental contribution to the growth of GDP, trade and international investment (see Summers 2000). The globalization of finance, like other watersheds in the evolution of the world economy, is the result of a set of factors inherent in the system, in part supported by decisions taken by governments, but essentially fuelled by technological progress and its application to the financial sector. Like the industrial revolution of the nineteenth century, the globalization of finance is here to stay, but the international community must learn how to manage its dysfunctions and excesses. The governments of the nascent industrial powers – in England, and later in continental Europe and the United States – soon had to cope with new problems such as inhuman working conditions at industrial factories, the deterioration of the environment, and monopolistic practices. They responded by drawing up a set of rules and establishing institutions that would enable them to exploit the positive effects of the industrial revolution, and eliminate or compensate the negative ones. National and international monetary authorities are now faced with a similar challenge.

NOTES

1. For a brief historical sketch of globalization, see IMF (1997, pp. 112–16). For an overview of the pros and cons of globalization see Stiglitz (2002), Bhagwati (2004) and Wolf (2004).
2. Globalization is a wide-ranging process that clearly goes beyond finance, involving also the production and exchange of goods and services with international economic and social implications for labour mobility and employment. Much has been written on these non-financial aspects of globalization: the main issues of economic policy are well identified by Rodrik (1997), IMF (1997) and Visco (2001) whereas IMF (2006b) focuses on the implications of globalization for inflation.
3. The Financial Services Authority (FSA) in the United Kingdom has identified a group of 15 LCFIs based on their ranking in two or more of the following activities: book runners of international bond issues, book runners of international equity issues, book runners of global syndicated loans, notional interest rate derivatives outstanding, foreign exchange revenue and worldwide custody assets. The group comprises: ABN Amro, Bank of America, Barclays, BNP Paribas, Citigroup, Crédit Suisse, Deutsche Bank, Goldman Sachs, HSBC, JPMorgan Chase, Lehman Brothers, Merrill Lynch, Morgan Stanley, Société Générale and UBS (see Bank of England 2001, pp. 80–81). Using similar criteria, the IMF has identified an additional group of 31 'internationally active' banks and securities houses generally headquartered in the United States, United Kingdom, Continental Europe, Japan and Oceania (see IMF 2004a, p. 75).
4. The information quoted is drawn from an article in *The Economist* (2007).
5. The history of the Carlyle Group is narrated in detail in Briody (2003).
6. Ferguson (1998, pp. 2 and 16) calls this anecdote a 'myth'.
7. Here again, nothing much is new under the sun as the analysis and management of risk has attracted the attention of philosophers, scientists and mathematicians since the seventeenth century, when Pascal and Fermat first established the laws of probability (see Bernstein 1996). For a broad survey of the applications of risk management techniques to various types of activities, see Celati (2004).
8. The most widely used methodology to manage the market risk of asset portfolios is the 'Value at Risk' (VaR) which determines the maximum potential loss by means of probabilistic simulations based on past patterns of interest rates and exchange rates. A more advanced technique, called eVaR, can be used to determine the 'expected shortfall', that is, the average of a given percentage – say 5 per cent – of the potential losses that could be incurred over a given time horizon. A similar methodology has been developed to manage credit risk (credit VaR) which uses historical data from credit rating agencies on the frequency of rating changes and defaults (see Hull 2006).
9. These low-probability events with a large impact inhabit – in the risk managers' jargon – the 'fat tails' of the curve of probability distribution.
10. The implications of the credit risk transfer market for the stability of individual intermediaries and of the financial system have been thoroughly examined by financial regulators (BCBS 2004). The report raises a number of issues, including whether participants understand the risks involved, and whether an undue concentration of risks is developing in the market; it also formulates a series of risk management recommendations for intermediaries and supervisors. The matter has been taken up again by Trichet (2007) who advocates 'market driven initiatives' to improve the transparency of a market in which the notional amount of CDS had risen by 52 per cent to $26 trillion in 2006.
11. The full story of this controversial item of the Washington Consensus is narrated in a report of the IMF Independent Evaluation Office (IMF 2005a) that also provides a comprehensive list of official and academic references.
12. Financial market failures have been the subject of countless books and papers. For a concise survey of the literature see Stiglitz (1994) and Mishkin (1997). On the overestimation of market liquidity, see Persaud (2003) and Borio (2004). For a severe critique of the behaviour of financial markets and of prevailing theories of finance, see Mandelbrot

and Hudson (2004). Similarly, Kay (2004, p. 319) warns that 'securities markets are better described as arenas for sophisticated professional gambling than as institutions which minimize the cost of risk bearing and allocate capital efficiently among different lines of business'.

13. The question of financial contagion following the Asian crisis was first analysed by the IMF (1999a, pp. 66–87). See also Goodhart and Illing (2002); Desai (2003, ch. 10).

14. The hypothetical sequence of events outlined here did in fact materialize in Argentina in early 2002 (see also Chapter 5 below).

3. Monetary and financial authorities

> Monetary and financial stability are of central importance to the effective functioning of a market economy. They provide the basis for rational decision-making about the allocation of real resources through time and therefore improve the climate for saving and investment. . . . In extreme cases, disruptions to the financial sector can have severe adverse effects on economic activity and even on political structures. Maintaining stability is thus a key objective of financial authorities.
>
> Andrew Crockett (1997, p. 1)

3.1 NATIONAL MONETARY AND FINANCIAL AUTHORITIES

Monetary and financial stability constitutes a shared objective that is pursued jointly by the authorities of each country, but with a clear separation of roles and instruments. 'Monetary stability' implies the absence of inflation or deflation in the prices of goods and services. In the majority of countries the responsibility for ensuring monetary stability is entrusted to the central bank, which conducts monetary policy accordingly. Price stability can also be pursued by means of administrative controls managed directly by government authorities, but these instruments generally prove ineffective in the medium term and provoke severe distortions in the functioning of the economic system and in the allocation of resources. In fact, price controls are typical of planned economic systems and have only been used by market economy countries in exceptional circumstances (for instance in wartime or after an oil price shock). The pursuit of monetary stability also depends on a country's general macroeconomic situation, for which government authorities are responsible through the setting of budgetary and income policies. 'Financial stability', on the other hand, implies the absence both of significant movements in the price of financial assets and of crises impairing the solvency of institutions operating on the banking and financial intermediation markets (or, put differently, that affect the nominal value of the assets entrusted to these intermediaries by their clients). The movements and crises that the authorities are expected to prevent are those that have significance for the stability of the financial system in its entirety, that is those that could hamper normal borrowing and lending operations, generate illiquidity in markets, or produce a chain reaction of bankruptcies among intermediaries. Any short-term volatility of asset prices or a crisis affecting a single financial institution are seen as physiological phenomena that testify to the vitality and regular functioning of markets and do not require the intervention of monetary authorities. The achievement of financial stability is the joint responsibility of government authorities and of specialized and independent agencies, usually operating under delegated authority from national parliaments. Generally, governments are in charge of setting the overall financial policy strategy, central banks are responsible for ensuring banking sector stability, and the supervision of stock exchanges is entrusted to special institutions such as the Securities and Exchange Commission (SEC) in the United States. Elsewhere, such as in the United Kingdom, Japan and Germany, the supervision of national banking, financial and insurance systems is carried out by a single independent institution. However, even in countries where central banks no longer perform banking supervision, they retain the function of 'lender of last resort', namely to provide financial support to intermediaries that are temporarily illiquid. Institutional differences aside, authorities use two instruments to pursue monetary and financial stability objectives – regulation and direct intervention – with different repercussions on the functioning of monetary and financial markets.

3.1.1 Regulation

The state's regulatory function consists essentially in the adoption of laws and administrative directives on the basis of which the relevant authorities issue rules that financial market participants must respect. Aside from the organizational and operational structure of markets, a wide range of transactions and operations carried out by market participants as part of their activities may be regulated. Regulations can concern: the 'birth' of the intermediary, for example by setting the requirements (legal, capital and so on) for establishing a bank or a financial company and for their admission to the market; the 'life' of the intermediary, influencing the conduct of its operations (the collection and investment of savings, the issue and trading of securities and so on) through disclosure obligations, authorizations and prudential requirements; and the 'death' of the intermediary, through the formulation of procedures for managing mergers and acquisitions, liquidation and bankruptcy. Implicit in the concept of regulation is the existence of a supervisory body whose job is to ensure the rules are respected.

Without going into the multiplicity of forms that the regulation of banking and financial systems has assumed in the experience of most industrial countries, it is possible to make a basic distinction between regulatory mechanisms that prevent or constrain the normal modus operandi of intermediaries and those that impose administrative requirements, which may affect how financial operations are managed, reported to authorities or disclosed to the public. The deregulation processes that accompanied international financial integration among industrial countries led to a gradual abandonment of restrictions of the first kind and to the simplification and rationalization of administrative requirements. For example, strict limits on domestic credit expansion by the banking system that were once relatively widespread (the 'corset' in the United Kingdom, '*encadrement*' in France or '*massimale*' in Italy) have disappeared. In the case of foreign exchange operations, obligations such as the requirement to balance daily exchange positions (whereby currency acquisitions must match sales, in order to avoid pressures on the exchange rate of the national currency) have been removed, as have bans or prohibitive penalties concerning certain kinds of foreign investment. In general, authorities are no longer confident in the ability of such restrictive measures to prevent adverse economic conditions or financial crises and there has been a growing consensus that they generate severe inefficiencies and distortions in the operation of the financial and economic system.

In parallel to the dismantling of these kinds of restrictive regulations, a new trend towards a market-friendly regulation has been set in motion in most industrial countries, largely in response to insolvency crises affecting banks, financial intermediaries and corporations (Padoa-Schioppa 2004a, pp. 1–13). This kind of regulation aims to strengthen the solidity of financial systems by imposing rules to ensure good governance, transparency, accountability and the adequacy of the capital base with respect to risks taken by the intermediaries. In the context of closer financial integration, the regulatory strategies of individual countries have been increasingly formulated within the framework of international cooperation among monetary and financial authorities (see section 3.2 below and Chapter 6). In this context, consensus has broadened among financial authorities in favour of the gradual closing off of regulatory loopholes; these can materialize in the supervisory network either because of the development of new types of intermediaries (such as hedge funds) or because of the establishment of offshore financial centres (OFCs), usually located in exotic islands, that attract financial intermediaries by offering shelter from regulation, supervision and taxation. Following the financial crises of the 1990s, the tendency to strengthen financial structures and supervisory networks has intensified and spread to emerging countries, as will be seen in more detail in Chapter 6 (page 153).

3.1.2 Direct Intervention

Direct intervention by authorities in monetary, financial and exchange markets aims both to achieve macroeconomic objectives of sustainable growth in output and employment and to maintain conditions of monetary and financial stability without which the achievement of these goals might be compromised. These interventions are generally carried out by government authorities, through the treasury or finance ministries, and by central banks.

Intervention by governments
Governments operate on financial markets primarily in order to fund the budget deficit. They collect private savings by issuing public debt securities on the domestic bond market, and in this way they also affect long-term interest rates. In fact, all things being equal, an expansion in the supply of government bonds will lead to a rise in interest rates and a contraction will lead to a decline. This is not an automatic effect. The underlying determinants of bond rates are linked to inflationary expectations and the risk premium that investors demand in order to protect themselves from the uncertainty implicit in medium- and long-term investments; in turn these factors are influenced by the expansion or contraction in the size of the public debt. If the government covers the state budget deficit by issuing foreign currency denominated bonds on international capital markets, it can also influence the foreign exchange market if it sells the currency proceeds on the market against the national currency, which will appreciate. Alternatively, it can sell the currency 'off-market' to the central bank, bolstering its official reserves, with a potentially positive effect on the quotation of the national currency. Another reason a state might resort to the market is in order to buy or sell assets. Governments can sell real or financial assets on the market as part of privatization schemes: in this case they drain liquidity from the market, that can then be used to reduce public debt (by repurchasing state securities) or to finance other spending programmes. The opposite effects occur in the case of nationalization, when the purchase of assets by the government increases the public debt and private sector liquidity. Because of the political relevance of their financial market activity, governments have a strong interest in ensuring that the markets in which they conduct their operations are the most efficient possible in terms of the cost of funding and liquidity. To ensure these conditions are met, governments endeavour to organize the government bond market in such a way as to take into account the needs of institutional investors and of major domestic and international market makers, using straightforward and transparent operational practices with fully automated platforms for trading and settlement of transactions.

Intervention by central banks

Direct intervention on the market by central banks for monetary and exchange rate policy purposes has the self-declared aim of influencing interest rate levels on the money market (namely the market for deposits or securities having a maturity up to three months) and exchange rate quotations on the currency market. These interventions consist in the purchase or sale of securities or currency against liquid assets (money) with market counterparts. If the central bank wants to adopt a more restrictive monetary policy in order to contain inflation and support the exchange rate, it will sell government bonds or foreign currency reserves, thus draining liquid assets from the market and replacing them with financial or foreign assets which are not immediately available for domestic payment purposes. All things being equal, this will lead to a rise in short-term interest rates and to the appreciation of the exchange rate. Similarly, if the central bank wants to pursue an expansionary monetary policy, it will act as a buyer of securities or foreign exchange on the market selling domestic currency: this will bring short-term interest rates down and lead to a depreciation of the exchange rate. The effectiveness of monetary policy interventions in influencing interest rates is ensured by the fact that in modern-day monetary systems the liabilities of central banks in the form of banknotes in circulation or of deposits of commercial banks, represent the 'monetary base' of the banking system. By means of their monopoly power to control the volume of the monetary base, central banks are able to control nominal interest rate levels in the short term. The market's awareness of the existence of this power means that any announcement of a change in the official discount rate (namely, the rate at which the central bank is willing to provide liquidity to money market participants against collateral) is enough to bring market rates in line with levels desired by central banks. Changes in interest rates are then transmitted to real economy variables (output, employment, prices), influencing their movement in the desired direction. Although this transmission process takes place in ways that even monetary theorists such as Benjamin Friedman (1999, p. 322) have called 'somewhat mysterious', economists agree that monetary policy is able to determine the general level of prices in the medium to long term and significantly affect income levels and employment in the short to medium term. This conclusion has not been invalidated, at least up to now, by the growing degree of concentration of global financial markets in favour of a smaller number of larger intermediaries.[1]

The development of information technologies, with their monetary and financial applications such as credit cards and electronic money, has also raised the question of whether it should be possible to conduct a 'monetary policy without money' (King 1999; Friedman 1999; Woodford 2000;

Goodhart 2000). The debate has been under way for some time and is far from reaching any unanimous conclusions. There is consensus, however, that the reason for the existence of central banks is not based on purely technical constraints, such as the use of paper money or the provision of monetary base for the final settlement of payments. According to Goodhart, the central bank exists for reasons of political economy, because of governments' decisions to endow the state with an institution, even an autonomous and independent one, capable of controlling interest rates. And governments will always be able to organize the financial system's structure in such a way as to make resort to the central bank necessary, irrespective of technological progress.

In the majority of contemporary banking systems, central banks have the exclusive power for the creation or destruction of the monetary base.[2] Even if, historically, central banks were established as 'banks of the sovereign' and therefore obliged to finance wars and plans for territorial expansion, over time they have been entrusted (following acts of parliament or government decisions) with conducting national monetary and exchange rate policies aimed at maintaining a currency's domestic and foreign purchasing power. In order to exercise these functions, the central banks are granted by law a high degree of independence from political power. The trend towards greater autonomy for central banks has grown as the globalization of finance has become more widespread. Laws safeguarding the independence of central banks were introduced by the United States Congress as far back as 1913 with the act establishing the Federal Reserve System; a similar law established the Bundesbank in Germany in 1948. The trend was confirmed in the 1990s when the Treaty of Maastricht included the independence of central banks among the convergence criteria that countries had to meet for admission to the EMU, obliging candidate countries to modify conflicting national laws by 1997. Partly in reaction to this trend, in 1997, the United Kingdom also sanctioned the independence of the Bank of England, discontinuing, however, its role as supervisor of the banking system. Lastly, in 1998, the Bank of Japan was granted full autonomy. Of course, the ways in which the independence of central banks is sanctioned and safeguarded vary from country to country and depend on the institutional and political context of each. Central banks' statutes are generally the object of a special law approved by parliament, which can be amended by normal legislative procedures. In the case of EMU, the independence of the European Central Bank (ECB) is sanctioned by a law having constitutional status, such as the Treaty of Maastricht, which can only be amended following the special procedures contemplated for the stipulation and ratification of international treaties. As a corollary of independence, central banks are called on to ensure transparency and accountability to parliaments and the public as regards the underlying motivations and the methods of conduct of monetary policy.

The fundamental reason for the independence of central banks, in representative democratic systems based on a division of powers between diverse bodies and on the interplay of 'checks and balances', is the need for a clear separation of responsibility among institutions with spending power and institutions with the power to finance expenditure. If a government wants to increase public spending, it must ask parliament for authorization. Parliament, in turn, will determine whether to finance the increase by taxation or by borrowing on the market (which effectively means simply postponing the tax increase). The autonomy of central banks is designed to prevent governments from forcing them to finance public spending through the 'printing of money'. Printing money takes place through direct lending by central banks to governments, the purchase of government bonds or, indirectly, through the adoption of expansionary monetary policies that facilitate the placement of public debt and make the state's repayment obligation less costly through inflation. Ultimately, the monetary financing of public deficits is seen as detrimental to monetary and financial stability. There are, moreover, economic reasons that support the option of giving responsibility for monetary policy to an independent technical body. The effects of monetary policy on output and inflation are only felt over a relatively long period of time, and this implies that the benefits of an anti-inflationary policy will be reaped only gradually, while the costs are immediate. Given this, a central bank controlled by political instances (be they governmental or parliamentary) may risk being overly conditioned by short-term considerations and therefore tend to conduct an inflationary monetary policy. This point has been confirmed by empirical evidence (Grilli et al. 1991; Eijffinger and De Haan 1996) and by the fact that in all countries a decision by the central bank to raise official rates, or its reluctance to reduce them, is invariably accompanied by protests from political leaders, who often highlight the 'democratic deficit' that they claim characterizes the 'unelected officials' whose job it is to set monetary policy.[3] The accusation is clearly a pretext, since it is democratically elected governments that appoint central bank governors; autonomy is granted to central banks by parliaments and central banks are accountable for their policy actions in ways prescribed by national law. But these controversies confirm the importance and sensitivity of monetary policy decisions even in leading democracies.[4] Indeed, it is a process with political and institutional implications comparable to those of the administration of justice by an independent entity such as the judiciary.

In a globalized financial system, central banks must be able to act independently not only of political power but also of markets. According to

Blinder (1998, pp. 54–62), an academic from Princeton University and Vice Chairman of the Fed from 1994 to 1995, there is in fact a risk that central banks will choose to 'follow markets' in order to avoid destabilizing them by making unexpected policy moves. Hence markets are supplied the interest rate that is already implicit in the prices of financial assets. Blinder believes this is a temptation that must be resisted because the financial markets 'tend to run in herds and to overreact to almost everything', making them 'susceptible to fads and speculative bubbles which sometimes stray far from fundamentals'; it follows that:

> If the central bank strives too hard to please the markets, it is likely to tacitly adopt the markets' extremely short time horizons as its own. This can create a dangerous 'dog chasing its tail' phenomenon wherein the market reacts, or rather overreacts, to perceptions about what the central bank *might* do, and the central bank looks to the markets for guidance about what it *should* do. (p. 61)

Central banks, however, cannot ignore the market's attitude because ultimately the effectiveness of monetary policies and their impact on the real economy depend on the market's reaction to changes in monetary conditions.

Monetary policy and global markets   Changes in short-term interest rates driven by monetary policy measures are reflected in bond and currency market conditions and have an immediate impact on portfolio decisions of global financial intermediaries. The development of information technologies makes it possible for central banks to communicate their decisions on official rates simultaneously to all major agencies responsible for disseminating and processing market data. The evolution of financial market techniques has induced the vast majority of central banks to rely on public auction mechanisms for the conduct of open market operations to inject or mop up liquidity. In this way, transparent conditions are ensured and all players are aware of the overall volume of liquidity being created or destroyed.

The level of interest rates on the money market is closely watched by intermediaries dealing in securities on a global scale. These typically fund themselves by borrowing at the short term, say over three months, and investing in five- or ten-year bonds, where the yield is normally higher. They make a profit on the interest differential by exploiting the normally positive inclination of the yield curve by maturity (the longer the duration of the investment the higher the rate). This type of operation allows intermediaries to earn by 'riding the curve', but it exposes them to the risk that short-term interest rates may rise, making the refinancing of the operation on maturity more costly. At the same time, there is the risk that if longer-term rates rise because of an expectation of higher inflation, bond prices will drop, causing a decline in the market value of the invested securities. These operations can also be carried out on markets in different countries. For example, dealers can borrow yen at three months in Tokyo where rates have been historically very low, sell yen against the dollar on the exchange market, and buy a ten-year dollar bond in New York. In this transaction, technically defined as a carry trade, investors are exposed both to the interest rate risk and the exchange rate risk because, were the dollar to depreciate against the yen, the value of the dollar investment would fall and the debt in yen to be repaid would rise. Of course, these risks can be hedged using derivatives, but this would significantly reduce the attractiveness of the investment. In practice, therefore, intermediaries accept a certain amount of risk but are ready to undo the operation at a moment's notice if the risk and yield conditions change. From this perspective, the evaluation of possible future behaviour by central banks with regard to official rates proves crucial. Typically, inter-mediaries hope that, through their policy actions, the authorities will vali-date the market's expectations that are incorporated in asset prices, but this does not always happen because central banks can assess the needs of the economy differently. Here, however, authorities must be ready to cope with negative market reactions or, in any event, reactions that appear to contra-dict the traditional 'laws' of the economy. If, for example, the market expects a rise in inflation in the future (implied by a very steep yield curve), a modest increase in official rates by the central bank will be judged inadequate and will provoke capital outflows from foreign exchange and bond markets, leading to a depreciation of the exchange rate and to a further increase in the long-term interest rate. This happens because the market considers that the central bank has fallen 'behind the curve'; as a consequence it then expects a further sizeable increase in interest rates and covers itself against the related risks. Conversely, if the central bank adopts a more aggressive monetary policy than expected by the market (positioning itself 'ahead of the curve'), traders will assume that inflation will fall and will increase their investments in the currency and bonds of that country, pushing the exchange rate up and long-term interest rates down.

In this context of actions, reactions, and changing expectations, the decision-making process and execution of monetary policy operations are meticulously analysed by market participants to obtain clues as to the future evolution of official interest rates, on which the cost of funding for intermediaries depends. The importance of market expectations in the evolution of interest rates has been vividly underlined by Mervyn King (2005), Governor of the Bank of England, in his 'Maradona theory of interest rates'. King recalls that, in the match against England in the 1986 World Cup in Mexico City, Diego Maradona of Argentina:

ran 60 yards from inside his own half beating five players before placing the ball in the English goal. The truly remarkable thing, however, is that Maradona ran virtually in a straight line. How can you beat five players by running in a straight line? The answer is that the English defenders reacted to what they expected Maradona to do. Because they expected Maradona to move either left or right, he was able to go straight on. Monetary policy works in a similar way. Market interest rates react to what the central bank is expected to do. (p. 3)

It is from the legitimate, but not always achievable, aim of knowing in advance what will happen next that pressures by market participants and academic economists are brought to bear on central banks to induce them to adopt a more readily intelligible and predictable reference framework for monetary policy.[5] Greater transparency in decision-making processes is considered necessary as the market wants to know in detail what economic and financial indicators and what standard criteria central banks refer to when formulating monetary policy. Moreover, intermediaries would like to have quicker access to the minutes of meetings of decision-making bodies in order to know what policy considerations were taken into account to justify a particular monetary stance. They also want to know whether the decisions were approved unanimously or by a narrow majority to gain an insight into possible future policy moves.

At an operational level, monetary policies can be more readily predictable when official interest rates are linked to the performance of some publicly available indicators. For example, central banks could commit to maintaining the rate of expansion of the money stock (variously defined as M2 or M3) within a fixed band of percentage increases, say from 3 to 5 per cent (a model usually referred to as monetary targeting). Since the statistics on the performance of monetary aggregates belong to the public domain, the market would be able to anticipate the moves of the central bank: if M2 or M3 grows by over 5 per cent, it will anticipate a rise in official rates; if it grows by less than 3 per cent, it will expect a cut. Another indicator that is frequently used is the exchange rate: central banks undertake to maintain a stable or fixed exchange rate of the national currency against other currencies (exchange rate targeting). If this rate tends to fall in value, central banks will increase official rates; if it tends to increase, they will lower them. This line of conduct implies de facto that the monetary policy of the country in question depends on the decisions made by the central bank to whose exchange rate the currency is pegged. The use of these kinds of indicators implies that central banks, given that the ultimate objective of monetary policy is price stability, modulate their interventions on the basis of an intermediate objective – a certain rate of increase of M2 or M3 or the stability of the exchange rate – held to be instrumental in achieving this final aim. The technical and institutional difficulties that arise as a result of using intermediate objectives have led economists and central bankers to believe it preferable that monetary policy should be guided directly towards the final goal – price stability – but quantified in an explicit manner and with reference to an indicator that is readily understood by intermediaries such as the index of consumer prices (inflation targeting). If the central bank defines price stability as a less than 2 per cent increase in consumer prices, the market will be able to anticipate its likely reaction should the index move significantly below or above the 2 per cent threshold.

Central banks have responded in various ways to market pressures for greater transparency. Some central banks publish the minutes of their decision-making meetings (the Fed and the Bank of England) and they do so a short time – around four weeks – after the meeting is held. The ECB holds a monthly press conference in which the President outlines the decisions taken by the Governing Council and provides information on the analytical considerations informing such decisions, but no indications are given on the position of individual board members. Irrespective of the operational model adopted, central banks provide information to market participants in periodic reports, as well as with statements and parliamentary hearings of key officials involved in the monetary policy decision-making process. The ECB also publishes a monthly bulletin containing a detailed account of its monetary policy decisions, in line with the practice of other central banks in leading European countries. The Fed publishes a quarterly bulletin, but its Chairman is also obliged by law to make periodic statements to Congress on the bank's monetary conduct. Japan's central bank draws up periodic reports on the state of the economy and its monetary policy, and reports to the Diet on a relatively regular basis. The role played by central bank communication in monetary policy formulation and in its transmission is increasingly subject to analysis and investigation.[6] The impact of central bank communication has been interpreted in various ways. For example, Friedman (1999) believes that:

> Central bankers' public utterances and other, more subtle signals . . . regularly move prices and yields in the financial markets, and these financial variables in turn affect non-financial economic activity in a variety of ways. Indeed, a widely shared opinion today is that central banks need not actually *do* anything. With a clear enough statement of intentions, 'the market will do the work for them'. (p. 1)

On the other hand, Padoa-Schioppa, the then member of the Executive Board of the ECB, was quoted in an interview with the *Wall Street Journal* on 15 July 2004 as saying: 'The danger that I see is that the market becomes lazy. . . . If it is spoiled to the point that it is told everything in advance, it relies not on its own analysis, but on the analysis of the central bank' (see Sims, 2004).

Central banks have been slower in responding to calls to make monetary policy less unpredictable. In the United States the Fed's policy-making body, the Federal Open Market Committee, has been granted maximum discretionary power with regard to the setting of official rates. US law does not mandate the Fed to pursue price stability exclusively but also to promote full employment. This is in line with the prevailing Keynesian philosophy that reigned in the years of the Roosevelt presidency and continues to permeate US economic legislation today. In Japan too, ever since the central bank was granted decision-making autonomy by the government, monetary policy decisions have been made on a discretionary basis. The situation in Europe is more varied. Prior to EMU, Germany's Bundesbank set itself an objective in terms of a monetary aggregate (M3) and managed official rates to maintain monetary conditions in line with this objective. In so doing, however, it exercised a high degree of discretionary power, reserving the right to evaluate case by case the causes and duration of the deviation of monetary aggregates from its ultimate objective before taking decisions on interest rates. The other European countries whose currencies were pegged to the German mark under the ERM of the EMS followed the moves of the Bundesbank with the discretionality allowed by the band of permissible exchange rate flexibility envisaged under ERM. In the period from 1979 to 1993, when exchange rates could fluctuate up to a maximum of 2.5 per cent around the fixed parity, the scope for action with respect to the choices of the Bundesbank was quite limited and could only be extended at the risk of devaluing the parity. There was greater scope for action following the crisis of the EMS in 1993, when the band was widened to 15 per cent below or above the central parity. In short, before EMU, monetary policy in Germany depended on a monetary target, while in other ERM countries it depended on an exchange rate target. Monetary policy in Great Britain was decided with the maximum of discretionary power by Her Majesty's government and uncritically applied by the Bank of England until November 1990 when sterling joined the ERM, implying the acceptance of an exchange rate target. After the 1992 crisis and the UK's abandonment of the ERM, the Bank of England adopted a strategy centred on an inflation target that remained in place even after the Bank was granted full autonomy in monetary policy by the government in 1997.

The advent of EMU ushered in significant changes in the monetary regime of countries that had chosen the euro as their national currency. In pursuing price stability as a priority objective, as sanctioned by the Treaty of Maastricht, the Eurosystem – that is, the ECB and the national central banks in the euro area countries – opted for an eclectic approach that reflected the very different experiences of the national central banks that were part of EMU. Having defined monetary stability as an increase in prices of less than 2 per cent, the Eurosystem bases its monetary policy decisions on two distinct elements or 'pillars' involving the analysis of a broad range of indicators of monetary and economic conditions. The monetary pillar involves the assessment of monetary conditions with respect to the reference growth rate for the money stock of the euro area (M3) and of the evolution of credit aggregates; the economic pillar involves the assessment of factors liable to influence the performance of prices in the short term (domestic and external demand conditions, wage developments, the performance of bonds and stock markets, the price of oil, the exchange rate of the euro and so on). This approach initially caused some puzzlement on the part of market participants and analysts; in particular, it was claimed that the use of two distinct indicators and the discretionary powers exercised by the Eurosystem in interpreting them prevented the market from accurately predicting future developments. In response to these criticisms the ECB provided the analytical motivations and institutional clarifications required for a better understanding of its actions.[7]

In conclusion, all the major central banks provide the market with a series of general indicators regarding their monetary policy objectives and their reaction function to the occurrence of certain events. Clearly, none of the central banks give the market any specific indications in advance about the timing, direction and extent of changes in official rates. This would merely have the effect of anticipating the bond price movements normally associated with a change in rates, only affecting the timing of those uncertainties that the pre-announcement was supposed to eliminate. In reality, the market as a whole would not derive any particular advantage or disadvantage from having even more precise advance information on the monetary authorities' plans, and most central bankers would consider a 'keep them guessing' approach to be the normal strategy vis-à-vis market participants. The minor drawback of this approach is that individual operators, who get their prediction of the central bank's behaviour wrong and incur losses, will then point the finger at the central bank, accusing it of scant transparency, obscure communication policies, and so forth. The situation would be different if *all* money market participants were misled by unclear central bank signals. In this case, the market would experience a sudden reversal when the true policy intentions of the central bank would become clear and this would increase uncertainly and volatility in financial markets, eventually raising the cost of capital for investors. In order to avoid these drawbacks, some central banks like the Fed and the ECB use 'code words' in their communications that should enable market participants to guess with some degree of accuracy the direction, if not the timing, of the next monetary policy measure.

Forced to operate in conditions of uncertainty with regard to the conduct of central banks, the market tends to formulate its own forecasts on the basis of data on past behaviour, or track record. Naturally, the longer the track record, the more reasonable and realistic the forecasts based on it will be. If, on the contrary, a central bank has a relatively short institutional history, the market will tend to exercise maximum caution when predicting future behaviour. The same caution will be exercised when a new governor is appointed, someone whose ability to make rapid decisions and react swiftly to events is not yet proven. This kind of stance also characterized the market's initial attitude to the ECB, whose track record was short, given that it was established on 1 January 1999. The fact that the ECB was the result of the merger of 12 national central banks, each with its own established analytical capacities and a long history of monetary rigour, was seen to be of little importance. As far as the market was concerned, the Eurosystem was a completely unprecedented institutional reality within which internal decision-making processes, the relationships between members of the Executive Board and the governors of the national central banks, and its ability to withstand external pressures, were unknown quantities. The market's initial apprehension about ECB's Governing Council processes was due in part to the fact that each member of the Council was entitled to one vote irrespective of the size of the country he or she represented. It was feared, for example, that the 'hawks' of the Bundesbank and other central banks in the mark area, which traditionally advocated a rigorous monetary line, might be forced into a minority by a coalition of reputedly overindulgent 'doves'. These early fears have now apparently been dispelled as the ECB has remained firmly committed to preserving price stability in the euro area, resisting calls for monetary relaxation that may have generated inflationary pressures or expectations.

Irrespective of the monetary regime that is adopted, it is inevitable that the conduct of monetary policy will continue to be characterized by a certain degree of discretionary power, with the risk that outsiders see this as arbitrary. In this sense Ralph Hawtrey's (1932) famous definition, according to which the profession of a central banker is more of an art than an exact science, remains as valid as ever. On deciding if, when, and with what vigour, measures should be taken to oppose inflationary pressures, the central bank must of necessity make a subjective assessment in uncertain conditions of an extraordinarily complex phenomenon influenced by factors that are difficult to quantify, such as the expectations of financial markets and the collective psychology of consumers or investors. In the same way as it is preferable not to entrust the delicate phases before touchdown in stormy weather entirely to an automatic pilot, it is unwise to tie the work of the central banker to any particular indicator or unchanging rule.

In both cases it is better to rely on the judgement, experience and prompt reactions of the person at the controls, and above all on their ability to take account in the decision-making process of every analytical element liable to contribute to a better assessment of what to do.

Exchange rate policy and global markets   Operations carried out by central banks on foreign exchange markets are closely linked to monetary policy decisions. In fact, the purchase or sale of a foreign currency on the market implies, respectively, the creation or the destruction of money in circulation. This is why, in the majority of jurisdictions, foreign exchange operations are left to the discretion of central banks. However, since foreign exchange policy operations influence the external value of the national currency, they have broad political implications above and beyond the specific competence of central banks. It is up to government authorities, therefore, to choose the exchange regime and determine the scope within which central banks can intervene on currency markets. As will be discussed in detail in Chapter 4, the regime can envisage either that the exchange rate be free to fluctuate on the market in relation to the supply and demand of foreign currency, in which case the central bank will not intervene at all, or that the exchange rate be maintained through intervention by central banks within limits decided on by governments or under international agreements, like Bretton Woods or the EMS. In countries with a floating exchange rate regime, government authorities are responsible for making decisions on occasional central bank interventions on the exchange market, since this implies, even temporarily, a regime change. In cases where foreign exchange operations are within the authority of central banks, they may be carried out in a discretionary manner, involving a degree of confidentiality, and therefore be less transparent. This is not the case where central banks buy or sell currency for monetary policy aims. In fact, these operations are conducted via public auction mechanisms of which the market is fully aware. On the other hand, the market will monitor closely exchange operations by central banks executed to influence the quotation of the national currency. Since interventions of this kind are often carried out with a single dealer as counterpart in a confidential transaction, other market participants may only guess that the 'central bank is on the market', if they spot a dealer acting against the prevailing trend. But even when the interventions of central banks are not covered by confidentiality, the market remains uncertain as to the extent of the intervention, its duration and ultimate purpose. And the doubt remains that the market's knowledge of an exchange intervention covers only a part of a much larger operation of which little is known. Furthermore, given that exchange transactions impact on monetary conditions, dealers may well wonder whether the effects of this kind of intervention will be neutralized or whether they will be allowed to influence the monetary base. In the second case, interventions could be a prelude to direct monetary action, for example a change of official interest rates.

Why do central banks intervene on foreign exchange markets?[8] There are many circumstances in which a central bank may deem it appropriate to influence the market price of the national currency. First, a central bank may decide to act to lessen what it sees as excessive daily fluctuations of exchange rates. This is especially true when national law or an international agreement oblige central banks to adhere to a fixed exchange rate or to maintain it within certain pre-agreed limits. In these cases, given that conditions of supply and demand on the market can be subject to considerable daily fluctuations depending on the performance of foreign trade, tourist flows and capital movements, central banks act as counterparts on markets where the supply of currency is either excessive or insufficient. If excessive, they will acquire foreign currency and increase official reserves; if insufficient, they will sell foreign currency reserves. In this way fluctuations that may be of limited economic significance, but nonetheless raise uncertainty and transaction costs, can be avoided. In principle, there is no particular reason for keeping this kind of intervention secret from the market. In fact, in many instances it is carried out publicly, at times on the stock exchange or at the headquarters of the central bank as part of a procedure for 'fixing' official exchange rate quotations. In conducting this kind of smoothing intervention the central bank will normally act as both buyer and seller, and such interventions tend to offset each other over time.

The situation changes when exchange markets show persistent excesses in the demand or supply of foreign currencies. Excess demand will result in an outflow of foreign currency and put downward pressure on the exchange rate, while excess supply will result in an inflow of foreign currency and put upward pressure on the exchange rate. In either case, the rationale behind intervention may simply be that of 'gaining time' in order to allow monetary authorities to analyse the evolution of the balance of payments and decide whether the outflow or inflow of foreign exchange is a temporary phenomenon or whether it reflects an imbalance requiring corrective economic policy measures. Central banks may decide that more time is needed to allow a strategy of balance of payments adjustment to start taking effect: if so, interventions may be useful to prevent exchange rate movements from hindering economic policy measures or rendering them ineffective. If, for example, the government and the trade unions agree to implement a wage policy aimed at containing inflation, a devaluation of the currency can significantly alter the expected performance of prices and negatively affect the unions' attitude vis-à-vis the agreement and jeopardize the policy's outcome.

When foreign exchange markets reflect a clear trend, interventions by central banks are necessarily unidirectional and, taken together over time, give rise to significant upward or downward variations in official reserves. In these cases, the central bank may intervene through private channels in order not to alarm dealers and to avoid the kind of counterproductive reactions the visible presence of the central bank on the market could engender. There is also the risk that, if news of the 'covert' intervention becomes known to dealers, concerns will be raised that exacerbate market tensions. In any event, the market can obtain confirmation of intervention by analysing the statistics on the volume of official reserves that the central banks periodically make available to the public, even if not immediately. The significance of data on official reserves can be lessened if the central bank simultaneously conducts financial operations that conceal the impact of interventions on reserves. Central banks may finance intervention sales from the proceeds of foreign currency debts incurred by the government or another public agency, or through a swap operation (involving the purchase of foreign currency against an agreement to resell it at a specified future date). However, if the central bank is seen selling currency and reserves do not fall, dealers will immediately guess that some other items in the country's 'consolidated balance sheet' must have changed, such as the state's foreign debt or the central bank's currency repurchase obligations. Broadly speaking, therefore, covert intervention in exchange markets is necessarily limited both in time and extent. When the intervention is undisguised, the central bank is exposed to the immediate judgement of the market, which may not agree with or understand its motives and the ultimate goal of its action. But in this way central banks have an opportunity to send an unambiguous signal to the market, spelling out their own reading of the balance of payments and exchange market situation. This message can be reinforced with an exhaustive illustration by monetary authorities of the economic reference framework and the economic policy strategy that lies behind the actions of the central bank. Dealers take due account of the signals and messages received from monetary authorities, but they reassess them on an ongoing basis to ascertain their consistency with subsequent developments and pre-announced economic policy strategies.

The role that market interventions can play in the context of strategies aimed at influencing exchange rates is a subject on which quite divergent opinions have been expressed. One view, in particular held among central banks participating in exchange rate arrangements, is that interventions are a monetary policy instrument which can be used pragmatically, with appropriate sterilization measures designed to offset the impact of interventions on the monetary base if needed, usually through purchases or sales of government bonds. Economists, especially those of the monetarist school, take the opposite view. Where the effects of interventions on monetary conditions are not immediately 'sterilized', economic analysis equates them with normal monetary policy measures. In other words, an unsterilized sale of foreign exchange against the national currency will have the same impact on exchange markets as the sale of government bonds, reducing the money stock and bolstering the exchange rate of the national currency. In the light of this equivalence, prevailing economic theory holds that it is useless, and even detrimental, to carry out monetary policy operations on foreign exchange markets. If, on the other hand, interventions on foreign exchange markets are completely sterilized, traditional empirical analysis tends to conclude that they will have no effect on exchange rates, because sterilization leaves monetary conditions unchanged.

Continuous reliance on sterilized and unsterilized interventions on the part of numerous central banks following the introduction of the floating exchange rate system has led analysts to rethink traditional theoretical conclusions and concede that even non-covert sterilized interventions may play an effective 'signalling' role as regards both the level of exchange rates and the stance of monetary policy. This is the thrust of the conclusions reached by empirical research conducted both within central banks (Catte et al. 1994; Fratzscher 2004b, 2005; Vitale 2006) and by academics (Dominguez and Frankel 1993; Sarno and Taylor 2001a; Dominguez 2003; Kubelec 2004). According to these views, intervention in foreign exchange markets signals that the central bank feels the quotation of a national currency is unjustified, and that it intends to take monetary policy measures in order to bring exchange rates back to a level it believes more appropriate. The signal helps modify dealers' expectations, their behaviour and, therefore, exchange rate quotations. Naturally, the market will constantly watch the monetary authorities of countries to see how trustworthy the 'signal' proves to be and how likely a change of monetary policy stance is.

The more the intervention reflects the opinion of all the main authorities involved, the stronger the signal broadcast to the market. If, for example, the Bank of Japan decides that the yen is overly depreciated against the US dollar, an intervention to buy yen against dollars will have a greater likelihood of success if there is a corresponding sale of dollars and purchase of yen by the US Fed. The market pays particular attention to these kinds of coordinated interventions, especially when accompanied by declarations of intent by the monetary authorities involved, spelling out the reasons and objectives of the course of action. This was the case of the coordinated rounds of intervention undertaken by the G7 from the 1980s onwards to influence the performance of the dollar with respect to the yen, the German mark or the euro, and which were preceded by official declarations by finance ministers and central bank governors (see Chapters 7, 9 and 11). At times monetary authorities have been led to believe that they can influence the course of exchange rates by resorting to 'oral' intervention only, not backed up by foreign exchange transactions or monetary policy measures. The impact of these purely communicational initiatives is usually modest and short-lived, but there has been a significant exception to this rule in the case of the United States. The dominant position of the American economy and of the dollar in the world economic and financial system is such that the market tends to adapt itself to indications on exchange rate movements when these emanate from the highest political and monetary authorities and when they are frequently repeated. This happened when the American government tried to 'talk the dollar down' in the second half of the 1970s and the early 1990s; and again in the late 1990s when the United States under President Clinton officially endorsed a 'strong dollar policy'. The evolution of the US dollar under the Administration of George W. Bush has clearly shown, however, that the mere announcement of a 'strong dollar policy' will not sway markets unless it is supported by consistent monetary and fiscal policies. Without these the dollar has 'strongly' depreciated in the early 2000s.

While the advent of a regime of generalized floating has not eliminated the need for monetary authorities to try to influence the performance of foreign exchange markets, the attitude of market participants with respect to strategies of exchange market intervention and the accompanying communication campaigns have begun to change. Intermediaries remain fundamentally sceptical about the effectiveness of intervention by central banks. However, they realize that such interventions cannot be disregarded since they can signal a change in monetary policy or a new economic policy strategy that could have a significant impact on market quotations and risk assessment by investors. And even though individual currency dealers at major international banks remain free to react as they see fit to interventions by central banks with respect to their own risk exposure, even 'going against' the indications of monetary authorities, global currency strategists in the same institutions would not exclude, in their medium-term scenarios, the hypothesis of a U-turn in the exchange rate trend of the currency that is the subject of official intervention. Translated into operational indications, this kind of scenario can go some way towards altering the choices of currency brokers and can help explain why, in many cases, the effectiveness of an intervention is only revealed after a certain length of time. On the other hand, intermediaries also attribute major significance to the absence of intervention by central banks when the currencies for which they are responsible are rapidly depreciating under a speculative attack; here, a non-interventionist strategy is interpreted as tacit acceptance of market movements or seen as a symptom of indecision within monetary authorities or in government, helping to reinforce the trend under way.

The debate over the effectiveness of interventions in exchange rates will run on, and the evidence for and against will continue to be partial and susceptible to multiple interpretations, particularly if the exchange rate relationships among the major currencies of the world remain as unsettled as they have been in the early years of the third millennium. What seems certain, however, in a regime of globalized financial markets where each item of information is carefully assessed by global players and taken into account in their decision-making processes, is the market's greater willingness to assess exchange policy strategies on a case-by-case basis, without being conditioned by the preconceptions of 'conventional wisdom'.

3.1.3 Intervention by Governments and Central Banks

The market assigns great importance in its assessments of the policy strategies of countries to the respective roles assigned to governments and central banks. As already noted, the market reacts positively to arrangements that distinguish clearly between the roles of the two institutions, whereby monetary policy is set autonomously. But the market also judges the 'policy mix' of monetary and fiscal measures as a whole, assessing their overall consistency and effectiveness. Its analysis focuses on the objectives of the strategy in order to determine whether the policies that have been adopted are compatible with the stated aims. One crucial element in this evaluation is the judgement on the strategy's sustainability over time. Sustainability is a concept that extends beyond mere economic concerns to include the political and social acceptability of measures envisaged under a particular strategy. Two examples can be considered. If a government decides to pursue an expansionary fiscal policy, leading to a larger budget deficit, and the central bank reacts by announcing a restrictive monetary policy, the market may regard the policy mix as balanced but will have doubts regarding its sustainability. This is because a rise in interest rates will end up making public debt repayment obligations more burdensome and therefore widen the budget deficit, necessitating a further increase in interest rates in a kind of vicious circle that only a reduction in public debt can break. In this case, the market's immediate reaction will be to push interest rates on government bonds up, in the expectation that inflation will increase. In the second example, a policy mix whereby both monetary and fiscal policies are restrictive in order to safeguard exchange rate stability may turn out to be unsustainable, given the negative effects this strategy could have on output and employment and, therefore, on political and social conditions. In this instance, the market will exert pressure on the exchange rate, in the expectation that monetary and fiscal policies will become less restrictive. The way in which monetary authorities respond to these initial pressures of the market will provide a further test of their credibility and of the sustainability of their strategy.

Another type of intervention by monetary authorities that is closely watched by the market is the 'bail-out' of banking and financial intermediaries or of other companies whose difficulties can threaten the stability of financial and foreign exchange markets. Operations of this kind have wide-ranging implications. In principle, the prevailing convention is that the fate of both banks and companies that prove unable to meet their financial obligations should be left to run its course: either they are expelled from the market through bankruptcy or liquidation, or taken over by another healthy company. In reality, even if monetary authorities accept this principle, they will inevitably worry that the failure of a major intermediary or corporation could have negative implications for the solidity of banking and financial systems and for the smooth functioning of the payment system. Managing systemic risk, either domestically or internationally, falls within the competence of monetary authorities. Specifically, in the case of a bail-out, the central banks will be involved due to the implications for monetary policy and the working of the payments system; the government will be involved due to the implications for the budget. A bail-out operation entails first and foremost an injection of liquidity into the system through the creation of money by the central bank, which grants credit to illiquid intermediaries or counterparts in difficulty owing to the inability of the former to meet their obligations. In this case, the market may fear that the creation of liquidity, albeit necessary in order to prevent a systemic crisis, may prove excessive with respect to the need to maintain price stability. Naturally, the central bank can always compensate for the monetary effects of the bail-out operation, but the market will want to be sure that this happens very quickly indeed or even simultaneously, and will react negatively if the sterilization happens gradually or is postponed for some time. An additional worrying aspect of bail-out operations is their impact on public finances. In fact, a government intervention using taxpayers' money would be required to make good the losses incurred if the illiquid intermediary turned out to be insolvent. Naturally, if the failure of the intermediary risks provoking systemic repercussions, then the public finance intervention will also be of systemic dimensions and therefore liable to have a negative impact on the national budget. As a result, corrective measures such as expenditure cuts or tax increases may well prove necessary.

Crises requiring bail-out operations have not been limited to developing countries but have involved all the leading industrial countries at one time or another. Among many examples, the crisis of the savings and loan associations in the United States in the 1980s stands out, as do the numerous interventions in support of banking and non-banking intermediaries in Sweden, Japan and France. The market's reaction to this type of intervention has been twofold: on the one hand, as noted earlier, it views with concern the implications of these bail-outs for monetary and fiscal policy and for the regular functioning of competition; on the other, investors see in the monetary authorities' commitment to preventing systemic crises a kind of implicit guarantee of invulnerability for major companies and intermediaries, be they private or public. Whoever is believed to be 'too big to fail' automatically becomes a low-risk client to whom the market is only too willing to grant credit, even at suboptimal conditions. And so an anomaly in the working of the market occurs, whereby the perception of the likelihood of intervention by monetary authorities produces a systemic underestimation of risk by financial markets leading to excessive risk-taking. The knowledge that the authorities will step in if necessary, even if motivated by public interest, can favour reckless behaviour by market operators, creating a 'moral hazard' with dangerous implications for the stability of the system.

3.2   INTERNATIONAL MONETARY AUTHORITIES

International monetary authorities exercise significant influence over the functioning of global finance. The role and functions of authorities operating at an international level are very different from those of authorities of individual sovereign states. Moreover, with the gradual emergence of financial globalization, the very concept of international monetary authority has been increasingly questioned, in parallel to the consolidation of a market-led international monetary system. That said, it was not until the twentieth century that the idea of conferring a certain amount of policy-making and supervisory powers on supranational institutions made any kind of headway in international relations among leading countries as a way to achieve a more binding and effective form of cooperation among independent sovereign states. It has been a slow process, with frequent stoppages and setbacks. The League of Nations, established in 1920 by the victorious powers of the First World War, is the earliest known international authority in the political sphere. The first act of institutional cooperation in the monetary sphere was the creation of the Bank for International Settlements (BIS) in 1930 by the central banks of the allied countries to manage the flow of war reparations owed by Germany. But the BIS was never endowed with truly supranational powers and essentially acted only as a central banks' bank and as a forum for informal monetary cooperation.

It was not until 1946, when the IMF was established, that a truly international monetary authority was created, an institution with its own statute ratified by the parliaments of member countries, granting it powers and financial resources. In reality, however, the IMF's authority has always been based more on the consensus of its leading stakeholders than on the exercise of the limited disciplinary powers at its disposal. The United States' abandonment, in 1971, of the fixed exchange rate system managed by the IMF heralded an abrupt erosion of its authority. Over time the Fund began to look increasingly like a multilateral surveillance forum where developments in the international monetary system were discussed, while its power to influence economic policies was gradually being restricted only to those countries that appealed to it for financial aid (Saccomanni 1988; James 1996). The IMF continues, however, to exert a high degree of influence over the trends and decisions of financial markets in a variety of ways. With 185 member countries, the IMF is the only institution of truly global proportions and is seen as the main non-partisan observer of the general performance of the world economy, particularly as regards the evaluation of the adequacy of economic policies pursued by leading countries, as well as their implications for growth, inflation and trade on a global scale. The Fund is also seen as an institution that has the power to issue a 'clean bill of health', or at least of 'good conduct', for emerging countries that intend to operate on the market. This role assumes special importance in times of financial crisis; together with the country concerned, the IMF is called on to devise and implement a strategy for the adjustment of financial and structural disequilibria. In these instances, the IMF acts on various fronts, drawing on its own resources to provide financial assistance, mobilizing funds from other official creditors, and calling on private financial institutions to keep existing lines of credit open. In this way, it functions as a 'catalyst', providing the financial resources required to halt the crisis and block the spread of contagion. Naturally, the IMF is by no means infallible and has, on more than one occasion, been accused of making errors of judgement both in the prevention and in the management of financial crises. Partly in response to such criticism, the Board of Directors of the IMF set up an Independent Evaluation Office to assess the performance of IMF management and staff in handling crisis situations.[9] Despite these difficulties, the market continues both to assign a high degree of credibility to judgements emanating from the IMF and to regard its role as being of vital importance.

The erosion of the IMF's authority has been accompanied by a growing role for informal groups from major industrialized countries, which have gradually become venues for mutual consultation and occasional economic cooperation in specific areas. In these settings participants cannot exercise direct decision-making powers, but they can agree on what stance they will take in competent institutional quarters such as in national parliaments or the Board of Governors of the IMF. To the extent that participants follow through in practice the decisions taken in informal cooperation groups, the role played by these 'unofficial' authorities can become quite important, especially in respect of financial markets. The origin of informal international cooperation is strictly linked with the history of the international monetary system. When in 1971 the United States dissociated itself from the rules of the IMF, it nonetheless recognized the need to preserve close relations with its European allies and Japan. This approach appeared warranted not only by the strong US trade deficit vis-à-vis precisely these countries, but also by emerging tensions on various international fronts, including: the worsening conflict in Vietnam; the energy crisis triggered by the quadrupling of oil prices decreed by the Organization of Petroleum Exporting Countries (OPEC); and pressures from Third World countries to bring about a 'new international economic order'. Taken together, these developments risked transforming the IMF from a technical body for the deliberation of specific monetary issues into a forum for political debates not unlike the United Nations General Assembly.

The quest for a more exclusive venue, where the major industrial countries could reach agreement on policies to be pursued collectively in the wider institutional fora, was not without difficulties. The ten main industrial countries in the world – the United States, Japan, Germany, France, the United Kingdom, Italy, Canada, the Netherlands, Belgium, Sweden (and subsequently Switzerland) – had already created in 1962 the Group of Ten (G10), with the aim of bolstering the IMF's resources through the establishment of a network of supplementary credit lines. It was in this forum that the finance ministers and governors of central banks negotiated the depreciation of the dollar in December 1971, after the declaration of its inconvertibility into gold the preceding August. But the United States grew to resent the presence of so many European states in the G10, often united in opposing US positions. In Europe, on the other hand, France believed that international monetary questions had become so important that they should be handled at the highest political level in a more restricted forum. It was a thesis that proved convincing, and President Valéry Giscard d'Estaing convened a meeting of the heads of state and government of the United States, Japan, Germany, France, the United Kingdom and Italy in Rambouillet in 1975.[10] From that point on, these countries, together with

Canada which joined later, made up the G7, becoming over time a kind of global economy 'directorate'. Despite the fact that it has retained an informal structure, backed by neither a treaty nor an international agreement, the G7 has in reality become institutionalized, with procedural rules and internal working arrangements that envisage an annual 'summit' meeting, chaired by each country in the Group in rotation and preceded by numerous technical-political meetings attended by finance ministers and the governors of the central banks.[11] In addition to adopting a common stance with respect to the major issues of international politics and economics at the summit, the G7 has also developed forms of cooperation aimed at achieving specific financial and economic targets that have a significant impact on market trends (Putnam and Bayne 1984). Some of the most important initiatives of the G7/G8 summits include: the review of the IMF's Articles of Agreement that sanctioned floating exchange rates (1975), the adoption of a coordinated strategy for economic recovery (1977), the management of the energy crisis (1978 to 1979), the correction of the overvaluation of the dollar (1983 to 1985), the management of the financial crisis in Mexico and its consequences (1995), the reform of the international financial architecture (IFA) and the management of the Asian crisis (1997 to 1999), the fight against poverty (2004 and 2005), and energy security (2006). On these matters, the G7/G8 acted by resorting to a wide range of instruments, promoting the adoption of economic and fiscal policy measures, coordinating interventions in exchange markets, granting financial assistance to countries in crisis, and adopting prudential regulation in the field of banking and finance.

Global financial players follow all the deliberations of the G7 very closely, deriving indications for their own activities, including the adoption of appropriate measures for 'hedging' against the risk of initiatives whose outcome is unpredictable. The market was most conditioned by what happened in the period from 1985 to 1987, when the G7 seriously considered the possibility of adopting a mechanism for the international coordination of economic policies based on the performance of the exchange rates of the respective national currencies. The idea was subsequently abandoned due to fundamental differences of opinion with regard to the political implications of such a mechanism,[12] but the G7 finance ministers and governors continued occasionally to express their view of the exchange rates of major currencies, sometimes pre-announcing monetary policy measures or intervention in exchange rates compatible with pre-set objectives. The relationship between the market and the G7/G8, however, has retained a certain amount of ambiguity on both sides. The heads of state and government of the Group's member countries want their deliberations to influence the market, but they often refrain from making any specific commitments on sensitive economic and monetary policy issues in an international forum lest they run up against subsequent opposition in the competent national institutions (parliaments for fiscal measures, central banks for monetary and exchange rate policies). Global market players, on the other hand, seem to expect nothing less than the birth of a 'world economic government' from every meeting, only to be severely disappointed, afterwards, by the scarcity of results or the inconsistency of the statements made.

While the G7/G8 has acquired a predominant role in informal cooperation on the major issues of economic and global financial management, other informal venues for cooperation have sprung up alongside the G7 to examine specific questions relating to international banking and financial activities. In the BIS, the central banks of the G10 countries have set up committees to coordinate their activity on an international level in various areas: the Basel Committee on Banking Supervision (BCBS), the Committee on Payment and Settlement Systems (CPSS) and the Committee on the Global Financial System (CGFS).[13] Similarly, supervisory committees for stock exchanges and capital markets (International Organization of Securities Commissions – IOSCO) and for insurance companies (International Association of Insurance Supervisors – IAIS) have also been established. These committees, and others that have been established to deal with more specific issues, have promoted the drafting of standards of 'good practice' for market participants. The standards cover a wide range of matters – from risk management to accounting, the dissemination of statistics and corporate governance – and end up becoming actual codes of conduct that aim in general to guide market participants towards soundness, accountability and transparency (more will be said on this in Chapter 6). Overall, this informal rule-making activity has given rise to a vast body of international law of a completely new kind: these are not regulations imposed under the binding instrument of 'hard law' but rather a kind of 'soft law', namely a set of suggestions whose adoption is at the discretion of the parties concerned.

The idea behind such codes of conduct is to reconcile systemic stability objectives with the interests of market participants, and efforts are made by 'standard setters' and international monetary authorities to ensure that the codes are adopted by the greatest possible number of intermediaries and countries. In this way, a kind of indirect collaboration between authorities and markets is achieved, thereby contributing to the effective adoption of sound, stability-oriented practices. The codes will eventually become part of the prevailing convention: the market will therefore reward those countries and businesses that adopt the codes, granting them more advantageous financial conditions, and penalize those that do not. In a sense then, the market may be seen as acting as agent of the authorities on whose behalf it encourages 'virtuous', and penalizes 'deviant', behaviour. Ultimately, this kind of soft law is an instrument that authorities may need in order to influence the general functioning of markets without recourse to direct intervention, which could create distortions and inefficiencies. While acknowledging the potential benefits of soft laws in an international context where no supranational legislative body exists, jurists doubt that regulations adopted on a voluntary basis, even when subject to the careful supervision of both national authorities and the market, can be 'resilient' enough to weather situations of major crisis in global finance (Giovanoli 2000).

NOTES

1. A survey conducted by the G10 confirms that financial sector consolidation has not had any significant impact on the channels for monetary policy transmission (G10 Deputies 2001, pp. 19–22).
2. A stimulating contribution on the role of the central banks remains the anthology edited by Ciocca (1987), which brings together the views of eminent central bankers from the main industrial countries. See also Goodhart (1988).
3. A good example of the perspective from which the activities of central banks are often seen and described is Stephen Solomon's book (1995), subtitled *How Unelected Central Bankers Are Governing the Changed Global Economy*; in it the author presents a detailed analysis of the disinflationary path embarked on by the central banks of the G7 in the 1980s. What followed, perhaps as a reaction to these concerns, was a debate on the advisability of rigidly limiting the autonomy of central banks to the sole exercise of monetary policy and reducing their sphere of influence. *The Economist* devoted ample attention to the issue in a special report, in which it claimed that 'central banks are now more powerful than ever before. They should enjoy their moment of glory: it will not last'. See the article by Woodall (1999, p. 3).
4. For a legal analysis of the relationship between central bank independence and accountability, see Zilioli (2003).
5. For an analysis of the evolution of the reference framework for monetary policies, see Cottarelli and Giannini (1997) and Borio (1997).
6. See Blinder et al. (2001). The topic is a subject of recurrent analysis in the ECB: see Fratzscher (2004a); Ehrmann and Fratzscher (2005a, 2005b).
7. See Issing et al. (2001) and García Herrero et al. (2001). For a comprehensive analysis and evaluation of the ECB policy strategy see Padoa-Schioppa (2004b, pp. 67–96). For an analysis of monetary policy predictability in the euro area see Wilhelmsen and Zaghini (2005).
8. This question was examined in detail within an ad hoc working group set up by the G7 in 1982–83 to analyse the effectiveness of exchange market interventions. As a former member of that working group representing the Bank of Italy, I believe the group's conclusions, which are summarized in Jurgensen (1983), are still valid.
9. See IMF (2003c). The role of the IMF in financial crises is described in Chapters 5 and 6.
10. See James (1997) on the origins of the G7.
11. Beginning with the Denver Summit of 1997 Russia had been included in the summit meetings of the Group, now formally known as the Group of Eight (G8). The first G8 meeting under Russian chairmanship took place in St Petersburg in July 2006. However, finance ministers and central bank governors of the original G7 have continued to meet

in the same format, occasionally inviting colleagues from Russia, China or other relevant countries to attend part of their meetings.

12. These questions are considered in more depth in Chapter 7.
13. See Padoa-Schioppa and Saccomanni (1994) on the potential for fostering cooperation between central banks under the aegis of the BIS.

4. The global market for foreign exchange

> The exchange rate is too important a price to be left wholly at the mercy of the exchange markets.
>
> Paul Krugman (1989, p. 100)

> The global foreign exchange market represents capitalism red in tooth and claw. This largely self-regulated trading system never sleeps and routinely transfers staggeringly vast sums of money around the world in seconds at the click of a mouse. In spite of its size and power the foreign exchange market has proved very adept at coping with change. It is immensely complicated but price transparency and intense competition ensure it operates on the tiniest of margins.
>
> *Financial Times* (2004)

4.1 A TRULY GLOBAL MARKET

The global foreign exchange market is the nearest thing to a model of a perfect competitive market ever to have been achieved on a global scale, given the very large number of participants, efficient processes for determining and disseminating quotations, and secure trading and settlement procedures.[1] Yet, it is only since 1989 that the scale and operation of global currency markets have been the subject of systematic research. Prior to that, only balance of payments statistics had been available on a country-by-country basis, and these did not provide indications on the size of the foreign exchange market or its organization in terms of currencies and instruments. Following an initial sample survey conducted on the London, New York, Tokyo and Toronto exchanges, a broader survey was carried out under the aegis of the BIS in 1989. The sample size was then gradually extended to 54 countries in 2007, based on a methodology approved by the respective central banks. Given the complexity and extent of the phenomena under examination, the survey was conducted only every three years and measured turnover levels for just the month of April of the reference year.

The surveys provide a truly startling picture of a market of gigantic proportions and explosive dynamism (see Table 4.1). The *daily* turnover recorded in April 2007, equal to $3210 billion, was – for the sake of comparison – about one-fourth larger than the *annual* GDP of Germany. Only

Table 4.1   Global foreign exchange market turnover[a] (daily averages in
            April, in billions of US dollars)

	1989	1992	1995	1998	2001	2004	2007
Spot transactions	317	394	494	568	386	621	1005
Outright forwards	27	58	97	128	130	208	362
Foreign exchange swaps	190	324	546	734	656	944	1714
Estimated gaps in reporting	56	43	53	61	28	107	129
Total turnover	590	820	1190	1490	1200	1880	3210
Memorandum item Turnover at April 2007 exchange rates[b]	680	880	1150	1650	1420	1950	3210

Notes:
a.   Adjusted for local and cross-border double-counting.
b.   Non-US dollar legs of foreign currency transactions were converted into original
     currency amounts at average exchange rates for April of each survey year and then
     reconverted into US dollar amounts at average April 2007 exchange rates.

Sources: BIS, *Quarterly Review*, December 2004; BIS, *Triennial Central Bank Survey*,
September 2007 (rounded figures).

with the introduction of the euro, which eliminated turnover between the
pre-euro currencies (absorbing highly active market segments like those of
the German mark–French franc and German mark–Italian lira), did the
relentless pace of the market stall, coinciding with a reduction in the number
of market participants and greater recourse to electronic trading systems.
The rising trend of the turnover resumed, however, in 2001–04, despite the
persistence of the factors that had determined the decline in 2001. The BIS
estimates a new key factor may have been the increased interest of money
managers and leveraged investors 'in foreign exchange as an asset class alternative to equity and fixed income' (Galati and Melvin 2004).The acceleration in turnover growth in 2004–07, according to a preliminary assessment
by the BIS (2007, p.1) is due to 'a significant expansion in the activity of
investor groups including hedge funds . . . and retail investors'.

The monitoring and regulation of the foreign exchange market is
conducted by the regulatory authorities of the major financial centres
(namely, London, New York and Tokyo) on the basis of their national
jurisdictions. In these centres, moreover, the authorities chair ad hoc
committees comprising representatives of the main financial institutions,
foreign exchange dealers and electronic broking firms, with the aim of

promoting 'best practices' through the establishment of guidelines or codes of conduct. On a global scale, the only widely accepted principles are those adopted by the international association of foreign exchange dealers.[2]

The interpretation of foreign exchange turnover data should not be stretched beyond the very concept of turnover, namely the sum of the amount of every purchase and sale of a currency against the national currency of the country carrying out the survey, net of double counting. Turnover should not be seen as an indicator of the market's speculative activity, actual or potential. In fact, foreign exchange dealers, in addition to buying and selling currencies on behalf of their clients for commercial and financial reasons, typically carry out a large number of daily transactions on their own behalf to make a profit from fluctuations in exchange rates, often investing the same amount of money in a chain of transactions. For example, a dealer with an initial amount to invest of one million euros can carry out a large number of transactions, moving the sum from one currency to another and closing the day by repurchasing one million euros in order to 'square' the exchange risk position, which is the most prudent and least speculative approach that can be recommended. At the day's close, he or she will have in their books an amount of one million euros, plus or minus the profit or loss made, but they will have recorded a *turnover* of as many million euros as the number of transactions carried out in the course of the day. In turn, the volume of transactions tends to be influenced by the volatility of market quotations. As it happened, conditions of uncertainty and tension prevailed in the market during almost all the periods chosen for conducting the foreign exchange survey: in April 1992, due to the deepening of the EMS crisis; in April 1995, due to the fallout from the Mexican debt crisis; and in April 1998, due to the contagion effects of the Asian crisis. Turnover declined in April 2001 when foreign exchange market conditions were relatively calm, but rose again in April 2004 due to the uncertainties created by the persistent weakness of the US dollar and the prospect of possible further declines. Yet the results are nonetheless astonishing and provide a series of snapshots of how the process of financial globalization evolved, using currency and derivative markets as the instruments and resources to fuel its rapid progress.

The release of these highly technical data into the public sphere is often accompanied by commentaries in which a simple comparison is made between data on the size of the market and the relatively modest volume of currency reserves held by central banks (see Table 4.2).

Although it is well known that it makes no sense to compare data on turnover over a given period with data on the volume of reserves at a given moment in time, the juxtaposition of these statistics may lead to the conclusion that it is impossible for monetary authorities to influence exchange

Table 4.2   Official reserves of the major groups of countries[a] (billions of US dollars; end of period stocks)

	1996	1997	1998	1999	2000	2001	2002	2003	2004	2005	2006
Industrial countries	791.7	783.0	772.5	810.6	853.8	868.7	1000.4	1222.4	1410.1	1343.1	1433.7
Oil exporting countries[b]	86.5	95.7	99.3	105.9	133.3	138.7	147.7	176.3	215.0	265.2	354.4
Non-oil developing countries	769.4	828.8	886.3	965.7	1035.4	1138.8	1377.3	1755.8	2242.0	2636.2	3303.1
Total official reserves	**1647.6**	**1707.5**	**1758.1**	**1882.2**	**2022.5**	**2146.2**	**2525.4**	**3154.5**	**3867.1**	**4244.5**	**5091.2**
Memorandum item											
Gold holdings at market prices[c]	408.9	315.7	310.3	312.7	291.7	291.2	357.0	427.1	441.1	506.7	621.0

Notes:
a. Excluding gold; totals may have discrepancies due to rounding.
b. Includes those countries for which oil exports represent at least two-thirds of total export earnings and at least 1 per cent of world oil exports.
c. Includes gold holdings of the IMF, the ECB and the BIS.

Source: IMF, *International Financial Statistics*, various issues.

markets, and therefore financial markets in general. For the purposes of this book, this particular item of conventional wisdom is especially misleading, because it implicitly assumes the only way in which monetary authorities can influence exchange rates is through interventions aimed at rebalancing the demand and supply of currency on the market. In reality, the issue is not so much the ability of monetary authorities to influence the exchange rate through the use of their official reserves, but rather the adequacy of the policy mix they are willing to adopt in order to pursue their exchange rate objectives. This in turn raises the question of what should be, in the context of the policy mix, the role of interventions in foreign exchange markets. Part III of this book will review how and with what results this question has been addressed by different countries at various times.

4.2   THE EXCHANGE RATE: A VERY SPECIAL 'PRICE'

Demand and supply in the global foreign exchange market determines the price at which different currencies are bought and sold. The price is the exchange rate, namely the amount of national currency needed to buy one unit of a foreign currency (or, vice versa, the amount of foreign currency needed to buy one unit of the national currency). The exchange rate plays a central role in the relationship between monetary authorities and global finance. This is the result of its complex nature and of the important implications that exchange rate movements can have for economic systems, financial markets and political and social stability. One might well wonder how it happened that a price, albeit a very special one, was assigned so many and such important roles in the daily life of even the largest and most developed countries. At the root of this fundamental issue is the fact that nation states – irrespective of their constitution or internal organization – have historically had different currencies. It follows that if residents of different states wish to do business and establish trade relationships among themselves, as has been the case since time immemorial, then it should be possible to determine the price of the currency of one state in terms of the currency of another. The reasons for the multiplicity of currencies are both historical and geographical, not unlike those for the diversity of languages. Distant populations separated by vast oceans and lofty mountains have scant need for communication or commerce; they tend to speak different languages and use different currencies, requiring neither interpreters nor money-changers. Neighbouring populations, instead, tend to speak or adopt a common language and to use the same currency. If, motivated by politics or national pride, they decide to adopt different currencies, they must govern foreign exchange rate relations in a clear and efficient manner. In short, the reasons for having different currencies are essentially of a non-economic nature, while the implications of their existence are intrinsically economic and touch on a vast range of sectors and markets in goods, services and financial assets.

With the development of international trade and investment, new roles and functions were gradually assigned to exchange rates. For commercial and financial operators, the exchange rate went from being a simple vehicle to access goods, services and capital markets in other countries to becoming an autonomous financial asset; one in which market players could invest, hedge and even speculate by availing of a variety of instruments from spot exchange to forward exchange, options, futures and swaps. For economic and financial analysts, the exchange rate has become a key indicator of the external position of a country; in fact, changes in real effective exchange rates (the weighted average of the exchange rates of a given currency vis-à-vis the other currencies of its trading partners, net of changes in the domestic price indices) provide important advance information on the competitiveness of an economy and hence on the sustainability of its external financial position and on the likelihood of foreign exchange tensions. For monetary authorities, the exchange rate has become a policy instrument used to pursue balance of payments adjustment or to stabilize inflationary expectations. For public opinion, and consequently for politicians, the exchange rate has become an essential yardstick for gauging the quality of a government's action and the relative robustness of the national economy. Nor could it be otherwise: a country whose currency is devalued grows poorer with respect to the rest of the world. In order to import the same amount of goods from abroad it is forced to export ever greater quantities of goods produced at home, suffering a decline in the value of its financial assets, real estate and companies.

The variety of roles played by the foreign exchange rate and the coming together of different and often conflicting commercial, financial, political and social interests around it, make this a beast that both economists and monetary authorities struggle to tame. This was true at the end of the gold standard era when, once individual national currencies had been cut loose from gold, neither economic science nor political wisdom proved able to recreate the conditions and mechanisms that had so effectively guaranteed monetary and currency stability for half a century. And in today's globalized system it is truer than ever before. The global foreign exchange market has grown to such proportions as to simultaneously appear incapable of being understood by economists and of being governed by monetary authorities.

Economists have invested vast amounts of intellectual resources in the analysis of exchange rates and the functioning of the foreign currency market, so far with only modest results.[3] A comprehensive survey of the economics of exchange rates (Sarno and Taylor 2002, p. 136), concludes that 'although the theory of exchange rate determination has produced a number of plausible models, empirical work on exchange rates has still not produced models that are sufficiently satisfactory to be considered reliable and robust'. In other words, these models on the whole have succeeded in identifying the fundamental factors that may influence the exchange rate between the currencies of two countries (real output, relative prices, interest rates and monetary aggregates) but fail to fully explain the behaviour of the exchange rate, particularly in the short run.[4] This unsatisfactory state of affairs has led such an eminent central banker as Alan Greenspan (2004) to observe that:

> No model projecting directional movements in exchange rates is significantly superior to tossing a coin. I am aware that of the thousands who try, some are quite successful. So are winners of coin-tossing contests. The seeming ability of a number of banking organizations to make consistent profits from foreign exchange trading likely derives not from their insight into future rate changes but from market making. (p. 1)

The market itself is also unable to predict exchange rate behaviour accurately: the three-month forward exchange rate quoted on the market, for example, provides an indication that is almost never confirmed by the spot market quotation once three months have elapsed. The conclusion that economists can draw from these theoretical and empirical analyses is that, while economic fundamentals may well 'matter' in the process of determining exchange rates, there are many other factors, including investors' expectations, the 'sentiment' of the global market, and prevailing conventions, that can significantly alter the causal links between the fundamentals and foreign exchange rates. Hence the suggestion to extend the field of research to new horizons using high-frequency data of foreign exchange market quotations (Goodhart and Figliuoli 1991) or by focusing on the microstructure of foreign exchange markets (Sarno and Taylor 2001b) to understand better the behaviour of market participants. Innovative models for determining foreign exchange rates that take account of new information and breaking news in guiding investor choices and the market's attitude are being developed along these lines (Tivegna and Chiofi 2004; Evans and Lyons 2004 and 2007). Charts depicting exchange rate performance are also being analysed in the hope they will be able to identify patterns of behaviour that could be used for operational and forecasting purposes; 'chartists' maintain they can identify the peaks and troughs at which there are 'resistance or support levels' and devise their trading strategies on the basis of such parameters. Empirical analyses (De Grauwe and Vansteenkiste 2001) indicate that the activity of chartists could have a dominant impact on the behaviour of foreign exchange markets.

Another implication of the inability to 'model' exchange rates with reliable econometric methods is the difficulty in arriving at a consensus on the role that changes in real exchange rates can play in correcting a country's balance of payments disequilibria.[5] In theory, an appreciation (depreciation) of the real exchange rate should bring about the adjustment of a balance of payments current account surplus (deficit) within a reasonable time horizon. However, a quick look at Figure 4.1, which shows the evolution of real exchange rates and current account balances in the United States, euro area and Japan, immediately reveals some puzzling patterns. The appreciation of the real exchange rate appears to have contributed to the increase in the current account deficit in the United States from 1995 onwards; however, the deficit has widened further despite the dollar depreciation since 2002. In Japan the marked real appreciation of the yen up until 1995 seems to have merely contained the growing structural balance of payments surplus for a limited period only; since then, the surplus has increased (decreased) in line with the real depreciation (appreciation) of the yen, while remaining constantly above 2 per cent of GDP. In the euro area, with the netting out of internal imbalances, a substantial degree of balance of payments equilibrium was maintained and changes in real exchange rates seem to have played a modest role overall. What is striking, however, is the unambiguous worsening of the balance of payments in the period from 1997 to 2000, despite the depreciation of the real exchange rate of the euro, and the marked improvement since 2002, despite the real appreciation of the euro. Although it would be wrong, from the theoretical and empirical contributions briefly surveyed in this section, to reach the conclusion that changes in real exchange rates do not play any role in the balance of payments adjustment process, it is fair to say that this role is of uncertain size and direction and may ultimately be influenced by other fundamental factors and policy measures.

4.3   CHOOSING AN EXCHANGE RATE REGIME

It is entirely legitimate for economists to affirm that there are no theoretical models capable of explaining the behaviour of exchange rates, recognizing as Krugman does, for example, that no economic controversy has ever been so ferocious and inconclusive as that between advocates of fixed or floating exchange rate regimes (see Krugman 1995). But this conclusion

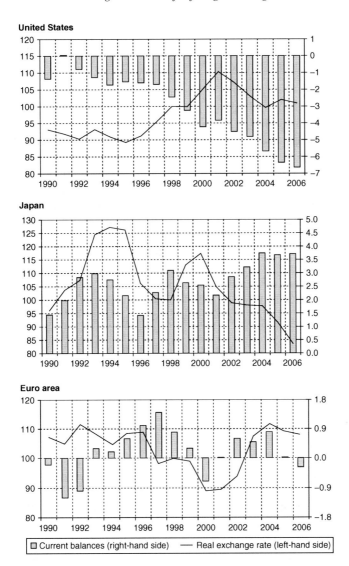

Notes:
a. Real effective exchange rates (base year 1998 = 100) for each area are calculated vis-à-vis
    61 trade partners (30 in the case of the euro area) based on relative producer prices (unit
    labour costs for the euro area).
b. Current account balance as a ratio to GDP; data for 2006 are partly estimated.

Sources: Bank of Italy, OECD and national statistics.

*Figure 4.1   United States, Japan, euro area: real exchange rates[a] and
    current account balances[b] (annual averages)*

does little to help monetary authorities meet the expectations of investors, businessmen and market participants, who need an exchange rate regime that facilitates the smooth functioning of international trade and investment, and does not result in excessive financial volatility or disastrous crises. In reality, the debate in leading industrial countries over the choice of foreign exchange rate regimes ended in the 1970s when the United States decided to let the dollar fluctuate freely, Japan adopted a managed floating exchange strategy for the yen, and the EU member states agreed to maintain stable exchange rates between their currencies whilst allowing them to float jointly with respect to the dollar and yen. It remains an issue, however, for all these countries to determine how much the floating regime should be 'managed' by the monetary authorities. For emerging countries, especially those that in the 1990s had 'graduated' into the international financial market and whose currencies were being included in financial portfolios managed by global players, the choice of the change rate regime became crucial.

The range of possible exchange rate regimes, traditionally limited for the sake of simplicity to the alternative between fixed and floating exchange rates (with nothing in between), was greatly expanded following the crisis of the Bretton Woods system. Nowadays, fixed and flexible exchange rate regimes represent the two extremes of a continuum, within which it is possible to identify a vast range of typologies. The main regimes are:

1. *Monetary union*   An arrangement whereby a group of countries use the same currency, such as the countries adhering to EMU that adopted the euro. EMU is a multilateral union, based on a strong institutional architecture and implying one central bank common to all member countries and mechanisms for multilateral economic and political cooperation. But there can also be unilateral monetary unions, in which one country adopts the currency of another and accepts the monetary policy decisions made by that country's central bank. This is the case of Panama, which adopted the US dollar. Elsewhere 'dollarization' or 'euroization' regimes have been implemented or proposed by some countries in Latin America or Eastern Europe. Monetary union is the most extreme form of a fixed exchange rate regime, but this does not mean that it cannot be dissolved as a result of political decisions bearing on a country's constitution, as happened in 1993 in Czechoslovakia when the country decided to split into two new nations with two different currencies.
2. *Currency board*   An institution that is similar to a central bank, but empowered to issue or withdraw national currency solely in exchange for reserve assets denominated in a foreign currency at a fixed rate of

exchange, sanctioned by law. This constitutes an automatic mechanism for adjusting balance of payments disequilibria given that surpluses or deficits trigger an equivalent contraction or expansion of the money stock and therefore of domestic spending. First conceived in the nineteenth century as an instrument for managing the issue of money in British colonies, currency boards experienced renewed popularity at the end of the twentieth century when they were adopted by Hong Kong, Argentina and some Eastern European countries that chose the dollar or the euro as the reference currency. It is possible for a country to abandon this kind of regime, but this step cannot be taken by monetary authorities and must instead be sanctioned by law.

3. *Fixed exchange rate agreements* Unilateral agreements according to which one country commits to maintaining a fixed exchange rate with a reference currency of another, with which it has strong political, economic and trade ties. Examples of this regime were the foreign exchange agreements linking the currencies of some states in Western Africa to the French franc (and now to the euro).

4. *Adjustable peg agreements* Agreements that envisage fixing the parity of a currency with the possibility of adjusting it under certain circumstances and according to predetermined procedures. This was the model adopted by the Bretton Woods system, in which parities were fixed in agreement with the IMF (and were adjustable only with its consent, when there was a fundamental disequilibrium in the balance of payments). Exchange rates were allowed to fluctuate within a band of ±1 per cent around the central parity. EU countries participating in the EMS adopted the same model, the only difference being that exchange rates were allowed to fluctuate by ±2.25 per cent around the central parity.

5. *Crawling peg* A regime that envisages the adjustment of the parity at regular intervals for modest amounts, determined in relation to the performance of the inflation differential. Some Latin American countries, such as Brazil and Chile, have adopted this model.

6. *Basket peg* Where exchange rates are fixed unilaterally in relation to the weighted average of a basket of foreign currencies that are important for the commercial and financial transactions of the reference country. A variant called BBC (Basket peg with a wide fluctuation Band and a Crawling parity) has been proposed by Williamson (2000), an early advocate of the crawling peg. The adjustment of the weighting of individual currencies in the basket lends a degree of flexibility to monetary authorities. Some small countries in Africa and Asia have adopted this regime, which seems to have been introduced also in China (see Chapter 12).

7. *Managed floating* A regime that implies the willingness of monetary authorities to intervene in the market to curb exchange rate fluctuations, but without defending any particular parity. This is the model adopted by some of the leading industrial countries such as Japan, Canada and the EMU countries. Goldstein (2002) has proposed a variant based on a managed floating regime that includes inflation targeting ('managed floating plus').

8. *Pure floating* A regime that permits exchange rates to fluctuate freely in relation to market forces and whereby the authorities abstain from all forms of intervention. This is the model the United States conformed to for a long period of time, apart from some sporadic episodes of intervention within the G7.[6]

The choice of the exchange regime has been the subject of a vast array of academic literature weighing the pros and cons of the various regimes.[7] Analyses focus on how exchange regimes affect systemic performance, both from a macroeconomic perspective (effects on national income, inflation and the balance of payments) and microeconomic one (effects on the behaviour of households, firms and intermediaries). One main line of research has focused on the crucial problem of assessing the extent to which different exchange rate regimes allow the exchange rate to reach its equilibrium level, namely the rate that ensures the equilibrium of the current account in the balance of payments in the medium term.[8] The difficulties involved, empirically speaking, in arriving at a single definition of the equilibrium exchange rate have induced economists to be cautious in evaluating exchange rate performance or in identifying situations of exchange rate misalignments (that is, of significant and lasting divergences from the equilibrium level).[9]

The indications offered to policy-makers by economic theory and empirical analysis on the question of which regime to adopt have not been clear-cut. As with many other fundamental issues, the response of economists has been 'it depends'. It depends, in this case, on: the underlying economic situation of a country; its geopolitical position; its stage of development; the final objectives that authorities assign to economic and monetary policies; and their ability to use the instruments at their disposal, including exchange rates, in a coherent manner. If pushed for a more precise response, the majority of economists, especially those of Anglo-American extraction, would declare themselves in favour of a floating exchange rate regime. However, with the advent of global finance, the creation of EMU in Europe and the rediscovery of currency boards, another school of thought began to emerge (Eichengreen 1994). This held that authorities could only chose between two extreme solutions, the only practicable ones available in a context of high capital mobility worldwide ('hollowing out of the middle'). At one extreme are monetary union and the currency board; at the other, pure floating. Intermediate solutions were to be rejected because of their tendency to create unsustainable tensions on foreign exchange markets (Goldstein 1995). As it happened, the prescription of extreme remedies also failed to obtain unanimous endorsement by economists, and the old debate between the advocates of fixed and flexible exchange regimes has turned into a contest between proponents of extreme and of intermediate solutions.

4.3.1 The First Polar Solution: Fixed Exchange Rates

At the outer extreme of fixed exchange rates are unilateral monetary unions (such as 'dollarization') and currency boards. From the standpoint of international economic relations, these regimes do away with uncertainties over the performance of exchange rates and therefore reduce transaction costs for international trade and capital movements. Less uncertainty is reflected in lower interest rates, with a positive impact on economic activity. Empirical studies have estimated the effects of fixed exchange rates on the volume of international trade as being positive but modest. More recently, however, research on the effects of monetary unions (Rose 2000; Frankel and Rose 2002) has revealed a strong positive effect on international trade among countries that adopt the same currency, although subsequent work by Baldwin (2006) has concluded that such trade effects are less sizeable than in the early estimates by Rose and others, but are still important. From a macroeconomic management perspective, a fixed exchange rate regime is theoretically seen as capable of making a fundamental contribution to a policy aimed at eradicating inflation, in so far as it guides the expectations and behaviour of households, companies and financial market participants towards price stability. Adopting a fixed exchange rate regime implies that the authorities will pursue monetary and fiscal policies compatible with exchange rate stability. It also implies that workers' and employers' unions will sign non-inflationary wage agreements linked to productivity gains and that the business sector will do all in its power to remove inefficiencies and cost factors that erode competitiveness and could cause a currency devaluation.

One might well ask whether the adoption of a fixed exchange rate regime would be truly necessary in the light of such virtuous behaviour on the part of authorities and market participants. The answer is that a specific official commitment to maintaining stable or fixed exchange rates entails a degree of credibility and visibility vis-à-vis economic agents that far exceeds that of generic pronouncements by authorities to pursue anti-inflationary policies. In fact, these policy intentions, even when reinforced by the announcement of an inflation target as a guiding parameter for monetary policies, are able to influence the expectations of only the most sophisticated economic players, those capable of independent assessment of the performance of price indexes with respect to the inflation target and the appropriateness of economic policy measures adopted to correct divergences. In any event, these assessments can only be made when the price indexes have been published, and therefore at some remove from when the anomalous pattern first occurred. The performance of exchange rates can, instead, be observed and understood by anybody, at any moment and in real time. The simplicity of the exchange rate as an indicator and its immediacy mean that signals sent by monetary authorities can be readily understood by a wider public, whose behaviour and expectations can in turn influence foreign exchange markets. For these reasons, fixed exchange rates play a key role in stabilization strategies adopted by countries that have experienced high and lasting inflation rates and where inflationary expectations and psychoses are widespread and deeply rooted.

When the commitment to maintaining fixed exchange rates is made under a currency board arrangement, the board's credibility is reinforced by its undertaking to adhere strictly to a monetary policy determined by the evolution of foreign exchange inflows and outflows with the rest of the world. This reassures market participants that interest rate decisions will no longer be at the discretion of monetary authorities and therefore at risk from political interference. In this sense, unilateral monetary unions should provide an even stronger guarantee than other regimes since monetary policy is managed by a foreign central bank with a solid anti-inflationary reputation. In fact, the introduction of currency board regimes by some Latin American and Eastern European countries strengthened the market's perception of the credibility of the monetary authorities' commitment to pursuing monetary stability and adopting the measures needed to achieve it. This greater credibility, especially as regards the degree and immediacy of interest rate adjustments in times of heightened tensions, has lessened the probability – while not entirely eliminating the risk – of speculative attacks against currencies linked to currency board regimes. Lessened, because a currency board does not guarantee that a misalignment of the exchange rate, for reasons external to the country, cannot occur. Even if this regime helps contain domestic inflation, countries can nonetheless register a drop in competitiveness because the reserve currency to which the board is tied becomes overvalued, or because the currencies of their main trading competitors depreciate. The emergence of a misalignment will not in itself trigger a currency crisis or a speculative attack, because market participants are only too aware that the regime's abandonment is a highly charged political decision that cannot be taken independently by monetary authorities and requires a parliamentary vote. In any event, such a move would have far-reaching institutional implications and could only take place in the context of a major political upheaval and as a result of a severe economic and social crisis. Having said this, the absence of exchange rate risk and a favourable interest rate differential (typically present in countries that adopt a currency board) can attract capital inflows of a speculative nature which are therefore particularly sensitive to any economic or political development that might foreshadow an abandonment of fixed exchange rates.

Relatively few countries have opted for a currency board to date, and the results of their experience vary widely: positive in the case of Hong Kong (see Chapter 10) and of some Eastern European countries; negative in the case of Argentina, where, despite having played a vital role in eradicating the 'hyper-inflation' of the 1980s, the currency board was jettisoned in dramatic circumstances at the beginning of 2002 (see Chapter 5). It seems fair to entertain some doubt as to the ability of currency boards to represent permanent arrangements, applicable to most emerging countries, as was fashionable for economists and policy-makers to claim for some time (Summers 2000; Mussa et al. 2000a). What is certain, however, is that for the authorities of countries wishing to adopt it, this extreme form of fixed exchange rate regime entails a series of difficult sacrifices from both an economic and a political point of view. Clearly, the surrender of the exchange rate instrument for adjustment implies the need to create efficient and flexible markets for goods, services and productive factors, in particular the labour market, and to maintain balanced public finances. The relinquishment of monetary sovereignty, aside from the purely political implications, also means giving up the possibility of providing financial assistance to the banking system in the event of a liquidity crisis. This in turn requires either very efficient banking supervision, capable of preventing situations of illiquidity, or the political will to permit a banking crisis to run its course, even if it may have systemic implications. Overall, the conditions imposed are quite severe and end up being acceptable only for countries that, for political reasons or due to institutional shortcomings, desperately need to re-establish the credibility of their economic policy in the eyes of their citizens and markets by accepting a fixed exchange rate commitment. The price for this credibility is the surrender of flexibility and discretionality.

4.3.2 The Other Polar Solution: Floating Exchange Rates

At the farthest extreme of exchange rate flexibility is the pure floating regime, in which exchange rates are permitted to fluctuate freely in relation to market conditions. Floating overcomes many of the inconveniences of fixed exchange rates, but it has drawbacks of its own and inevitably imposes constraints on economic policies. The arguments in favour of floating exchange rates were developed with great analytical and polemical vigour by Milton Friedman (1953) when the Bretton Woods system was at the height of its glory and fixed exchange rates had been adopted by all the leading industrial countries, including the United States. Friedman argued that the rate of exchange was a price and that its level of equilibrium, like that of any other price, should be determined by the free interplay of market forces, that is by the demand and supply of foreign exchange. Claims by monetary authorities to know better than the market and to be able to identify the equilibrium exchange rate would only lead to distortions and inefficiency in the allocation of resources. With flexible foreign exchange rates, instead, balance of payments equilibrium would be automatically guaranteed, allowing economic policies to concentrate on 'domestic' objectives such as the growth of national output and employment. Friedman's position ought to be considered in the context of the ongoing debate in those years over how to manage America's current account deficit in its balance of payments, a debate that in the 1960s would ignite and spill into the international arena. Friedman contended that the United States should have allowed the dollar to fluctuate, ignoring the current account deficit (whose financing could be assured by capital inflows or by increasing dollar liabilities vis-à-vis non-residents) and expanding domestic demand to support income levels and employment.

The history of events as they unfolded from 1973 onwards, with the switchover to a floating foreign exchange regime by the majority of industrial countries, allows a balanced assessment of the functioning of this regime across a broad spectrum of countries with different economic, political and institutional situations. One aspect that has become particularly important in the context of financial globalization is the fact that floating exchange rates keep the perception of risk alive, something which is instead 'anaesthetized' to a certain extent in fixed exchange regimes. The perception of exchange rate risk influences the investment decisions of market participants, who must equip themselves with appropriate forms of risk hedging or predetermine the necessary strategic adjustments in relation to changes in exchange market trends. These factors have tended to curb the volume and duration of investment in countries where exchange rates are highly volatile. Exchange rate risk has also been taken into due account by national market participants when deciding whether to incur foreign currency debt: the prospect of a depreciation of the national currency makes this kind of financing more costly, and the hedging of exchange risk can cancel the benefit of this option compared with borrowing in domestic currency. It follows that countries with floating exchange rates are less likely to experience the kind of excessive foreign currency inflows that a fixed exchange rate tends to encourage. Moreover, a floating exchange rate does not offer easy opportunities for profit to speculators, and this reduces the risk that a floating currency becomes the target of a speculative attack. From a macroeconomic perspective a floating exchange rate regime certainly enhances the freedom of monetary policy to pursue domestic objectives; it avoids the erosion of external competitiveness and facilitates the adjustment of balance of payments disequilibria. But these benefits are by no means certain, particularly as regards their intensity or duration, because, in a system of financial globalization, exchange rates do not respond exclusively to incentives and impulses of a domestic nature. Moreover, as has been mentioned earlier, a floating exchange rate regime does not appear to be able to correct structural current account imbalances in a country's balance of payments, nor does it provide a full guarantee against the risk of misalignments. The fact that monetary policy is not tied to the objective of exchange rate stability has often generated expectations of higher inflation. To remedy this, other forms of 'anchorage' have been associated with a floating regime, such as setting an inflation target for monetary policy, as in the case of Canada, the United Kingdom and Sweden, or delegating the task of ensuring price stability to a central bank with full decision-making independence, as in the case of EMU.

From a systemic perspective, floating exchange regimes have resulted in greater volatility and variability of exchange rates, increasing uncertainty and transaction costs. The volatility of the exchange rates of the principal currencies against the dollar has increased from practically zero in the Bretton Woods era to a range of 5–20 per cent in the period between 1973 to 2002 (IMF 2003b, p. 67) but does not appear to be on a rising trend. Economists have long debated the question whether the volatility of exchange rates has a negative effect on international trade and investment. Traditional empirical analyses tend to rule out the existence of a negative effect, given the availability on the market – even if at non-negligible costs – of efficient instruments to cover exchange risks. On the other hand, there is a vast store of anecdotal evidence regarding investors who are powerless in the face of abrupt and large changes in exchange rates that wipe out the modest profits achievable with productive activities. Other stories speak of the need for multinational corporations to reconsider localization decisions for production plants in the light of exchange rate trends. This was reportedly the case of Japanese industries with plants in the United Kingdom, following the strong rise of sterling against the euro in the early 2000s, which negatively affected exports to continental European markets.

The most worrying aspect of floating exchange rate regimes, made more evident by the working of global finance, is their propensity to generate one-way trends in which the movements of market quotations feed on themselves, overshooting exchange rate equilibrium levels. In an overshooting scenario, fluctuations in a currency's exchange rates can be so wide and steep, and an inversion of the trend so improbable, that the exchange market effectively grinds to a halt. In the case of a downward overshooting, exchange dealers will continue to bid increasingly depreciated quotations for that currency, but no transaction will take place at those prices because they will be considered in any event insufficient to induce holders of foreign currency to sell. This, for example, is what occurred in Indonesia during the financial crisis of 1997–98.[10] These kinds of scenarios can also occur on stock markets, in which case the supervisory authorities can suspend trading in a security when an excessively steep drop in the share price occurs, allowing operators a pause for thought before trading resumes. Unfortunately, this cannot happen on currency markets, and even the most extreme and anomalous variations of exchange rates are free to influence the domestic prices of all internationally traded goods and services. The result of this propensity to overshoot is to increase the likelihood of misalignments of exchange rates, as well as to make their correction by monetary authorities more difficult and costly in terms of time and resources. It follows that even a floating exchange rate regime needs to be supported by consistent economic policies. A country that wants to correct a disequilibrium in its balance of payments, say a surplus, through an appreciation of its exchange rate, may rely on the price mechanism (raising the cost of exports and decreasing the cost of imports), but it must also adopt an expansionary monetary policy to offset the restrictive effect on global demand that the appreciation of the exchange rate entails. Similarly, a depreciation of the exchange rate designed to correct a deficit must be accompanied by monetary tightening to compensate the inflationary impact of the devaluation. Without supportive economic policies, the authorities risk losing control of exchange rate movements, triggering destabilizing capital flows and setting in motion an overshooting trend.

4.3.3   Intermediate Solutions

Out of the broad spectrum of intermediate exchange rate regimes, the adjustable peg and the crawling peg stand out. As in the case of extreme fixed rate regimes, the main motivation for adopting an adjustable peg is to provide an anchor for monetary policy and guide the expectations of market participants towards price stability. The positive contribution of adjustable peg regimes in the fight against inflation has been demonstrated by the long phase of worldwide price stability during the Bretton Woods years in the 1950s and the 1960s. The experience of Italy in the EMS is another case in point. Its monetary authorities adopted a stabilization strategy at the end of the 1970s to cope with strong inflationary pressures stemming from the perverse interaction between a constantly depreciating exchange rate and a highly reactive wage indexation mechanism. As a result of its entry in the exchange rate mechanism of the EMS and its adoption of a monetary policy consistent with the exchange rate objective, the rate of inflation in Italy gradually dropped from 22 per cent in 1979 to 5 per cent at the end of the 1980s. The stabilizing influence of the lira's entry into the EMS on inflationary expectations took effect despite the fact that the parity of the lira was gradually devalued through periodic modest 'realignments' in the course of the decade.

But it is precisely this proven ability of fixed exchange rates to influence market behaviour and expectations that makes the adjustable peg regime vulnerable unless it is accompanied by consistent economic policies. Generally speaking, the adoption of an adjustable peg can soften the perception of exchange rate risk among market participants. These tend to view a commitment to maintaining the peg as a guarantee of unlimited protection against exchange risks. So, while they are aware that this commitment can be reneged on at any moment since the parity is indeed adjustable, they remain convinced that they can disengage from exchange rate risk on time. In a country with high inflation, the adoption of a parity generates market expectations of a reduction in interest rates that encourages investors to purchase fixed income financial assets denominated in the national currency with the prospect of making a capital gain and earning the interest differential. This will give rise to capital inflows that tend to sustain the exchange rate and bolster the country's official reserves. At the same time, given the perceived reduction of exchange rate risk, domestic market participants will deem it more convenient to borrow foreign currency at lower interest rates than those available on the domestic market, generating more inflows of capital and further strengthening the exchange rate.

In the context of an appreciating exchange rate, falling interest rates, easy access to foreign borrowing and rapidly increasing official reserves, it is highly likely that the authorities' determination to pursue policies of austerity and structural adjustment will weaken. At the same time, if inflation in the country in question (despite a downward trend) remains higher than in its main trading partners, then a stable or appreciating exchange rate will result in a loss of external competitiveness. This will have a negative impact on the balance of payments and, in the long run, on employment. To some extent, the loss of competitiveness can be reabsorbed through increases in labour productivity, improvements in the quality of export products and the adoption of more effective marketing strategies. Beyond a certain limit, however, unless the exchange regime is supported by adequate measures for containing domestic demand through fiscal and wage policies, the loss cannot be made good. Without these accompanying measures the deterioration of the country's competitive position will ultimately provoke a misalignment and a higher perception of exchange risk by financial players both at home and abroad, who will then take steps to cut back on their foreign currency debts and financial investments in that country. In both cases, this will give rise to a capital outflow, a reduction in official reserves and a downward pressure on the exchange rate.

It is in circumstances such as these that adjustable peg regimes can trigger or even provide incentives for speculation against the parity. In these regimes, monetary conduct remains at the discretion of central banks, but they commit to intervene by buying and selling national currency against foreign currency at predetermined prices set at levels more or less close to the parity they aim to maintain. The ability of a central bank to withstand downward pressure on the exchange rate depends on the volume of official reserves it can dip into in order to intervene to counter the pressure and on its willingness to adjust interest rates to combat speculation. If the market comes to believe that these instruments are not available due to 'lack of ammunition', or for political reasons, market participants will speculate that the country's monetary authorities will be obliged either to devalue the parity or to abandon the pegged regime, letting the exchange rate fluctuate. In both cases, a profit opportunity materializes that can be exploited through speculative activities. This essentially entails borrowing the national currency and selling it immediately back on the market against a foreign currency at a price that will be quite close to the parity level thanks to the interventions of the central bank. The cost of the transaction is given by the differential between the interest paid on the national currency and that earned on the foreign currency, while a profit is made only if the national currency is devalued. In that case, speculators can resell the foreign currency at a higher price than the one they originally paid, reimburse the loan and pocket the difference. The central bank can make speculation more costly by increasing the interest rate on the national currency, but if the market expects a relatively sharp devaluation, the interest rate necessary to counter speculation effectively would have to be extremely high, and therefore incompatible with the fundamental requirements of the economy.[11] The experience of Sweden during the EMS crisis of September 1992 is often cited as a case in point, when an increase in interest rates to 500 per cent was insufficient to halt speculative attacks on the krone. The market guessed, correctly, that a similar degree of monetary restriction could not have lasted long without damaging the economic system, and speculation continued apace until the exchange rate was devalued and interest rates lowered.

The long history of currency crises is peppered with similar stories and this has contributed to the consolidation of the convention that adjustable exchange rate regimes are always destined to become an easy target for speculation, and will inevitably succumb to an attack. In reality, this is true only when a misalignment of the exchange rate has emerged and monetary authorities cannot or will not pursue economic policies that dovetail with the objective of maintaining stable exchange rates. Speculation, in other words, does not attack an exchange rate parity for the same reason George Mallory famously gave in the early 1920s, when asked what had inspired him to climb Everest: 'because it's there'. Speculation is triggered by inconsistent economic policies and penalizes attempts by authorities to use the exchange rate regime to attain credibility on the market without wanting to abide by the market's rules.

To sum up, intermediate foreign exchange regimes can make an important contribution to strategies of disinflation and financial adjustment, but they place strict constraints of consistency and continuity on the conduct of economic policies. If these constraints are respected, the stability of foreign exchange rates will help speed up the achievement of strategic objectives, decreasing their costs in economic and social terms. If the constraints are not respected, the rigidity of the exchange rate will become a source of economic distortion, weakening the competitive position of the country and exposing its currency to speculative attacks. In practice, in the context of the relationship between monetary authorities and the market, this alternative is less stark: the market will react negatively only where inconsistent policies result in losses of competitiveness deemed to be unsustainable. This may allow the authorities to pursue deliberately a strategy of contained competitive loss to encourage stability-oriented behaviour by the corporate sector and consumers. In this case, they must be ready to modify the parity quickly before the market decides that the loss has become unsustainable and the crisis becomes unmanageable. In any case, the adjustment of the parity, even when not accompanied by a currency crisis, provides an opportunity for reconsidering the adequacy of strategies to adjust payments imbalances and may facilitate a return to consistency in economic policies.

4.4 WHAT TO DO?

The answer an economist might give a policy-maker who asks which regime is best is aptly summed up in a paper written by Jeffrey Frankel titled: 'No single currency regime is right for all countries or at all times' (1999). In it, Frankel effectively dismisses the theory that in the current era of financial globalization only polar regimes are suited to all countries at all times. He settles instead on a more open-minded approach that views all exchange rate regimes as being potentially useful depending on the underlying economic conditions of individual countries, their geopolitical position and the objectives they intend to pursue. Hence, a floating currency regime may be the best option for major industrial economies, but it will need to be managed with occasional interventions to avoid misalignments. A rigidly fixed currency regime may be the answer for small open economies with a history of hyperinflation or for countries whose monetary conditions are wholly dictated by the decisions of a major foreign central bank. In these instances, a currency board or even a unilateral monetary union (dollarization or euroization) might represent the best solution. According to Frankel, however, even intermediate exchange rate regimes can be useful in countries that are not yet fully integrated into the international financial system, or for major emerging countries in certain stages of their economic development such as the monetary stabilization phase. In this case adjustable peg regimes may be used to pave the way for an eventual 'unpegging' of the exchange rate and for the adoption of an alternative reference anchor for monetary policy. Williamson (2000) took a similar stance when he supported the 'revival of the intermediate option' for major emerging countries, highlighting how this could prevent the most glaring exchange rate misalignments that both extreme solutions can trigger. Moreover, empirical research (Calvo and Reinhart 2002) has shed light on the 'fear of floating' that can be observed in many emerging countries and induces them to adopt managed float regimes. Put simply, when a nation's economy is in good shape, a floating exchange rate tends to become overvalued due to the inflows of capital from abroad, eroding the competitive position of the country. When the economy is performing badly, the exchange rate depreciates, triggering an increase in the burden of foreign currency debt that these countries are virtually obliged to accumulate in order to finance economic development and investments in infrastructure. There are also indications that intermediate exchange rate regimes will continue to play an important role in the processes of economic and monetary integration at regional levels, both in Europe and in Asia (see Chapter 14).

Economists at the IMF have also been moving gradually towards a 'middle of the road' position. It is considered likely that the intensification of the processes of financial globalization will be accompanied by a tendency to abandon the adjustable peg regimes, but not necessarily result in the adoption of the two more extreme versions, and that the more flexible among intermediate regimes, such as the crawling peg or managed floating will continue to be both useful and used (Mussa et al. 2000a; Fischer 2001). More recently, a comprehensive IMF study (Rogoff et al. 2004, p. 49), analysing exchange rate regimes adopted by IMF member countries over the period 1940–2001, confirms that intermediate exchange rate regimes of various kinds continue to be widely used and that 'the view that intermediate regimes are an endangered species is belied by their persistence, while their performance is not dominated by either of the polar regimes'.

All signs, then, are that the choice of currency regime must be made on a case by case basis, whilst recognizing that the decision, whatever it may be, has many implications for a country's economic policy strategy. In other words, the terms of the question may be summed up by the following three statements:

1. Every exchange rate regime must be managed: there is no regime that runs on 'automatic pilot', leaving the authorities free to busy themselves with more important things;
2. Policies do matter: the quality of economic policies must be high in any exchange rate regime, given that none of them can compensate for policy errors;
3. Exchange regimes do matter: if the regime is right, economic policies will be more effective and sustainable.

NOTES

1. Sarno and Taylor (2002, p. 1) note, however, that empirical analysis shows that the foreign exchange market is not an efficient market, one where 'prices fully reflect information available to market participants and it should be impossible for a trader to earn excess returns to speculation'.
2. ACI–The Financial Market Association, a private, self-regulated entity, was founded in 1955 and draws its 15 000 members from over 80 countries. In 2000 it drafted 'The Model Code – The International Code of Conduct and Practice for the Financial Markets' (www.aciforex.com). The Code has been widely adopted by market participants and has been endorsed by supervisors and regulators in many countries.
3. The literature on exchange rate economics is enormous and the references made reflect my personal inclinations without any pretence to comprehensiveness (Mundell 1968; Dornbusch 1980; Kenen 1988; Krugman 1989; Isard 1995; Taylor M. 1995; McKinnon 1996; Sarno and Taylor 2002).
4. In recent empirical studies there is some emerging consensus that the purchasing power parity (PPP) (namely, the exchange rate equating national price levels in two major countries) could be a long-run equilibrium condition for real exchange rates among major industrial countries (Sarno and Taylor 2002, p. 2).
5. Krugman (1991) provides a good summary of the theoretical clashes between those who affirm and those who deny the effectiveness of exchange rate changes.
6. A detailed explanation of the US approach to exchange rate policy is provided by Taylor J. (2007, pp. 278–82).

7. Among the most comprehensive reviews of the literature see: Corden (2002), specifically devoted to the choice of exchange rate regimes; and Sarno and Taylor (2002, pp. 171–207), especially Chapter 6 on 'currency unions, pegged rates and target zone models'.
8. See, in particular, the broad analytical survey by Gandolfo (2001) and the contributions included in the collection of essays edited by Williamson (1994).
9. On exchange rate misalignments, see Chapter 5, section 5.2.4.
10. During that crisis the exchange rate went from around 2500 rupiahs per US dollar in early 1997 to over 15 000 rupiahs per US dollar in mid-1998. It subsequently stabilized at around 7000 rupiahs (IMF–IEO 2003, p. 71).
11. If investors believe that devaluation will take place in a matter of days, the cost of borrowing may be very high in percentage terms but will only have a marginal influence on the potential profit of the speculative transaction.

PART II

Global finance between crisis and reform

5.   The crises of global finance

Madamina, il catalogo è questo. [Madam, this is the catalogue.]
Lorenzo da Ponte (1787) from the *libretto* of Mozart's Don Giovanni

Financial markets are markets in information, and information by its nature is asymmetric and incomplete. It arrives on an unpredictable schedule and when it arrives markets react. Inevitably, then, sharp changes in asset prices – sometimes so sharp as to threaten the stability of the financial system and the economy – will occur from time to time.

Barry Eichengreen (2002, p. 4)

5.1   HOW MANY CRISES?

Financial crises with international repercussions have occurred throughout the history of the world economy, well before the word 'globalization' was coined and circulated in print.[1] International lending, sometimes with unpleasant consequences for the institution providing the credit or for private investors, is nothing new. The examples abound.[2] In 1343 the Florentine banks of Bardi and Peruzzi failed after King Edward III, to whom they had lent large sums of money, refused to honour the Crown's obligations, producing the first case of sovereign insolvency with international implications.[3] In 1720 the financial 'bubbles' generated by the South Sea Company in England and by the Mississippi Company in France burst, precipitating severe crises in the London and Paris stock markets and sending out international shockwaves.[4] A more systematic analysis of crises from the inception of the Gold Standard (around 1880) to the end of the twentieth century reveals that episodes of severe financial turbulence, affecting the exchange rate, the banking system or both, have been a recurrent feature in a broad sample of countries under different international monetary systems. However, the analysis also shows that 'since 1973 crisis frequency has been double that of the Bretton Woods and classical gold standard periods and matched only by the crisis-ridden 1920s and 1930s. History thus confirms that there is something different and disturbing about our age' (Bordo et al. 2001, p. 72).

The disquiet deepens if one broadens the definition of financial crisis to cover episodes of significant movements in the price of assets (broadly defined to include bonds, stocks, foreign currencies and real estate), accompanied by problems of market illiquidity. Indeed, the foreign exchange and banking crises of emerging countries of Latin America and Asia are only part of the story of financial instability in the last two decades of the twentieth century, when the roots of globalization burrowed deeper and deeper. A fuller account would include other key chapters covering the episodes of volatility and illiquidity in international bond markets during the 1990s; the misalignments of real exchange rates of the major world currencies in the 1980s and 1990s; and the 'bubbles' affecting stock markets and real estate markets in Japan in the 1980s and the United States and several other industrial countries in the 1990s.

Economists have paid varying degrees of attention to these types of financial instability. The financial crises of emerging countries have been the subject of countless papers and books which have provided extensive empirical evidence about the causes and the channels of propagation of disturbances on a global scale.[5] The cases of illiquid bond markets and of exchange rate misalignments among the major currencies have attracted considerably less attention by academic economists – with the notable exceptions of McKinnon (1996) and Obstfeld and Rogoff (2000) – and have been analysed mostly in the periodical reports issued by the IMF and the BIS. Bubbles in stock and real estate markets have only recently been the subject of renewed attention by analysts. After the 'Great Crash' of 1929, only the sudden and short-lived fall on Wall Street in October 1987 was thoroughly investigated by regulators, but mostly because of the role played by electronic broking systems in triggering and amplifying the downfall. The Japanese bubble of the 1980s was studied mostly by Japanese economists as was judged to be largely the result of structural problems specific to the economy of Japan (see Shiratsuka 2005). The boom of the US economy in the 1990s, associated with the information and communication technologies (ICT) revolution and the development of the 'new economy', generated bubbles in the US stock and real estate markets with significant international repercussions and led to a revival of interest in the subject.[6]

The vast economic literature on financial crises fails to shed any light, however, on an issue that is central for the purposes of this book: whether the various typologies of financial instability might be regarded as originating from a common cause and whether this cause has anything to do with the workings of global finance. In a survey article on financial instability, Eichengreen (2004), having defined a financial crisis as 'a sharp change in asset prices that leads to distress among financial market participants', goes on to analyse the main causes of financial instability. Eichengreen's survey identifies four main determinants of financial crises and instability: (1) unsustainable macroeconomic policies; (2) fragile financial systems;

(3) institutional weaknesses; and (4) flaws in the structure of international financial markets. All these factors have been at play in the debt crises of emerging countries. The first three categories relate mostly to causes of domestic origin, pointing to the inconsistency of monetary and fiscal policies with the exchange rate regime and the liberalization of capital movements, the inadequacy of prudential supervision of banks and financial institutions, and the lack of effective governance in the corporate sector. The fourth category includes exogenous causes originating from the operation of global financial markets, where information asymmetries, herd behaviour and competitive pressures combine to generate situations of boom and bust in capital flows, with attendant contagion effects. Although lately, increasing attention has been devoted in the literature to this last category of systemic dysfunctions, particularly as regards the activity of hedge funds,[7] the analysis of the primary causes of market dysfunctions is still insufficient.

Economists and historians have worked closely to identify the economic, social and psychological factors that have consistently contributed to the generation of crises. The interpretative model of financial, national and international crises, devised by an acute theorist of financial instability, Hyman Minsky (1972), and confirmed by the research of an eminent economic historian, Charles Kindleberger (1978, 2000), seems to me entirely applicable also to the pathologies of global finance.[8] According to this model, at the root of crisis is an event that is external to the macroeconomic system – to use Minksy's word, *a displacement* – that induces market participants to expect an increase in the price of both financial assets (such as shares, bonds and currencies) and real assets (land or buildings). In the past, these displacements consisted primarily of wars, the discovery of new territories, or inventions. In the age of financial globalization, in addition to technological innovations, displacements could include political and institutional changes, such as the fall of the Berlin wall or the creation of EMU. Whatever its cause, the displacement triggers an economic boom that is financed through credit expansion, generating an increase in money supply. The boom creates a climate of euphoria on the markets and an acceleration of financial transactions (overtrading), where the overestimation of expected profits translates into a sustained increase in prices. Euphoria, however, makes the upswing vulnerable to sudden changes in expectations as soon as the prices no longer appear sustainable, and this in turn persuades some participants to cash in the profits made up to that point. In a climate like this, it is possible that a massive closure of positions will follow, with a strong negative impact on prices. This, in turn, slows down the entry of new buyers into the market and sows panic among investors, precipitating a headlong rush to sell. The generalized panic of the market participants triggers heavy capital losses, bankruptcies and crises. The Minsky–Kindleberger model assigns a crucial role to the set of rules and institutions that govern the processes of monetary and credit creation, which I would define using the all-encompassing term 'monetary constitution'. In every country, the monetary constitution is the outcome of the decisions made at a national level by the various political and institutional bodies, but also of external obligations arising from the prevailing international monetary system. In the Bretton Woods era, members of the IMF were obliged to adopt a monetary constitution aimed at maintaining stable exchange rates by pursuing appropriate interest rate policies and, if necessary, imposing restrictions on capital movements. The current global financial system leaves countries free to choose their own monetary constitution, but exerts strong pressure in favour of floating exchange rates and the liberalization of currency and capital transactions (see Williamson and Mahar 1998). In this context, it is conceivable that strong and rapid interactions can materialize through the operation of global finance between the monetary policies pursued by the major countries, the fluctuations of the exchange rates of reserve currencies, and the direction of international financial flows.

The remainder of this chapter will be devoted to the analysis of the episodes of financial instability that have been recorded in the last two decades of the twentieth century to determine whether historical developments are compatible with the Minsky–Kindleberger model. In particular, it will examine whether conditions of excessive financing and 'overtrading' have materialized in response to 'displacements' of various kinds.

5.2   THE CAUSES OF FINANCIAL INSTABILITY

5.2.1   The Economic Background

The overall economic background against which recurrent episodes of financial instability have been recorded is surprisingly benign (see Table 5.1). Global real output between 1985 and 2006 grew on average between 2 and 5 per cent a year, with a low of 1.7 per cent in 1991 and a high of 5.4 per cent in 2006. Except for Japan, where a prolonged phase of stagnation has been recorded since the early 1990s, real growth in the rest of the industrial world has, on average, hovered between 2–4 per cent in the United States and between 1–3 per cent in the European Union. There have been very few years of recession or markedly low growth: 1991 in the United States, 1993 in the European Union. In emerging and developing countries, real output in 1985–2006 grew on average between 3.5 and 6.5 per cent a year, with a

Table 5.1 World output growth and inflation (%)

	1985	1986	1987	1988	1989	1990	1991	1992	1993	1994	1995
Real output growth											
World	3.8	3.7	4.0	4.7	3.8	2.9	1.7	2.4	2.5	3.9	3.7
Advanced economies	3.7	3.3	3.6	4.7	3.9	3.1	1.5	2.3	1.4	3.4	2.8
United States	4.1	3.5	3.4	4.1	3.5	1.9	−0.2	3.3	2.7	4.0	2.5
Euro area	2.5	2.7	2.7	3.9	3.6	2.6	1.1	1.0	−0.2	2.8	2.9
Japan	5.1	3.0	3.8	6.8	5.3	5.2	3.4	1.0	0.2	1.1	1.9
Developing countries	4.0	4.3	4.6	4.8	3.6	2.6	2.0	2.7	4.1	4.6	5.1
Consumer price index											
Advanced economies	5.4	3.2	3.2	3.6	4.5	5.1	4.7	3.5	3.1	2.6	2.5
United States	3.5	1.8	3.7	4.1	4.8	5.4	4.2	3.0	3.0	2.6	2.8
Euro area	6.4	4.4	4.4	6.4	18.2	26.6	10.8	11.4	7.0	4.6	4.3
Japan	2.0	0.6	0.1	0.7	2.3	3.1	3.2	1.7	1.3	0.7	−0.1
Developing countries	29.4	23.7	29.7	43.8	59.7	65.5	52.6	104.4	97.9	76.3	34.1

Table 5.1 *(continued)*

	1996	1997	1998	1999	2000	2001	2002	2003	2004	2005	2006
Real output growth											
World	4.1	4.3	2.8	3.7	4.8	2.5	3.1	4.0	5.3	4.9	5.4
Advanced economies	2.9	3.4	2.6	3.5	4.0	1.2	1.6	1.9	3.3	2.5	3.1
United States	3.7	4.5	4.2	4.4	3.7	0.8	1.6	2.5	3.9	3.2	3.3
Euro area	2.0	2.9	3.0	3.0	3.9	1.9	0.9	0.8	2.0	1.4	2.6
Japan	2.6	1.4	-1.8	-0.1	2.9	0.2	0.3	1.4	2.7	1.9	2.2
Developing countries	5.8	5.4	3.1	4.1	6.0	4.3	5.0	6.7	7.7	7.5	7.9
Consumer price index											
Advanced economies	2.4	2.0	1.5	1.4	2.2	2.1	1.5	1.8	2.0	2.3	2.3
United States	2.9	2.3	1.5	2.2	3.4	2.8	1.6	2.3	2.7	3.4	3.2
Euro area	3.5	2.6	2.1	1.1	2.1	2.4	2.3	2.1	2.1	2.2	2.2
Japan	0.3	1.7	0.6	-0.3	-0.4	-0.8	-0.9	-0.2	–	-0.6	0.2
Developing countries	17.6	11.3	11.1	10.3	7.1	6.7	5.8	5.8	5.6	5.4	5.3

Source: IMF, *World Economic Outlook*, various issues.

low of 2.0 in 1991 and a high of 7.9 per cent in 2006. Inflation has been generally declining in advanced economies, from 4.5 per cent on average in the mid-1980s to 2.0 per cent on average in the 2000s; among emerging and developing countries the rate of disinflation has been even more remarkable, falling from an average of over 70 per cent a year in 1990–95 to an average of around 6 per cent in 2002–06.

The pattern of payments imbalances among industrial countries and between them and the rest of the world has been much more disturbing (see Figure 5.1). The key destabilizing factor has been the US balance of payments deficit: after a decade of relative equilibrium following the devaluations of the dollar in 1971 and 1973, the current account balance deteriorated sharply in the mid-1980s reaching a deficit of over 3 per cent of GDP in 1985–86. In 1991 it returned to near equilibrium following the coordinated adjustment strategy adopted within the G7 (which will be analysed in detail in Chapter 7). It then began deteriorating again during the 1990s, reaching a record deficit of $848 billion or 6.5 per cent of GDP in 2006. The counterpart of the US current account deficits has been the surplus of Japan and of the European Union until the end of the 1990s, and of emerging and developing countries since 2000 (with the EU surplus gradually being reduced to near balance). Against this background, the monetary policies of the three key-currency centres have been mostly influenced by domestic developments in output and inflation, and exchange rates have been left to the interplay of market forces (see Figure 5.2). It is indeed remarkable that in a scenario of significant price stability, good growth performances and sound monetary and exchange rate policies, financial instability has found so many opportunities to manifest itself, affecting in turn all regions of the world and all segments of the main asset markets.

5.2.2 The Debt Crises of Emerging Countries

The financial crises that struck the major emerging economies in the 1990s can be grouped into three distinct phases, characterized by different global economic scenarios. The first phase began with the Mexican crisis that struck at the end of 1994, highlighting the role played by global financial players in the sudden and massive turnaround of capital flows.[9] The second phase started with the crisis in Thailand (July 1997), rapidly spreading to nearby Asian countries such as Indonesia, Malaysia, the Philippines and South Korea (December 1997), and revealing how international contagion operated in the global financial market. The third phase originated with the collapse of the rouble in August 1998 and Russia's subsequent default on its external debt. This phase induced global players to reconsider the

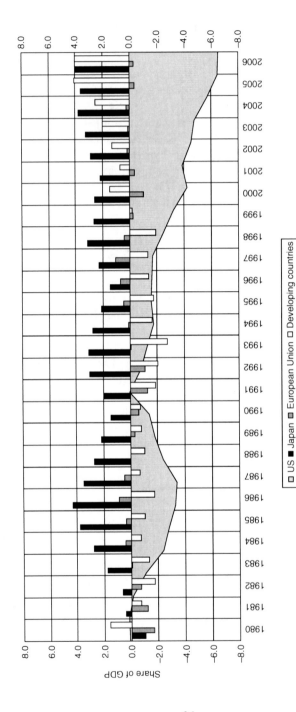

Source: Bank of Italy elaboration from IMF, *World Economic Outlook*, various issues.

Figure 5.1 Current account balances

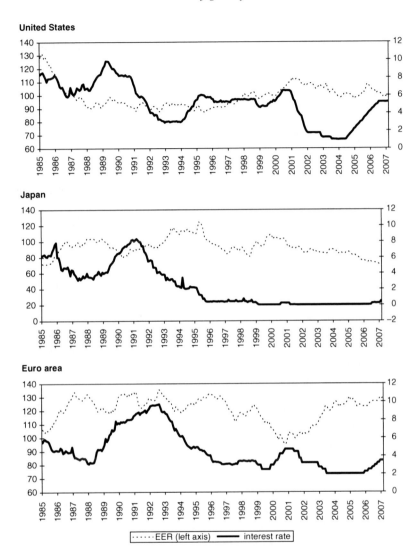

United States

Japan

Euro area

······ EER (left axis) ——— interest rate

Sources:
Real effective exchange rates (EER): for the United States and Japan deflated with producer prices (source: Bank of Italy); for the Euro area deflated with consumer prices (source: BIS). Index base year: 2000 = 100.
Interest rates: Board of Governors of the Federal Reserve System (effective federal funds rate; monthly averages of daily figures); Bank of Japan (collateralized overnight call rate; end of month); Euro area: Bundesbank (overnight money market rate; monthly average for 1985–1998), and ECB (interest rates for main refinancing operations; end of month for 1999-to date).

Figure 5.2   United States, Japan, euro area: real effective exchange rates and policy interest rates (monthly averages)

sustainability of exchange rate pegs in a number of countries on a global scale. The reassessment resulted in a new round of financial turbulence affecting Brazil (January 1999), Turkey (February 2001) and Argentina (December 2001).

Although these various cases presented a broad range of pathologies (a collapse of the exchange rate, illiquidity or insolvency of banks, corporate bankruptcies, and so on), the key determinants of the crises were the financial markets' doubts about the ability of the countries concerned to service their external debt. In some cases, the crisis involved an outright default on the sovereign debt (Russia and Argentina); in all other cases, the default was avoided through a more or less voluntary restructuring of the debt (involving a rescheduling of repayments of principal and interest) or via the concession of large refinancing packages by official and private creditors.

The Mexican crisis

The causes of the Mexican crisis were both endogenous and exogenous. Domestic imbalances and structural weaknesses combined with unfavourable developments in the economic situation in the major industrial countries, especially the United States, paved the way for deep financial turbulence. The US economy slid into recession in 1991 after a long period of strong growth in the 1980s. In 1992 deceleration also started in other industrial economies, more sharply in Japan, where the effects of the bursting of the stock and real estate bubble were beginning to be felt, more gradually in Europe. The monetary policy response in the United States and Japan was quick and aggressive. The Fed cut official rates from 8 per cent at the end of 1990 to 3 per cent in mid-1992, and kept them at this level until the beginning of 1994. The Bank of Japan lowered the discount rate from 6 per cent at the end of 1991 to 1.8 per cent in mid-1993, maintaining this level until mid-1995. The stance of monetary policy in Europe remained on the whole restrictive to counter the inflationary impact of German reunification. Official rates did not decline until after the EMS crisis of September 1992 (see page 119).

Against this background, private capital flows tended to move from the United States and Japan towards areas with higher interest rates: to Europe and emerging economies and in particular to Latin America and Asia. During 1990–93 Mexico recorded a net private capital inflow of $97 billion (see Table 5.2), two-thirds of which, according to IMF estimates (IMF 1995b), comprised portfolio investments. Mexico appeared highly attractive to foreign investors for a number of reasons. As an oil-producing country the market expected it would enjoy a comfortable balance of payments position; moreover, the Mexican economy was expected to benefit

Table 5.2   Mexico: net capital flows (billions of US dollars)

	1990	1991	1992	1993	1994	1995	1996	1997
Private capital								
flows, net	13.3	23.5	24.9	35.0	19.1	−19.6	14.6	28.5
Direct invest-								
ments, net	2.6	4.8	4.4	4.4	11.0	9.5	9.2	12.8
Portfolio invest-								
ment, net	−3.9	12.1	18.1	26.7	7.2	−9.8	12.4	4.2
Other flows	14.6	6.6	2.4	3.9	0.9	−19.3	−7.0	11.5
Official capital								
flows, net	−4.8	1.5	2.1	−1.5	−2.9	11.1	−2.7	−5.9
Reserve assets*	−3.5	−7.4	−1.0	−6.0	18.4	−9.6	−1.8	−10.5
Memorandum item								
Current account								
balance	−7.5	−14.6	−24.4	−23.4	−29.7	−1.6	−2.5	−7.7

Note: * A minus sign indicates an increase.

Source: IMF, *World Economic Outlook*, various issues.

considerably from participation in the NAFTA agreement signed at the end of 1992. Mexico had borrowed heavily from foreign lenders to implement an ambitious domestic investment programme, but this was considered sustainable for two reasons. First, because of the low level of US interest rates and, second, because of the weak trend of the dollar, which became evident towards the end of 1993 as the American monetary authorities carried out the delicate exercise of 'talking the dollar down' in the context of the trade negotiations with Japan (about which more will be said in the section 'The yen misalignment' – page 120). Financial markets did not seem to be overly concerned with the Mexican sovereign debt risk, the spread on which fell sharply until mid-1994 in line with the prevailing trend in other Latin American countries.

The situation changed suddenly at the beginning of 1994 when the Fed unexpectedly decided to tighten monetary policy to counter a possible overheating of the business cycle. Between February 1994 and the beginning of 1995 the federal funds rate rose from 3 to 6 per cent in a sequence of small changes that fuelled expectations of further increases, with negative repercussions on international bond and foreign exchange markets (see page 111). In Mexico, the deterioration of the domestic political situation (including the murder of the ruling party candidate in the 1994 presidential elections) produced a climate of growing uncertainty and had a negative impact on market sentiment towards Mexican risk. Doubts about the stability of the exchange rate led to large capital outflows, which the monetary authorities tried to counter by issuing short-term treasury bills denominated in pesos but indexed to the dollar exchange rate (the *tesobonos*). Towards the end of the year, difficulties in funding maturing *tesobonos* on the market generated a widespread crisis of confidence, which led to the abandonment of the currency peg on 20 December 1994, with very serious repercussions on the stability of the banking and financial system. Left free to float, the peso depreciated by 53 per cent until March 1995, when Mexico received a $51.6 billion financial assistance package from the United States and other industrial countries of the G10 as a bridge to loans to be provided by the IMF and the World Bank in support of a programme of macroeconomic adjustment. Subsequently the exchange rate stabilized (IMF 1995c, pp. 53–69). The massive injection of funds allowed Mexico to repay as much as $16 billion in *tesobonos* held by foreigners. This averted a default on sovereign debt but the bail-out of foreign *tesobonos* holders raised moral hazard implications for the working of the global financial system.

The tequila crisis, as it was immediately dubbed, did not trigger similarly acute episodes in other emerging countries, but did have a considerable impact on spreads on international bonds and exchange rates. The widening of the spreads resulted in a de facto closing down of the market for emerging countries' bonds for several weeks from January to March 1995 (IMF 2001c). Surprisingly, the impact of the tequila crisis was also felt by industrial countries. At the beginning of 1995 the US dollar weakened considerably in exchange markets for fear that Mexico's illiquidity would generate difficulties for American banks; tensions were also felt on the spreads of European countries such as Italy and Spain, belonging at the time to the group of 'high yielders' that were somehow linked to the emerging countries in the investment strategies of global players.

The Asian crisis
The macroeconomic and financial backdrop against which the Asian crises of 1997 materialized was heavily influenced by the prolonged stagnation of economic activity and private consumption in Japan and by the structural weaknesses of the Japanese banking and financial system. Monetary policy in Japan had already become strongly expansionary in the course of 1995, when the discount rate was lowered to 0.5 per cent to counter the strong appreciation of the yen (see Chapter 9). The provision of liquidity through expansionary policies was continued for several years, bringing market interest rates to zero. This opened up ample opportunities for global financial players to borrow in yen at low interest rates and invest in higher

interest rate countries (the yen carry trades), earning a large positive spread with minimum foreign exchange risk due to the prospect of a weakening yen. In Europe too, monetary policies were becoming more expansionary following the abatement of inflationary pressures in Germany and progress towards the establishment of EMU: short-term rates declined to about 3 per cent in Germany and to 4 per cent in other main European countries. In the United States a relatively more restrictive stance was maintained, with rates stable at around 5 per cent.

In these circumstances, international capital flows tended to move from Japan, Europe and Latin America towards the emerging countries of Asia and Eastern Europe. During 1993–96 the five Asian countries that would be hit by a crisis recorded a combined net inflow of private capital totalling $197 billion (Table 5.3). Foreign investors were attracted to the Asian 'dragons' by the spectacular performance of their economies, with high growth rates, rising productivity, low inflation and reasonably sound macroeconomic policies. In particular, Lamfalussy noted (2000, p. 28), these countries underwent a phase of 'over-investment' (reminiscent of the 'over-trading' of the Minsky–Kindleberger model), which resulted in substantial excess capacity in electronics, home appliances, automobiles and real estate. Institutional factors, such as the liberalization of capital

Table 5.3   Asian countries:[a] *net capital flows* (billions of US dollars)

	1993	1994	1995	1996	1997	1998	1999	2000	2001
Private capital flows, net	30.8	35.4	56.8	74.3	−5.6	−31.6	−13.9	−15.7	−16.2
Direct investments, net	6.7	6.5	10.3	11.7	10.2	11.5	14.6	14.3	8.3
Portfolio investment, net	25.0	13.3	18.6	26.9	8.9	−9.0	11.6	7.0	3.2
Other flows	−0.8	15.6	27.9	35.7	−24.7	−34.1	−40.4	−36.9	−27.7
Official capital flows, net	3.2	0.7	8.8	−4.7	13.7	17.0	−2.2	6.6	0.6
Reserve assets[b]	−20.0	−6.5	−17.5	−4.8	40.6	−46.9	−38.2	−22.4	−11.7
Memorandum item									
Current account balance	−13.5	−23.2	−39.8	−53.1	−25.5	69.7	62.7	47.1	32.6

Notes:
a.   Indonesia, Malaysia, Philippines, South Korea and Thailand.
b.   A minus sign indicates an increase.

Source: IMF, *World Economic Outlook*, October 2001 and April 2002 (rounded figures).

movements or the 'graduation' of Korea to membership of the OECD, also contributed to positive market sentiment with regard to extending credit to these countries. However, both global players and the monetary authorities of the countries concerned paid insufficient attention to the final destination of the funds borrowed on international capital markets, often used to finance large projects with very long time horizons and a very limited capacity to generate earnings in foreign exchange.

The triggering factors of the Asian crisis are hard to pinpoint. In Thailand, where the crisis began, it is unclear why foreign investors suddenly became concerned about the sustainability of the country's balance of payments, which had recorded large current account deficits for a number of years, to over 8 per cent of GDP in 1996. The outlook for Thai exports may have been negatively influenced by the appreciation of the US dollar, to which the Thai baht was pegged, or by the deepening recession of the Japanese economy. Be that as it may, domestic and foreign market participants began to liquidate their baht-denominated assets in the early months of 1997, forcing the central bank to intervene to maintain the stability of the exchange rate. As rumours about the adequacy of the central bank's official reserves began to circulate in the market, the outflow of capital intensified, leading to the floating of the baht in July, which precipitated a sharp devaluation. In the second half of 1997 the outflow of capital from Thailand via the banking system was in the order of $18 billion (Lamfalussy 2000, p. 32). The Thai crisis induced global players to review the sustainability of the external position of other countries in the region. Tensions spread quickly to Indonesia and the Philippines during the summer and finally to Korea in December, again resulting in the sharp depreciation of the exchange rate and insolvency of financial intermediaries and private corporations.[10] Only in Malaysia and Hong Kong were the authorities able to contain the market pressures by reintroducing capital and exchange controls and by adopting innovative but unorthodox market intervention techniques to counter speculative attacks on the exchange rate (see Chapter 10). For the five countries most seriously affected, the crisis opened a five-year period of sustained capital outflows, totalling $100 billion (Table 5.3). After the outbreak of the crisis, Thailand, Korea and Indonesia applied for financial assistance from the IMF. The three countries received a total of $117 billion from the IMF, the World Bank, the Asian Development Bank (ADB) and from G10 governments (Lamfalussy 2000, pp. 33–4). The official financing allowed Asian countries to repay to some extent the obligations incurred by domestic private banks and corporations vis-à-vis foreign financial institutions and investors, thus raising again moral hazard implications. In the case of Korea, the IMF package involved a debt rescheduling and a plan for commercial banks to roll-over credit lines to Korean borrowers. In the end, the plan entailed conversion of bank debts into Korean government bonds for a total of $24 billion (Desai 2003, p. 126).

The Asian crisis was the first case of turbulence in the era of financial globalization in which contagion effects unfolded with great intensity and rapidity throughout a large region of the world, affecting the lives and economic fortunes of tens of millions of people. The channel through which the contagion spread was essentially foreign trade, as the devaluation of the Thai baht was seen as a key negative factor for the competitive position of Thailand's main trading partners in the region. There is little doubt, however, that the Thai crisis acted as a 'wake-up call' for global players, inducing them to reassess the risk on their total financial exposure to the region as a whole.[11]

Russia–Brazil–Turkey–Argentina

Following the Asian crisis, four significant episodes were recorded in the period 1998–2001, affecting countries in different regions of the world and with different economic and financial profiles. To consider these episodes as additional outbreaks of the Asian contagion would be misleading. In fact, several months elapsed between the end of the Asian crisis (December 1997) and the Russian default (August 1998) and the triggering factors of the crisis were quite different. Indeed, Russia was regarded by global financial players as a superpower with huge natural resources and attractive profit opportunities, while its obvious structural and institutional weaknesses were seen as manageable in the context of the transition from a socialist to a market economy system. Contrary to other emerging countries, for a number of years before the crisis Russia had a current account surplus in its balance of payments, thanks to oil and gas exports. At the same time, considerable capital inflows from foreign investors, attracted mostly by the privatization process, were almost entirely offset by domestic capital outflows, mainly through banking channels, as residents were obviously sceptical about the outcome of the transition and the stability of the exchange rate (see Table 5.4). Foreign direct and portfolio investment flows to Russia were encouraged by the strong political support the Russian government seemed to enjoy in the West, as witnessed by the decision to associate Russia to the G7 Summit meetings in 1997, and substantial IMF lending. The underlying factor that upset this precarious balance was the decline in the price of oil and gas, more than the activity of global financial markets (Lamfalussy 2000, p. 45). The declining trend of oil prices, already clear in 1997, accelerated in early 1998 when London Brent was quoted at $17 per barrel and fell to less than $12 in August. Still, it took a letter by George Soros to the editor of the *Financial Times* published on 13 August 1998 to precipitate the

Table 5.4 Net capital flows: selected countries (billions of US dollars)

	1993	1994	1995	1996	1997	1998	1999	2000	2001	2002
Argentina										
Private capital flows, net	9.8	13.1	4.2	10.7	16.4	16.3	12.1	6.9	−16.5	−9.0
Direct investments, net	1.1	2.5	3.0	4.8	4.6	4.6	7.1	7.3	2.0	2.8
Portfolio investment, net	6.1	9.5	2.3	9.6	11.0	8.8	−6.8	−2.6	−9.5	−4.6
Other flows	2.6	1.1	−1.1	−3.7	0.7	2.9	11.8	2.2	−9.0	−7.1
Official capital flows, net	3.3	0.6	3.5	1.5	1.1	2.1	1.6	1.8	11.1	−2.3
Reserve assets*	−4.4	−0.6	0.1	−3.8	−3.1	−3.4	−1.1	0.4	12.0	4.4
Memorandum item										
CA balance	−8.0	−11.0	−5.1	−6.8	−12.1	−14.5	−11.9	−9.0	−3.8	8.7
Brazil										
Private capital flows, net	12.9	10.0	30.4	34.6	25.0	18.8	11.6	26.2	19.0	−3.5
Direct investments, net	−0.4	0.9	3.3	11.3	17.9	26.0	26.9	30.5	24.7	14.1
Portfolio investment, net	14.2	10.0	8.5	21.5	12.9	18.0	0.3	3.0	−3.9	−6.2
Other flows	−0.9	−0.9	18.6	1.8	−5.8	−25.2	−15.7	−7.3	−1.8	−11.4
Official capital flows, net	−2.5	−1.4	−1.9	−1.1	0.8	10.9	5.2	−7.2	7.9	12.2
Reserve assets*	−8.7	−7.2	−12.9	−8.3	7.9	7.6	8.2	3.4	−2.9	−2.0
Memorandum item										
CA balance	−0.6	−1.7	−18.4	−23.5	−30.5	−33.4	−25.3	−24.2	−23.2	−7.6

Russia

Private capital flows, net	5.9	−16.3	5.3	−13.3	−8.2	−13.2	−14.4	−29.5	2.8	13.3
Direct investments, net	0.9	0.4	1.5	1.7	1.7	1.5	1.1	−0.5	0.2	−0.1
Portfolio investment, net	5.0	0.1	−1.6	2.1	1.3	0.3	−0.8	−9.9	−0.2	3.3
Other flows	0.0	−16.8	5.5	−17.1	−11.2	−15.1	−14.7	−19.1	2.7	10.0
Official capital flows, net	−3.6	−11.5	−4.9	−5.7	−2.2	−0.7	−4.6	−4.4	−4.3	−9.9
Reserve assets*	−4.9	3.4	−4.9	6.1	−0.4	10.6	−5.4	−18.9	−12.0	−12.9

Memorandum item

CA balance	2.6	7.8	7.0	10.8	−0.1	0.2	24.6	46.8	33.9	29.1

Turkey

Private capital flows, net	9.9	−3.1	6.3	6.4	7.5	0.4	6.9	9.8	−14.3	13.7
Direct investments, net	0.6	0.6	0.8	0.6	0.6	0.6	0.1	0.1	2.8	0.9
Portfolio investment, net	0.2	0.7	0.9	−0.9	0.3	−6.5	−0.2	0.0	−0.9	−2.6
Other flows	9.1	−4.4	4.6	6.7	6.6	6.3	7.0	9.7	−16.2	15.4
Official capital flows, net	−0.9	−1.1	−0.2	−0.9	−0.5	−1.2	−1.5	3.1	9.9	−6.2
Reserve assets*	−0.8	−1.5	−6.2	−5.9	−3.9	−0.2	−5.7	−0.4	2.7	−6.2

Memorandum item

CA balance	−5.5	4.0	−0.5	−2.1	−2.1	2.0	−1.3	−9.8	3.4	−1.5

Note: * A minus sign indicates an increase.

Source: IMF, *World Economic Outlook*, various issues.

crisis. Soros, the famous hedge fund manager who had successfully led the attack against sterling in the ERM in 1992, simply questioned the sustainability of the exchange rate peg of the rouble in the light of the deteriorating outlook of the balance of payments and the willingness of the G7 countries to support an expansion of IMF financial assistance to Russia without clear commitments by the authorities to address its structural imbalances. As pressures mounted on the foreign exchange market, Russia decided on 17 August to let the rouble float and declared a unilateral moratorium on the servicing of its rouble-denominated debt (a large share of which had been underwritten by foreign investors).

The Russian crisis had major international repercussions that posed a serious threat to the stability of the global financial system in the last quarter of 1998 (see page 113 below). Once the shock was absorbed, however, significant changes of a more durable nature were reflected in the attitude of financial markets towards emerging countries. A sharp reduction in the 'appetite' for this type of risk resulted in a steep decline in the net flow of private capital to emerging markets. After a peak of $228 billion in 1996, private flows dropped to $192 billion in 1997 following the Asian crisis, before falling to $76 billion in 1998 and hovering around that level until 2002 (see Table 5.5). In the context of an overall strategy of risk aversion, global players singled out major emerging countries that continued to adopt pegged exchange rate regimes. This attitude resulted in what some observers called a 'serial killer approach' whereby pressure was exerted in succession on each of the main currency-peggers until they eventually let the exchange rate float freely. It is important to note that this change in market sentiment took place in the context of a generalized loosening of monetary policies to counter recessionary trends in all the major industrial countries and especially in the United States, a condition that in previous years had provided the stimulus for a reorientation of global capital flows towards emerging and developing countries in pursuit of higher returns. The key factor guiding the strategies of global players after the Russian crisis was, instead, the search for 'quality' of risk, attracting funds towards 'safe havens' like the United States. This explains why, at the same time as interest rates were brought to record low levels in the United States, the dollar and the Wall Street stock market both recorded strong gains.

The first victim of this new approach was Brazil, forced to float the real in January 1999. In fact, as can be seen from Table 5.4, Brazil had enjoyed a considerable net inflow of capital in the second half of the 1990s, mostly in the form of direct and portfolio investment. The pressure came mostly from foreign banks, concerned about the sustainability of the exchange rate peg in the presence of a persistent deficit in the current account balance of payments (other flows in Table 5.4 turned negative from 1997 onwards). In

Table 5.5 Emerging market and developing countries: net capital flows (billions of US dollars)

	1994–96	1996	1997	1998	1999	2000	2001	2002	2003	2004	2005	2006
Private capital flows, net	156.4	228.3	191.7	76.2	74.6	56.7	70.2	88.3	173.3	238.6	257.2	255.8
Direct investments, net	98.5	109.5	146.2	158.6	177.4	168.6	182.8	152.2	165.3	190.0	266.3	266.9
Portfolio investment, net	65.0	94.6	60.8	42.6	60.1	11.4	−80.5	−90.9	−12.1	25.0	29.4	−76.3
Other flows	−7.0	24.2	−15.3	−125.0	−162.9	−123.4	−32.1	26.9	20.1	23.5	−38.5	65.2
Official capital flows, net	15.2	−2.8	28.4	56.0	22.4	−34.2	6.6	2.3	−44.5	−57.8	−122.6	−143.8
Reserve assets*	−97.3	−109.9	−105.2	−34.8	−98.2	−131.2	−120.6	−198.9	−358.9	−508.2	−590.1	−738.4
Memorandum item												
Current account balance	−88.7	−90.4	−82.6	−51.6	34.4	123.5	86.8	132.3	229.4	299.7	511.6	638.5

Note: * A minus sign indicates an increase.

Source: IMF, *World Economic Outlook*, various issues.

the new climate that had emerged in global financial markets, the Brazilian monetary authorities decided to abandon the exchange rate peg without risking a fully-fledged financial crisis.

The markets' attention then turned to Turkey and Argentina towards the end of 2000, which in turn suffered substantial capital outflows. Turkey decided to let the lira float in February 2001, resulting in a significant depreciation of the exchange rate. In Argentina, the situation was further complicated by the existence of a currency board regime linking the peso to the US dollar, which did not allow for the un-pegging of the exchange rate except with the approval of parliament through an ad hoc legislative measure. Political uncertainties, related to the outcome of presidential elections, and sharply deteriorating domestic economic conditions further aggravated the situation, eventually leading in December 2001 to the suspension of the currency board and to Argentina's sovereign debt default. Argentina's bankruptcy had an enormous impact on global market sentiment regarding emerging countries in general and contributed to accelerating the 'flight to quality' by financial intermediaries and investors.

Bad debtors or bad creditors?

What lessons can be drawn from the debt crises of emerging countries? In all countries the crisis was preceded by massive net inflows of foreign capital in the form of bank loans, portfolio investment (bonds and shares) and direct investment. In all cases, incoming foreign funds were used to finance broad and deepening current account deficits, of between roughly 3 and 8 per cent of GDP, in the three years prior to the crisis. In line with the Minsky–Kindleberger model, in all cases the crisis was triggered by net outflows of bank credit and/or portfolio disinvestment. In all cases, the crisis led to massive currency devaluations (often unduly amplified by the overshooting of floating exchange rates), the suspension of foreign, public and/or private debt repayments, and the insolvency of companies and financial institutions (Mussa et al. 2000b).

While excessive foreign credit was clearly one of the root causes of the debt crises, it must also be asked which other external factors led to the occurrence of the 'displacement' and subsequent improvement of the credit rating of these countries. The common factor was the advent to power of political forces that supported the implementation of economic liberalization programmes, privatization, international trade and integration in the global capital market, in line with the prevailing 'Washington Consensus'. All the major industrial countries gave their political backing to these changes, with the full analytical support of the IMF (see IMF 2005a). Market participants considered that the nature of the 'displacement' could somehow overshadow the widely acknowledged gravity of the structural weaknesses in the economic, banking and financial systems of these countries. Above all, there was an underestimation of the risks of exposure towards countries that lacked efficient banking and financial supervisory structures. There was also a collective overestimation by the market of the degree of liquidity of loans granted to these countries, with the result that individual market participants underestimated the risk of insolvency of the debtor, trusting in their own ability to disinvest without incurring losses.

A crucial role was played by the exchange rate regime chosen by emerging economies in creating the conditions for excessive recourse to foreign loans. In all of the countries hit by crisis, monetary authorities kept exchange rates either rigidly fixed or oscillating within narrow margins. The choice of a stable exchange rate was a crucial ingredient in lending credibility to the monetary stability strategies adopted by the authorities and in rapidly eradicating the inflationary psychology that had produced irrational behaviour among producers and consumers. Yet the commitment to maintaining stable exchange rates also generated irrational behaviour; domestic borrowers and international financiers mistook this as an implicit guarantee against exchange rate risk. For borrowers, the guarantee meant access to foreign loans at a rate of interest that was much lower than that applied to loans denominated in the national currency. Creditors, meanwhile, could count on a higher margin of return for their investments than that available on their own market. In short, a kind of collusive agreement was formed between creditor and debtor whereby the possibility for both to make a profit was based on a dubious assumption, namely that the exchange rate would remain stable indefinitely and irrespective of changing circumstances. Moreover, strong inflows of foreign capital led to an excess of domestic liquidity and fuelled domestic demand, bringing with it problems of inflation and monetary control. The inflows also created a climate of euphoria in which concern for the correction of structural disequilibria and the strengthening of the banking and financial systems diminished.

This line of thinking – shared by most analysts – lays the blame for the crises of emerging countries at the doors of the countries themselves: they failed to pursue macroeconomic policies that were consistent with the choice of a fixed exchange rate regime; moreover, they freed up capital movements without having first installed supervisory and risk management structures in their own banking and financial systems. Indirectly, however, the IMF is also blamed for not having provided emerging countries with the necessary guidance on the policy strategy to deal with the impact of financial globalization.[12] The only blame that can be ascribed to the global market is of not having adequately priced credit risk and of having overestimated its ability to manage its own investments. Market participants, however, partly reject the accusation, claiming that the errors committed in assessing risk were mostly due to the lack of transparency of debtor countries regarding both their real economic situation and the adequacy of government and market institutions and the judicial system. There is broad consensus, however, that after the outbreak of the crises, the markets displayed destabilizing behaviour, leading to both an excessive correction of disequilibria and the spread of tensions to other countries.

I believe that this reading of the events does not give a proper weight to the role that, in a global financial system, is played by the interdependence between the policies and performances of major industrial countries and the external position of emerging economies. As noted by the IMF (2001c, p. 79), this issue has been comparatively neglected by research. Clearly, however, global markets are influenced by the transmission of impulses through the channels of international trade and global finance, in particular by changes in exchange and interest rates.[13] The impact of movements in interest and exchange rates of the major countries can be rapidly transformed into a crisis factor for emerging market economies that have a structural current account deficit offset by a net inflow of foreign capital. These countries must import the capital goods needed to fuel the growth process and incur debts to finance the necessary investments. Once their productive base has been broadened, they will become net exporters and will be able to repay the debt. The market is quite willing to finance these deficits so long as they are 'sustainable', or remain at least relatively stable with respect to GDP, and are the result of an increase in productive investments. However, since the foreign debt is denominated in one of the major reserve currencies,[14] the financial position of the indebted country can be significantly affected, either positively or negatively, by changes in interest rates in the creditor countries and fluctuations in the exchange rates of their own currencies. In practice, the net impact of these effects turns out to be negative for debtor countries more often than not. If the currency in which the debt is expressed (say, the dollar) depreciates, it is likely that the interest rates on the borrowed funds will rise as a result of monetary policy tightening (by the Fed), and the advantage of having a less burdensome principal debt is offset by the higher interest payments. Moreover, a stronger exchange rate will lead to a slowdown in exports from the debtor to the creditor country. In the opposite case, when the currency of the creditor country appreciates, it does not always follow that interest rates will fall (as was the case in the United States in the second half of the 1990s when the rising dollar was accompanied by high interest rates as a result of a Fed policy). Even less certain is the incentive effect on exports, given the frequency with which creditor countries adopt protectionist regimes targeting products from emerging markets (food and textiles). In conclusion, when the net effect is positive for the debtor country its foreign debt position is made only marginally easier to manage, while when the net effect is negative, the implications can be much more serious. The line of demarcation between payments disequilibria that the market believes to be sustainable, and is therefore willing to finance, and those it believes to be unsustainable is actually very blurred. All other things being equal, changes in the exchange or interest rates of the major currencies can, in fact, tip countries from one category into another in a matter of – literally – hours. If this happens, the credit flow is abruptly interrupted, with serious consequences for the debtor countries' exchange rate and balance of payments and even for their solvency. The conclusion is supported by recent evidence quoted by Williamson (2005, pp. 7–8),[15] which underscores the importance of 'the state of liquidity in the markets of the developed countries' as a factor in explaining the transition from boom to bust in emerging countries.

5.2.3 The Liquidity Crises in Bond Markets

The debt crises of emerging countries provided a backdrop against which episodes of severe tension in the financial markets of leading industrial countries took place, giving rise in some cases to serious illiquidity problems for major intermediaries. Two episodes, in particular, stand out for their global nature and systemic implications: the simultaneous collapse of the major bond markets in 1994; and the sudden drop of liquidity and a generalized increase in risk premia in the second half of 1998 (see Figure 5.3). In both cases, the tensions can be traced back to excessive credit, both through bank lending and fund raising from financial and derivative markets, accompanied by a widespread underestimation of market risks.

Bond market collapse in 1994
During 1994, global bond markets recorded capital account losses estimated by the BIS (1995, pp. 94–117) at about $1.5 trillion, equal to almost 10 per cent of GDP in the OECD countries, the biggest loss in over a decade and among the biggest losses of the post-war period. The collapse of government and corporate bond prices and the consequent sharp rise in long-term interest rates began in February 1994 when the Fed, which was concerned about the re-emergence of inflationary tensions in the United States, raised official interest rates. The episode is significant because of the rapidity of the reaction of market rates to the change in official rates, and the strong correlation between the movement of yields on the American market and on the markets of a great number of other countries. In Europe, for example, market rates rose in line with US yields, despite the fact that the monetary policy of the central banks of the EMS (following the period of major contraction linked to the currency crisis of 1992–93) continued to

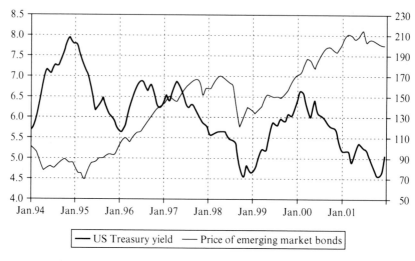

Notes:
a. Yield on 10-year US Treasury notes.
b. JP Morgan's emerging market government bond index EMBI-plus (price index base:
    January 1994 = 100).

Sources: Thomson Financial-Datastream; JP Morgan.

Figure 5.3   Yields of US government bonds[a] (left-hand scale) and prices
*   of emerging market bonds[b] (right hand scale)*
            (monthly averages)

be set along expansionary lines. Moreover, the extent and intensity of the markets' reaction contrasted with the widespread climate of low inflation that prevailed in most industrial countries, with the exception of the United States; the Fed's abrupt tightening appeared to have transformed, radically and without warning, the markets' forecasts for world economic growth and global inflation (see Table 5.1).

In practice, the very particular circumstances in which the trend of rising bond yields was inverted can be largely explained by looking at how financial markets operate. According to the BIS, the sharp rise in yields was the result of an excessive drop registered in 1992–93 that had seen bond market rates fall to unjustifiably low levels, which were therefore unsustainable in the long term. In essence, the inversion of the trend was so abrupt precisely because it represented the correction of a previous collective overshooting by markets. The tendency of bond markets to overshoot in one direction or the other can be explained by the ease with which global intermediaries can open major speculative positions on fixed-income securities by recourse to financial leverage (in other words, by borrowing) or through derivative instruments, with only a modest investment of their own capital. Moreover, it is precisely this widespread dependence on borrowing to finance speculative financial positions that leads to their rapid liquidation as soon as developments alter the risk profile. Both these factors played an important part in the collapse of the bond markets in 1994. The availability of loans induced an ever-greater number of intermediaries to assume that the increase in bond prices would gradually affect bond markets worldwide, from the United States to Europe to emerging countries. Often the purchases involved long-term bonds (typically with a maturity of ten years) and were financed using short-term credit that enabled operators, in the event the investment proved successful, to profit not just from capital gains but also from positive interest rate spreads. The increase of official interest rates made the financing of speculative positions more costly and generated expectations of a fall in bond prices, inducing intermediaries to close positions. This made the downward pressure on prices more acute, often through the triggering of automatic mechanisms for the sale of securities once they had reached a predetermined level. The need to limit the maximum amount of losses as rapidly as possible arose also from the fact that the reversal of the trend had become apparent at the beginning of the year, when investors had not yet made enough profits to absorb the losses without jeopardizing their quarterly statement of accounts to shareholders and, more in general, to the market. As a result of these rapid liquidations, between the beginning and end of 1994, government bond yields rose on average by between 2 and 3 percentage points in industrial countries, with peaks of between 3 and 4 percentage points in Italy, Spain and Sweden. In emerging markets, the increase was in the order of 6 to 8 percentage points.

What happened in the bond markets in 1994 confirms that a financially globalized system tends to produce not only widespread and sharp fluctuations in prices on bond markets, but also misalignments in long-term interest rates with respect to the fundamentals of the economies involved. While fluctuations in prices are certainly an intrinsic characteristic of markets, the misalignments of bond rates imply greater potential costs in terms of the inefficient distribution of resources; according to the BIS (1995), misalignments increase the probability of sudden and disorderly corrections of trend and the risk of global financial instability.

Financial market illiquidity in 1998

In the two months following Russia's declaration of insolvency on 17 August 1998, a turbulence on international financial markets occurred, which the BIS (1999) described in its annual report in rather dramatic terms:

During this brief spell, financial markets around the globe experienced extraordinary strains, raising apprehensions among market participants and policymakers of an imminent implosion of the financial system. As investors appeared to shy away from practically all types of risk, liquidity dried up in financial markets in both industrial and emerging economies, and many borrowers were unable to raise financing even at punitive rates. Prices for all asset classes except the major industrial country government bonds declined and issuance of new securities ground to a halt. (p. 82)

This episode of severe tension cannot be considered a mere 'coda' of the Asian crisis in the summer of 1997. Rather, it was the financial collapse of Russia, a country that up to few years earlier had been believed to be a world superpower capable of standing shoulder to shoulder with the United States, that was perceived by the market as a potentially devastating global event. There could be no alternative explanation for the mass stampede of every category of intermediaries – institutional investors and professional portfolio managers leading the field – from all types of risk and their equally feverish quest for liquidity that was increasingly hard to secure. The effect of this global rush towards quality was to widen to unprecedented levels the spread between the yields of securities perceived as being more liquid and secure and those of all the other financial instruments in both industrial and emerging economies. Yet even when choosing securities issued and guaranteed by the state, investors favoured the most recent issues (on the run) because they believed them to be more liquid than those that had been available on the market for longer. In Europe, spreads widened between securities issued by governments that had already been admitted to EMU and those that had not. In Italy, the interest rate differential between the 10-year Treasury bond and the comparable Bund issued by the German government, which had fallen to roughly 20 basis points after the decision to include the lira in the single European currency, rose to 50 basis points between September and October 1998. Similar trends were recorded in France and in the other 'hard core' EMU countries.

The increase in spreads proved ruinous for global players that had built convergence trades around the hypothesis of a gradual narrowing of credit margins. With market participants already reeling from the losses incurred in the Asian crisis, the unusual increase in spreads spelled trouble for many intermediaries, forcing them to meet payments the magnitude of which even sophisticated risk-management models based on historic trends had failed to anticipate, precisely because of their exceptional nature. All attempts to curb losses by closing positions only helped sharpen market tensions and fuel fears of a possible collapse of the global financial system. It was against this background that Long Term Capital Management (LTCM), a hedge fund which had accumulated liabilities for a total of over

$125 billion against assets of roughly $4 billion, became illiquid and sought assistance from the US monetary authorities.[16] The Fed arranged a refinancing of LTCM by a group of creditor banks on 23 September 1998, and reduced official interest rates the following 29 September. It was feared that an overly hasty liquidation of positions of the large LTCM exposure would have brought unsustainable pressures to bear on other intermediaries and across the entire US financial market, with serious international repercussions. The intervention of the Fed reassured the market about the timeframe and procedures for the management of LTCM liabilities, and the reduction in official interest rates provided confirmation that the Fed would supply liquidity if the market needed it. Despite these interventions, turbulence on the market persisted until mid-October, also giving rise to moments of unprecedented tension and volatility on the foreign exchange markets of the major currencies, in particular the dollar and yen. The losses many operators made on convergence trades persuaded them to anticipate the repayment of yen liabilities (borrowed at low interest rates) incurred to finance investments in dollar bonds (yielding high interest rates). One contributing factor in the decision to 'unwind' the yen carry trade was the expectation of a depreciation of the dollar against the yen which could have significantly reduced the return on these transactions. This triggered a strong upward trend for the yen, which rose by 12 per cent against the dollar in just two days (from 7 to 8 October), the highest increase recorded since 1971. It was not until the end of the month, when it became clear that the failure of LTCM had not been the beginning of a chain reaction of insolvencies in the banking and financial system, that the tensions subsided, enabling a gradual return to normal working conditions on financial markets.

5.2.4 Exchange Rate Misalignments

The transition to the floating exchange rate regime during the 1970s saw a significant increase in the short-term volatility of exchange rates among the main currencies, with large medium-term swings between the dollar, yen and European currencies in both nominal and real terms (see Figures 4.1 and 5.2). A key issue on this subject, from both an analytical and policy point of view, has been whether it is possible to determine when exchange rate trends might be regarded as a 'misalignment' and therefore as being likely to lead to international payments imbalances and macroeconomic instability. Despite the well-known conceptual and statistical difficulties involved, the IMF (Mussa et al. 2000a; IMF 2000a, p. 15) identified as a misalignment a number of situations in which exchange rates persistently deviated from equilibrium levels by over 10–15 per cent. The first misalignment identified using this empirical method was the appreciation of the nominal and real exchange rate of the dollar with respect to all the other principal currencies in the period from 1983 to 1985. In the 1990s, these episodes became more frequent: there was the appreciation of the real exchange rate of European currencies against the German mark that led to the crisis in 1992–93; the appreciation of the yen against the dollar in 1994–95; and finally, the depreciation of the euro against the dollar and the yen in 1999–2000.

Since the beginning of the third millennium the concept of exchange rate misalignment has not been mentioned in IMF official documents.[17] This is probably because it implies a value judgement on specific currencies and may incite speculative pressures. However, the external imbalances that are in many cases related to exchange rate misalignments have, unfortunately, not disappeared. Thus, the issue is currently being dealt with by estimating the change in real exchange rates that may be required, in addition to other policy measures, to adjust a given external imbalance (IMF 2002, pp. 65–81; IMF 2005b, pp. 109–28; Obstfeld and Rogoff 2005). Irrespective of the terminology used, there is broad consensus that, notwithstanding a partial correction, over the period 2000–2006 a substantial overvaluation of the US dollar has persisted, alongside a possible undervaluation of the Chinese renminbi and of other Asian currencies. In all the cases of misalignment under review, the evolution of exchange rates has been heavily influenced not only by changes in trade and current account balances but also by international capital flows. Speculative factors and bandwagon effects have played a significant role.

The 'mother of all misalignments': the dollar overshooting of 1983–85

The first and most important exchange rate misalignment of the post-Bretton Woods era originated in the early 1980s. At that time the world economy was struggling to cope with the consequences of the second major oil shock (following OPEC's decision to raise the price of crude oil by roughly 60 per cent in 1980), which was igniting inflationary tensions and simultaneously reducing the purchasing power of households. The 'stagflation' was apparent in rates of inflation of over 10 per cent in most industrial countries and 30 per cent in developing countries, coupled with a sharp drop in the growth of GDP. In 1982 the volume of international trade fell by 2 per cent and GDP in the G7 countries declined on average by 0.4 per cent, contracting by as much as 2.9 per cent in the United States. Meanwhile balance of payments disequilibria between oil-producing and oil-consuming nations widened. Monetary policies were uniformly restrictive across all the major industrial countries, while fiscal policies were moderately expansionary due to the effect of automatic stabilizers (resulting in a drop in tax revenue and a rise in unemployment spending). This was not the case of the United States, where the tax cuts imposed by the Reagan administration more than doubled the federal budget deficit forecast for 1982 (from $45 to $111 billion). Yet despite the predicted worsening of the 'twin deficits' of the balance of payments and the budget in the United States, the dollar performed strongly on foreign exchange markets. This was thanks to substantial inflows of funds attracted by high US interest rates (over 12 per cent); better growth prospects (the United States was still an oil producer, even if it had to import oil to meet domestic demand); and the trust of international investors in the 'safe haven' that America tradit-ionally represented in times of political uncertainty and economic and financial turbulence. The dollar began to appreciate in the spring of 1980 and three years later its effective exchange rate had risen by roughly 25 per cent. The strong dollar caused problems for the EMS, leading to five realignments of the parities of European currencies in the period. At the same time, conditions of stagflation persisted in Europe due to the com-bined effect of high interest rates and currency devaluations.

It was in these circumstances that monetary authorities in the other G7 countries became increasingly convinced that the dollar's performance was not justified by the underlying conditions of the US economy. They regarded the strength of the dollar as a reaction of financial markets to an unsustainable combination of US economic policies, where the govern-ment's excessively expansionary fiscal policy had obliged the Fed to respond with a tough monetary restriction. This policy mix was judged detrimental both to the US economy, in as much as it aggravated the twin deficits, and to the global economy, by jeopardizing the adjustment of international trade imbalances and a return to non-inflationary growth. The Reagan government, by contrast, remained persuaded that an expan-sionary fiscal policy would support growth, helping to reduce the debt-to-GDP ratio, and blamed Japan and Europe for hampering the recovery of their economies through government interventions and protectionist poli-cies that widened the American trade gap. As far as the dollar was con-cerned, Reagan's attitude was that exchange rates were determined by the free market, on the basis of investor confidence, and that a strong exchange rate helped combat inflation. The Reagan administration therefore dis-missed any possibility of intervening on exchange markets to halt the swelling of the speculative bubble. This deep disagreement regarding the operational choices of international economic policy strategy ultimately required the involvement of the highest political instances of the G7 and the issue was put at the top of the agenda of the summit attended by the heads of state and government in Versailles in June 1982. But, despite strong pressures exerted by President Mitterrand, the summit's host, Reagan refused to give ground and would only concede the approval of a 'statement on international monetary undertakings' in which the G7 accepted a 'a joint responsibility to work for greater stability of the world monetary system' and declared themselves willing to strengthen cooperation with the IMF in its activities of multilateral surveillance of the main currencies. It was also agreed, if necessary, 'to use intervention in exchange markets to counter disorderly conditions' (IMF 1982). To make up for the absence of any concrete undertakings in these declarations, President Mitterrand persuaded other members to approve the establishment of a group of experts from finance ministries and central banks of the G7 charged with analysing the effectiveness of interventions on currency markets from an empirical standpoint and drawing up a report on their findings in time for the next summit.

To some extent the report's conclusions (Jurgensen 1983) were forgone, because the US representatives made it clear they would not approve a text that confirmed the effectiveness of interventions and recommended their use. Despite this, the debate within the group provided ample analytical food for thought as well as plenty of information on the decision-making processes and reaction functions of monetary authorities with respect to market developments. This was also thanks to the more open attitude of the Fed, which, as Volcker recalls (Volcker and Gyohten 1992, Chapter 8, p. 237), cooperated with representatives of continental European countries to ensure that the report's conclusions were not entirely negative.

The Jurgensen Report was discussed at the G7 Summit held in Williamsburg in May 1983, but the stalemate on exchange rate policies persisted. The dollar continued to appreciate, but the recessionary cycle of the G7 economies had come to an end and inflation was falling; monetary issues began to appear less pressing even though European countries, and France in particular, continued to call for a comprehensive review of the functioning of the international monetary and financial system. The most that the 'interventionists' succeeded in obtaining from the summit was a general commitment to stabilize currency markets that would take account of the conclusions of the Jurgensen Report, as well as a directive to finance ministers to 'define the conditions for improving the international monetary system'. A period of broad-based discussions within the G10[18] followed, but progress was very slow because the US government did not want the negotiations to end up with an 'indictment' of its economic policy on the eve of the Presidential elections of 1984. The markets interpreted this laissez-faire approach as yet another demonstration of the economic and political muscle of the United States and used it to justify moves to drive the dollar up further, ignoring the increasing internal and external disequilibria in the US economy. In 1983 the budget deficit reached 4 per cent of GDP and in the course of 1984 the trade gap doubled, climbing to $120 billion. Eventually, the misalignment was corrected not by market forces but by the coordinated foreign exchange interventions of the G7, which will be analysed in detail in Chapter 7. Here it will be sufficient to note that the action to stop the upward overshooting of the dollar obliged financial markets to reassess their outlook for the US currency, leading them to unwind rapidly their long dollar positions. This in turn induced significant capital outflows from the United States, eventually turning the necessary devaluation of the dollar into a downward overshooting.

The EMS crisis

The EMS crisis of 1992 to 1993 is described in the literature as essentially due to a competitiveness gap between the German mark and the other European currencies, exacerbated by problems stemming from the reunification of Germany in 1990 and the vicissitudes of European monetary integration (Collignon et al. 1994; Buiter et al. 1998). The emphasis is once again on exchange rate policies, this time of the countries belonging to the EMS. Following the realignment of ERM parities in 1987, all the EMS countries kept their nominal exchange rates unchanged with respect to the mark, despite having higher inflation than Germany. The resulting appreciation in real exchange rates and heavy losses in competitiveness, which were not offset by increases in productivity, were seen as the trigger for the currency crisis. Subsequent analyses (Eichengreen 2000) focused more on the role of capital markets in generating the crisis. The financial market had initially ignored imbalances in competitiveness, banking on the fact that the transition to EMU would strengthen the process of real convergence between the economies of the member countries. In fact, the successful negotiations for a treaty on EMU during 1991 led to a widespread expectation by the market that interest rates on government bonds issued by the EMS member countries would converge around the level of yields in Germany, barring a modest spread to cover the difference in credit ratings. It was also expected that the exchange rates of EMU candidate countries would remain stable. These expectations translated into mass purchases of securities issued by countries like France, Italy and Spain, whose currencies were considered certain participants in EMU together with Germany, but whose interest rates were much higher than German rates. A survey carried out on behalf of the G10 finance ministers and central bank governors in April 1993 (G10 Deputies 1993) estimated net inflows of capital in these countries, in the two and a half years from the beginning of 1990 to halfway through 1992, to be in the region of $150 billion. The majority of the inflows were linked to transactions betting on the convergence of exchange and interest rates and were carried out by major international banks and financial institutions. In the

United States in particular, in the two years 1990–92, convergence trades in the EMS currencies created a new segment in the financial services industry. Hedge funds mobilized $25 to $30 billion to carry out, also with the help of derivative instruments, convergence trades in multiple amounts with respect to their capital base. Subsequently, the upward pressure on interest rates in Germany, due to a revival of inflationary expectations connected to the expenditure for the rebuilding of East Germany, persuaded the markets that a parallel tightening of monetary policies could not be sustained by other European economies. Market participants therefore doubted the sustainability of the parities of currencies such as the French franc, lira, pound sterling and peseta. In 1992, when uncertainties grew over the ratification of the Treaty of Maastricht by Denmark and France, the market perceived that the EMS cooperation mechanisms could not be fully applied due to Germany's reluctance to loosen its restrictive monetary policy. The result was the 'coordination failure' which, according to Padoa-Schioppa (1994), was the root cause of the EMS crisis. Mass outflows of capital followed from 'weak' currencies towards the mark precipitating, in September of the same year, the exit of sterling and the lira from EMS and their sharp depreciation. The crisis spread to other European currencies and culminated in August 1993 in the French franc crisis that necessitated the broadening of the fluctuation band around EMS exchange rates from 2.25 to 15 per cent.[19]

The yen misalignment

The third episode of misalignment relates to the strong rise of the yen against all the major currencies, and in particular against the dollar, in the period 1994–95, when the effective exchange rate of the yen appreciated by over 20 per cent (see Figure 5.2). This development has to be placed in the context of the deep stagnation of the Japanese economy, following the bursting of the asset price bubble at the end of the 1980s (described in greater detail in the section 'The Japanese bubble' – page 126). The misalignment was actually part of a long-term upward trend of the yen that began at the end of the Bretton Woods era and was rooted in Japan's large, deep and lasting structural current account surplus. The surplus, which averaged nearly 3 per cent of GDP per annum in the period 1973–93, was offset by capital outflows in the form of financial and direct investment (see IMF 2001b, 2006b). This helped to brake, but not prevent, the appreciation of the yen. The persistence and magnitude of the surplus fuelled expectations on the exchange market that the yen's appreciation would also persist: this influenced foreign exchange hedging transactions by major Japanese exporters and significantly contained capital outflows, putting more upward pressure on the yen. The result was the creation of what

McKinnon and Ohno (1997) would later refer to as the 'syndrome of the ever-higher yen', further hindering efforts to lift the Japanese economy from stagnation.

This was the backdrop for the complex economic and financial interplay of relations between the United States and Japan, which was transformed into a serious confrontation over the dollar–yen exchange rate.[20] Despite the expansionary monetary policy adopted by the Bank of Japan to avoid the emergence of an interest rate differential on the money market that would favour the yen, the tensions pushed the yen up even higher against the dollar. The upward trend continued well beyond the moment in which a broad interest rate differential in favour of the dollar emerged, in the early months of 1995, fueled by massive inflows of capital into Japan, supported by the expectation that the appreciating trend would continue. During 1995, net capital outflows dropped to a little over half of what they had been in 1994 (from $131 to $75 billion), forcing the Bank of Japan to mop up a significant amount of the current account surplus ($35 billion) to prevent any further appreciation of the exchange rate. The trend was not inverted until 1995, following a series of coordinated interventions by the monetary authorities of the G7 (see Chapter 9). The uncommon prospect of a weakening yen redirected capital flows towards the dollar, supported also by a fall-off in forward trades by Japanese exporters no longer obliged to hedge against exchange rate risk. Since that time the syndrome of the ever-appreciating trend seems to have disappeared, although it did resurface in 1998–2000, at a time when the Japanese economy was experiencing severe stagflation.

The undervaluation of the euro
The fourth episode of misalignment, that between the dollar and the euro, occurred in 2000 (IMF 2000a, pp. 15–16), when the value of the euro measured against medium-term economic fundamentals appeared to be misaligned by 25 to 30 per cent with respect to the dollar and the yen. In the third quarter of 2000, the effective nominal and real euro exchange rate dipped under the historic low registered in 1984 by the currencies that would switch to the euro. The euro's weakness was also seen as a reflection of the growing misalignment of the dollar, whose exchange rate continued to get stronger despite the widening American balance of payments deficit (which had reached over 4 per cent of GDP in 2001) and the strong deterioration (to 23 per cent of GDP in 2000) in the net debtor position of the United States (Obstfeld and Rogoff 2000). The existence of a misalignment of the euro was subsequently confirmed by the ECB using a broad spectrum of models to gauge equilibrium exchange rates (Maeso-Fernandez et al. 2001).

The causes of the euro's excessive depreciation against the dollar have been the subject of a lively debate among economists, market observers and politicians. From the list of possible factors those most often highlighted are of a bilateral nature, such as the superior cyclical performance of the United States with respect to the European Union, the interest rate differential in favour of the dollar, and the positive impact of the 'new economy' on productivity and therefore on medium-term growth prospects in the US economy. Delays in the EU's structural reform process and the liberalization of domestic markets were also cited as possible causes. These factors were apparently at the root of strong capital outflows, principally for investment in manufacturing and financial activities, from the European Union to the United States. An in-depth analysis of the issue conducted by the IMF (Meredith 2001), however, concludes that many of these explanations were not borne out by events or by subsequent developments. For example, the dollar continued to perform strongly against the euro even after the emergence of an interest rate differential in favour of the euro in 2001 or after the decline of US economic growth to a rate below that of the euro area. Even the EU structural weaknesses argument (rigidity of the labour market, excessive regulation, and so on) was found to be invalid because these flaws did not become more pronounced in the period of the euro's decline. On the contrary, measures were already being taken to remove or mitigate them. The IMF's analysis highlighted, instead, the influence of financial factors operating on both sides of the dollar-euro relationship. The dollar benefited from the structural reduction in the risk premium in equities, mostly related to the development of the 'new economy', which gave rise to an exceptional increase in stock prices from the mid-1990s and acted as a magnet for foreign capital inflows. Moreover, the euro exchange rate was affected by changes in the behavioural patterns of international financial markets due precisely to the introduction of the new single European currency. The euro's introduction was accompanied by a sharp rise in bond issues denominated in euros by residents to take advantage of the depth and liquidity of the new market, and by non-residents because interest rates were lower than on the dollar market.[21] This increased supply was not matched by an equivalent demand for funds denominated in euros by non-resident issuers, who normally converted the proceeds of the issue from euros into their own currency, thereby putting downward pressure on the euro exchange rate. Moreover, among resident investors there was demand for a greater diversification of portfolios in favour of non-euro area currencies to make up for the re-denomination of investments carried out in national currencies due to make the changeover to the euro.

Another possible negative influence in the performance of the euro was the sudden change in expectations of foreign currency dealers regarding the impact of the new currency's introduction on global exchange rate relationships. Ever since the creation of EMU in May 1998, and well before the introduction of the single currency, the widespread expectation on markets had been that the euro would bring about a rapid and massive diversification of the portfolios of intermediaries and institutional investors and in the official reserves of central banks. It was taken for granted that there would be a reduction, in favour of the euro, of the dollar's share (McCauley 1997; Bergsten 1999) and a dollar depreciation was widely anticipated. Prompted by forecasts of this kind, dealers opened speculative positions that favoured the euro for the entire second half of 1998, recording a significant appreciation of currencies due to make the changeover to the euro (see Figure 5.2). When international portfolios failed to diversify rapidly in favour of the euro, operators began to close their speculative positions that bet on a rising single currency: the result was a one-way market in the supply of euros, in which downward speculation became consistently profitable. It is indeed surprising that these expectations were able to influence the global foreign exchange market. The empirical evidence on the processes that lead a country's currency to become an 'international currency' and an official reserve asset shows, in practice, that such processes develop very gradually and that there is strong resistance to change by economic agents. The long-standing hegemony of sterling until the outbreak of the Second World War is proof of this, as is the substantial resilience of the dollar's share after the Second World War, despite several bouts of pronounced weakness in the 1970s against other reserve currencies such as the German mark and the yen. Further confirmation was provided by the scant success of attempts to replace the dollar with an 'artificial currency' such as the Special Drawing Rights (SDR) created by the IMF (Mussa et al. 1996; Eichengreen and Frankel 1996; Padoa-Schioppa and Saccomanni 1996). Also in the case of the euro, the evidence gathered by the ECB five years after its introduction 'supports the view that changes in the international role of currencies are slow and gradual' (ECB 2005a, p. 62).

A new misalignment of the dollar?
Exchange rate developments in the 2000s have not followed uniform patterns. Until early 2002, the US dollar continued to appreciate in nominal and real terms along a trend that had begun in 1995 and which had been strongly supported by the large private capital inflows, attracted by the euphoria surrounding the 'new economy' and the ICT bubble on the stock market. Some time after the irrational exuberance subsided in Wall Street, the dollar began to depreciate, a development that was also linked to the turnaround of the downward overshooting of the euro in 2001. The dollar decline continued until the end of 2004, when it was trading some 22 per

cent below its peak in January 2002 in real effective terms (see BIS 2002, p. 78). Over the same period, the euro appreciated by 23 per cent and the yen was at the same level as three years earlier. Since January 2005 the dollar has appreciated again vis-à-vis most currencies, despite a growing current account deficit in the US balance of payments that stood at over 6 per cent of GDP in 2005. The dollar resumed a downward trend at the end of 2005 and in 2006 as a whole depreciated by 4 per cent in real effective terms, with no consequence on the size of the current account deficit. The downward trend of the dollar has continued in the first quarter of 2007. Since the end of the stock market bubble, the US current account deficit has been financed to a growing extent by purchases of US Treasury bonds by central banks of Asian countries (China and Japan especially, but also by other Asian emerging countries). The massive accumulation of claims on the United States by these central banks is the result of intervention purchases of dollars in the foreign exchange market in order to prevent the appreciation of their currencies.

The debate about whether there is a dollar misalignment in view of the large and persistent US current account deficit has continued without reaching unanimous conclusions. Here it will be sufficient to recall that the overwhelming majority view among economists is that the deficit will not be sustainable and will not be corrected in the absence of a sizeable depreciation of the real exchange rate of the dollar, in the order of 20–35 per cent.[22] The position of the US authorities has been that the deficit is basically due to the strong and persistent demand for US dollar-denominated assets by the rest of the world economy (see US Administration 2006). Bernanke (2005) had earlier taken a more elaborate position, arguing that the increase in the US current account deficit was due to the emergence of a 'global saving glut' related, *inter alia*, to the shift that had transformed developing and emerging market economies from borrowers on international capital markets to large net lenders. Given the underlying sources of the US deficit, Bernanke expressed the view that the adjustment would take place gradually and smoothly. A similar view has been taken by Caballero et al. (2006), who argue that emerging countries would not easily find a safer alternative than the United States for the investment of their surplus savings. The IMF has been reviewing the issue in its periodic surveys of the world economy, using simulations of various adjustment scenarios based on its Global Economy Model. The starting assumption in IMF projections has been that a depreciation of the real exchange rate of the dollar in the order of 15 per cent would be required to correct the deterioration of the US external position. In September 2006 the IMF (2006d, pp. 24–7) examined three possible scenarios for the achievement of this objective: a 'no policy scenario' in which the imbalances are unwound through gradual changes in private sector saving behaviour and orderly movement in exchange rates; a 'disruptive scenario' in which the dollar depreciation is abrupt and disorderly as a result of a sudden reduction in the world's appetite for US assets; and a 'strengthened policies scenario' in which a set of cooperative policies will be implemented by the main actors, including a fiscal consolidation in the United States, greater exchange rate flexibility in emerging Asia, structural reforms in the euro area and Japan, and additional spending by oil exporters. The first scenario envisages a decline in the US deficit from 6.5 per cent of GDP in 2006 to 4 per cent in 2015. By the same year its net debtor position will have deteriorated from 30 to 55 per cent of GDP. According to the second and third scenarios, in the same period, the deficit will shrink to 2.5 and 1 per cent of GDP respectively and its net debtor position will not have exceeded 40 per cent of GDP. In its most recent forecasting exercise (IMF 2007c) the IMF seems to have somewhat changed its assumptions about the 'no policies scenario' as 'the US current account deficit is projected . . . to remain around 6 per cent of GDP in 2012' implying a renewed build-up of 'the US net external liability position' (p. 13). The current account surplus of China is projected to increase to 10 per cent of GDP by 2012, while the surplus of oil-exporting countries is expected to decline moderately. In the end the IMF urges caution:

> Thus far, the capital inflows needed to finance the large US current account deficit have been forthcoming, but over time the composition of the flows has shifted from equity to debt, and within debt away from Treasuries to riskier forms. These shifts suggest an increasing vulnerability to changes in market sentiment, particularly if returns on US assets continue to underperform returns elsewhere. Hence, the concern remains that at some point more substantial adjustments will be needed to ensure that the global pattern of current account positions remains consistent with the willingness of international wealth-holders to build up net claims on the United States. (p. 14)

Based on these projections and assessments it seems fair to conclude that what had been identified as a misalignment of the euro in 1999–2000 has in fact evolved into a misalignment of the dollar (and, possibly, of the renminbi).

5.2.5 Asset Price Bubbles

Unsustainable increases in asset prices, followed by sharp declines, have been a recurrent feature of the operation of stock and real estate markets since the end of the Second World War. Equity holdings and property are the largest component of households' wealth in developed countries and their values tend to move together over long periods. In a study of the consequences of the bursting of bubbles in a sample of 19 major industrial countries, the IMF (2003a, pp. 61–94) found that in the period from 1959–2002:

> Equity price busts on average occurred about once in every 13 years, lasted for about 2 1/2 years and involved price declines of about 45 per cent. . . . Housing prices busts on average occurred about once every 20 years, lasted about 4 years and involved price declines of about 30 per cent. While only one-fourth of equity price booms were followed by busts, about 40 per cent of housing price booms ended in busts. Both types of busts were highly synchronized across countries. (p. 74)

According to this study, the most 'virulent crashes' in equity markets occurred in the 1970s, following the breakdown of the Bretton Woods exchange rate regime and the first oil shock, when the average equity price decline amounted to 60 per cent. With the accelerating pace of financial globalization during the 1980s, the magnitude and repercussions of the asset prices boom–bust cycles have increased significantly. The two major episodes are: (1) the equity and real estate bubble in Japan that inflated during 1985–90 and burst in 1990–92; (2) the global equity and housing bubble that originated in the mid-1990s, affected most industrial and emerging countries, and burst in early 2000 for the equity component while continuing well into the decade for the housing component.

The Japanese bubble

The process leading to the development of the bubble in Japan is fully consistent with the assumptions of the Minsky–Kindleberger model: indeed, as noted by Calverley (2004, p. 43) 'the drivers for Japan's bubble were, as usual, optimism and liquidity'. In the 1980s, a 'displacement' affected the Japanese economy as perceived both by domestic economic agents and by the international community. Japan was enjoying strong growth and low inflation, the yen was constantly appreciating and the trade balance was recording growing surpluses as Japanese consumer goods and technologies flooded the global market. Japanese financial institutions were consistently at the top of the 'league tables' in all areas of capital market activity, while Japan was becoming the largest creditor country of the world and Tokyo was acquiring the status of a major international financial centre. In these circumstances, 'overconfidence and euphoria' played a vital role in inflating the bubble (Shiratsuka 2005, p. 44). But the bubble could not have reached major proportions without the contribution of expansionary monetary policies. These took the form of a series of discount rate cuts by the Bank of Japan (five times from 5 to 2.5 per cent between January 1986 and February 1987) accompanied by massive interventions in the foreign exchange market, which braked the appreciation of the yen against the dollar through the injection of yen-denominated liquidity. Bank lending grew by more than 10 per cent in both years and was used mostly to finance purchases of stocks and real estate. As noted by Gyohten (2004, p. 1) 'The only item Japan could not produce more was the land. When people believed in an everlasting growth of the economy, the price of land . . . was bound to rise. . . . As the market value of collateral kept going up, banks could expand their loan assets with virtually no credit risk'.

Despite clear signs of an overheating economy, the expansionary monetary policy stance of the Bank of Japan was kept unchanged until early 1989, partly in response to international pressures to stimulate domestic demand and appreciate the yen in order to reduce the trade surplus, particularly vis-à-vis the United States. At the same time, Japanese exporters were putting pressure on the government to halt the appreciation of the yen, which had sharply accelerated following the Plaza Agreement among the G7 countries to reverse the upward overshooting of the dollar. To deal with such conflicting pressures, the Bank of Japan continued to pursue an accommodating monetary policy while stepping up its foreign exchange interventions to prevent a further appreciation of the yen. This policy mix received international support in February 1987 in the context of the G7 Louvre Agreement to stabilize the US dollar (see Chapter 7 below). The sharp decline recorded by Wall Street in October 1987 had no impact at all on the Nikkei, perhaps providing policy-makers with indications of the soundness of the Japanese equity performance or in any case with a good reason to delay a possible tightening of monetary policy.

In this procyclical policy environment, land prices in Japan trebled between 1985 and 1988 while equity prices rose fourfold (see Figure 5.4). The stock market bubble burst in December 1989 after the Bank of Japan had sharply reversed its monetary policy stance, raising the discount rate five times from 2.5 in May 1989 to 6 per cent over a period of 15 months. Land prices peaked in January 1991. The bursting of the bubble precipitated a recession of the Japanese economy that lasted for over a decade, and well into the new millennium, with outright deflation (that is, with negative GDP deflators) during 1998–2005. The recession exposed the until then well-concealed structural weaknesses of the Japanese economic and financial systems, while the sharp decline in equity and real estate prices resulted in widespread situations of illiquidity and insolvency in the corporate and banking sectors, requiring massive bail-outs by the government.

With the benefit of the hindsight afforded by the 'lost decade', an experienced insider like Toyoo Gyohten (2004, p. 3) concluded that: 'All in all, we could not prevent the birth of the bubble because we could not distinguish

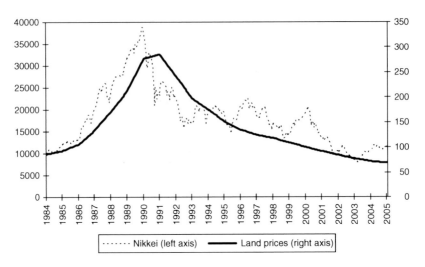

Source: Thomson Financial-Datastream.

Figure 5.4   The Japanese bubble

the real risk in the economy, because we set a wrong target for economic policy, because we chose the wrong policy instrument and because the timing of our policy implementation was wrong'.

This stern indictment puts the blame for the bubble on the entire policy-making structure of Japan, from the prime minister to the ministry of finance and the central bank. While the Bank of Japan was blamed for not having acted early enough to prevent the formation of the bubble and for having perhaps overreacted when it did tighten monetary policy, the government was criticized for not having carried out the structural reforms needed to prevent the emergence of the bubble during the boom years. Moreover, the ministry of finance refused to use fiscal policy measures to stimulate the economy and promote import demand, shifting the burden of the adjustment onto monetary and exchange rate policies. And finally, both the ministry and the central bank failed to recognize the vulnerability of the banking and financial systems as a result of their reckless lending policies and inadequate risk management strategies.

The global equity/housing bubble
In the second half of the 1990s, equity prices began rising rapidly in the United States and in other major industrial and emerging countries. In the United States the trend began in the context of a strong economic performance, sustained productivity growth and massive investment in new ICT

companies. The bull equity market was supported by an accommodating monetary policy stance by the Fed, which kept official interest rates stable or slightly declining from early 1995 to mid-1999, and by the 'strong dollar' policy constantly advertised by the Clinton administration. The trend accelerated in 1998–99 as the Fed's earlier concerns about the 'irrational exuberance' of the US stock market (voiced by the then Fed Chairman; see Greenspan 1996) were replaced by optimistic statements about the sustainability of the 'new economy' created by the ICT revolution and the structural nature (that is, unrelated to the business cycle) of the rising trend of productivity. In this increasingly euphoric climate the Dow Jones index of major US stocks rose from 3600 in 1994 to over 10 000 in March 1999, peaking at 11 723 on 14 January 2000. According to the BIS Annual Report for 2001 'the price rises appeared to be driven largely by a mutually reinforcing process of investor optimism and herding' (BIS 2001, p. 103). The climate is vividly described by Robert J. Shiller (2005) in his classic analysis of the equity (and housing) bubble.[23]

The rising trend of equity prices became a common feature in most industrial and emerging countries, despite very different underlying macroeconomic conditions (see Figure 5.5). Even in Japan, where the stock market had been depressed because of the impact of the bursting of the earlier bubble, equity prices rallied in 1999 in line with global trends. The boom was especially strong in the ICT sector, where prices in countries like Sweden rose sixteen-fold between 1994 and 1999, because the performance of the sector was considered immune to possible monetary policy tightening given the structural nature of the ICT revolution.

The equity bubble burst in every stock market of the world during the year 2000. The decline in stock prices took place in two phases, the first one between April and May 2000, the second, between September 2000 and the first quarter of 2001. As clearly explained in the BIS Annual Report for 2001: 'The most notable aspect of the first round of price declines was the lack of identifiable and significant new information that could account for the sudden fall in prices. In this respect the episode was similar to the global market declines of October 1929 and October 1987' (BIS 2001, p. 104). In fact, markets had been increasingly volatile since 1999 because the continuing strong performance of the US economy was fuelling expectations of an increase in interest rates by the Fed, causing uncertainty as to how this would affect stock valuations. Some tightening of monetary policy was indeed introduced by the Fed in the second half of 1999, but it was accompanied by repeated assurances that the central bank would provide all the liquidity needed by the financial system to overcome any possible malfunctioning in information technology (IT) systems owing to the transition to the third millennium (the Y2K factor). The perception among market

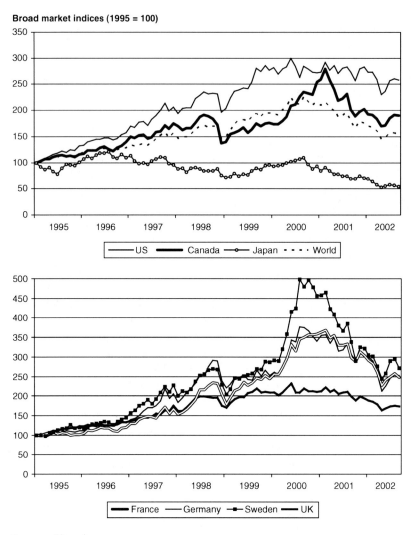

Broad market indices (1995 = 100)

Source: Bloomberg.

Figure 5.5   Stock market indicators

participants worldwide was that some sort of implicit guarantee existed that the Fed would not allow a sharp decline of the stock market for fear of its possible implications for the real economy (the 'Greenspan put' that Shiller (2005, p. 40) mentions). In these circumstances the sharp decline in technology stocks in April 2000 appeared to be, again in the view of the BIS, 'prompted solely by a shift in investor sentiment' (BIS 2001, p. 105).

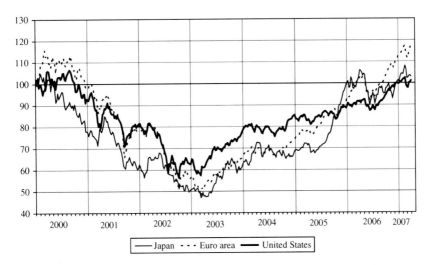

Note: Stock indices: for Japan TOPIX; for the Euro area Datastream; for the United States S&P 500 composite.

Source: Thomson Financial-Datastream.

Figure 5.6 *Stock market prices* (weekly averages; base: 1st week of January 2000 = 100)

The second round of price declines instead took place against the background of negative information on corporate profits and other indicators projecting a more rapid slowdown of economic activity than had earlier been anticipated. The turnaround in prices was highly synchronized across major stock markets in both industrial and emerging countries (BIS 2004, p. 107). In the ICT sector, markets appeared to assign an anchor role to the NASDAQ index of technology stocks, and price changes everywhere were strictly correlated to its performance. The decline continued for three years until March 2003, amid temporary rallies triggered in January 2001 by a 50-basis-point surprise reduction in official interest rates by the Fed and in September 2001 by investors' reaction to the terrorist attack on the World Trade Center in New York (Figure 5.6). The market was negatively influenced by the collapse of the energy trading company Enron in December 2001 and by the restatement of financial accounts by WorldCom in June 2002, raising doubts about the reliability of the information supporting the operation of US financial markets. A further rally by the US equity market in November 2002 proved short-lived as expectations about corporate earnings and overall economic activity were not confirmed by subsequent events. While the Fed continued to lower interest rates to counter the deflationary impact of the bursting of the bubble (bringing them to an historic low of 1 per cent in June 2003), the bear equity market ended in March 2003, giving way to a market rally which lasted for about 12 months. In the same period monetary policies in other major financial centres continued to be accommodating. All in all, according to estimates of the BIS, 'In the downturn from April 2000, equity markets worldwide had lost $13 trillion in capitalization. . . . In the 12 months to March 2004, the markets recovered $10 trillion of that loss' (BIS 2004, pp. 106–07). Since then equity markets have, on the whole, achieved a moderate rise, at a faster pace since mid-2006 (Figure 5.6). In April 2007, the Dow Jones index rose above 13 000.

The boom–bust cycle in global equity markets was closely connected with developments in housing markets in major industrial countries, albeit with some significant differences in timing and origin (see BIS Annual Report 2003, pp. 116–19; Calverley 2004, pp. 73–86; Shiller 2005, pp. 11–20). Although using different databases, most analyses concur that the rising trend in housing prices as a global phenomenon began around 1997, two years after the start of the equity bubble. Contrary to established patterns of asset price movements, housing prices continued to rise well after equity prices began to fall in 2000, as investors shifted funds from the stock market into real estate and households were encouraged by histori- cally low mortgage rates to buy property. Using its own comparable house price indexes for 20 major countries over the period 1997 to the first quarter of 2005, *The Economist* (2005b) estimated that:

> The total value of residential property in developed countries rose by more than $30 trillion over the past five years, to over $70 trillion, an increase equivalent to 100 per cent of those countries' combined GDPs. Not only does this dwarf any previous house price boom, it is larger than the global stock market bubble in the late 1990s . . . or America's stock market bubble in the late 1920s . . . In other words, it looks like the biggest bubble in history. (p. 62)

The increase in house prices was unevenly spread among countries, ranging from 244 per cent in South Africa, to around 150 per cent in Great Britain and Spain, 114 per cent in Australia, around 85 per cent in France and Sweden, and 73 per cent in the United States. However, while in some countries prices had already begun to decelerate by around 2005 (most notably in Great Britain and Australia), in other countries they have slowed only in the second half of 2006 (United States and France). In the United States, the accelerating trend has apparently been affected only gradually by the tightening of monetary policy carried out by the Fed since June 2004; according to IMF estimates, at least 18 states were experiencing housing booms in 2005, raising concern about the sustainability of the trend and the implications of a possible reversal (IMF 2005c, pp. 19–20). In a broad historical survey of the behaviour of real housing prices in industrial countries, the OECD noted that 'a number of elements in the current situation are unprecedented: the size and duration of the current real house price increases; the degree to which they have tended to move together across countries; and the extent to which they have disconnected from the business cycle'. Moreover, the historical record suggests that if housing prices were to adjust downwards 'the drops (in real terms) might be large and . . . the process could be protracted given the observed stickiness of nominal house prices and the current low rate of inflation. This would have implications for activity and monetary policy' (OECD 2005, p. 123).

The eventual outcome of the current global bubble is impossible to predict at the time of writing (spring 2007). However, there is sufficient evidence available to draw a few conclusions about the origin and development of the global bubble. As envisaged in the Minsky–Kindleberger model, the bubble begins with a 'displacement', represented in this case by the ICT revolution and the 'new economy' in the United States. The bubble inflates in the stock market benefiting from low interest rates. Profit expectations attract funds from international capital markets, pushing up the dollar exchange rate; the increase in stock prices combines with the foreign exchange capital gains in attracting further investor attention and capital. This pattern is replicated in stock markets worldwide, benefiting from abundant international liquidity. As market sentiment changes and the stock market bubble bursts, investors seek alternative sources of profit in the property markets, where the bubble regains strength, living a life of its own seemingly disconnected from the business cycle and immune to changes in the stance of monetary policy – until the next change in market sentiment.

5.2.6 An 'Integrated' Overview

Through the long catalogue of episodes and tensions in the global financial system in the last two decades of the twentieth century I have attempted to shed light on the common causes of these events, singling out in particular the role played by monetary policies in the major industrial countries and by the operation of global financial markets. These common factors have interacted with specific events affecting individual countries, amplifying and propagating the impact of economic policy measures adopted by national governments or of business strategies of corporations and financial intermediaries. The tendency of analysts to examine disturbances separately (debtor insolvency, market illiquidity, exchange rate misalignments and asset price bubbles) may have somewhat obscured the connections among the various episodes that have to be fully understood in order to devise any international strategy to manage global financial instability. It may be useful, therefore, to conclude the survey by briefly reviewing the episodes of tension, this time in chronological order and with a focus on international linkages.

The choice of a starting point for the sequence of 'stylized facts' that are important for the analysis of instability in a global financial system is necessarily an arbitrary act. As explained in previous chapters, my view is that financial globalization started in the early 1980s when the process of deregulation and liberalization took off in the United Kingdom and the United States, spreading into continental Europe towards the end of the decade. Indeed the policies introduced by Margaret Thatcher and Ronald Reagan can be regarded as the 'displacement' that set the stage for the tensions which have since reverberated across the global financial system and the world economy. Here is the catalogue:

- The euphoria generated by *tax cuts in the United States coupled with a restrictive monetary policy* induces large capital inflows leading to the overvaluation of the dollar (1983–85);
- The *G7 coordinated exchange market intervention* provokes a sharp turnaround of the trend, causing a downward overshooting of the dollar requiring additional stabilization interventions by the G7;
- The stabilization of the dollar/yen exchange rate is achieved by a *strongly expansionary monetary policy in Japan*, which fuels an asset price bubble in the real estate and equity market at the end of the 1980s;
- The adjustment of the US twin deficits and the correction of the dollar overvaluation lead to a recession in the United States, which is countered by a *strongly expansionary monetary policy by the Fed* in 1990–92, resulting in the depreciation of the dollar vis-à-vis the yen and the German mark;
- *Monetary policy is also relaxed in Japan* in 1990–92 to counter the effect of the bursting of the bubble;
- At the same time *monetary policy is tightened in Germany* to cope with the inflationary impact of German reunification and in other EMS countries to maintain exchange rate stability within the ERM;
- Global financial markets respond to these policy changes by *shifting funds from the United States and Japan into higher yielding countries* in Europe (mostly for the convergence trades on ERM currencies) and emerging countries in Asia and Latin America (especially in Mexico);
- Uncertainties about the progress towards EMU induce *large capital outflows from ERM countries and speculative movements* that result in

a severe crisis in the EMS with the devaluation of several currencies between September 1992 and August 1993. After the crisis, monetary policies are loosened in Europe, favouring the reflow of funds towards emerging markets;

- The strong recovery of the United States economy, accompanied by renewed inflationary pressures, sets the stage for *an abrupt change in the stance of monetary policy by the Fed* in the course of 1994;
- Taken by surprise by the Fed move, *bond markets throughout the world incur record losses* and bond yields are quickly adjusted upwards;
- Following the increase of bond interest rates, markets question the sustainability of Mexico's external position, and large capital outflows eventually lead to *the devaluation of the peso in December 1994 and the ensuing debt crisis*;
- The ongoing crisis of the Japanese banking system and the threat of an ever-appreciating yen lead to a *highly expansionary monetary policy in Japan, with interest rates close to zero* in 1995. Monetary policy becomes more accommodating in the European Union and to a lesser extent in the United States;
- In the context of a generalized easing of monetary policies in major industrial countries, *a boom of financing to emerging markets* is recorded in Asia, Latin America and Eastern Europe in 1995–96;
- As markets question the sustainability of the external position of major emerging countries in Asia, *large capital outflows provoke a regional financial crisis* in the second half of 1997 with a strong destabilizing impact on exchange rates, banking systems and the external debt of Thailand, Indonesia, Korea, Malaysia and the Philippines;
- Following the Asian crisis, *markets show a reduced appetite for risk in currencies that peg their exchange rates*: Russia (1998) is obliged to float the exchange rate and to declare insolvency; the Russian default has major negative repercussions on credit markets with widespread situations of illiquidity, leading to the failure of an important US hedge fund. In subsequent years, Brazil (1999), Turkey (2001) and Argentina (2001) will also be forced to float their currencies in the context of severe external debt crises;
- The outflow of funds from emerging countries from 1997 onwards takes place during a concomitant phase of *'irrational exuberance' in equity markets* in industrial countries and especially in the United States, where funds are attracted by favourable expectations concerning the profitability of the ICT business and the appreciation of the dollar, in the context of a generally accommodating monetary policy;

- A shift in market sentiment in 2000 provokes the *bursting of the equity bubble* in the United States and in other major markets. The Fed adopts a strongly expansionary monetary policy, while the dollar depreciates considerably vis-à-vis the euro and the yen. Monetary policies in the European Union and Japan remain expansionary;
- Outflows from equity markets lead to *a boom in investment in real estate markets* in a large number of industrial and emerging markets over the period 2001–05, in a context of abundant international liquidity and record low interest rates;
- Despite a gradual *tightening of monetary policies in the United States, the European Union and Japan* over the period 2004–06, liquidity in international financial markets remains abundant, exerting a downward pressure on credit spreads;
- Improved economic conditions in emerging markets lead to a *strong rise in private capital flows to these countries* in 2004–06, for amounts larger than those recorded before the Asian crisis (although mostly in the form of foreign direct investment, heavily concentrated in China and other Asian emerging countries).

The conclusion that can be drawn from this description of the connections among the episodes of instability in the era of global finance is that there is indeed a common pattern in the development of disturbances. A displacement in the sense explained by Minsky and Kindleberger is at the origin of most cases, be it the deregulation of the Thatcher–Reagan era, the graduation of emerging markets, the new European monetary order, the 'new economy', the ICT revolution or the 'peaceful rising' of China. Global financial markets are only too eager to fund the displacement: in a regime of globalized finance, monetary policy impulses emanating from the major countries immediately influence liquidity conditions on monetary and financial markets as well as the lending strategies of global intermediaries. Fierce competition between global players, the uniformity of their reactions in the face of changing market conditions (such as changes in interest and exchange rates), information asymmetries especially regarding the creditworthiness of borrowers, the existence, real or presumed, of 'safety nets', and herding behaviour by intermediaries and investors, are all factors at play in creating credit booms leading to excessive financing and 'overtrading'.

The factors that have turned booms into busts are obviously different in each episode. Political and/or economic events in a country – or countries – have interacted in many different ways, helping to turn euphoria into panic. But these differences are irrelevant for the purposes of understanding the causes of disturbances: they are merely triggers that help detonate mines that have been hidden in the soil of the global financial system. This is not to say that globalization is the primary determinant of crises and instability. Still, globalization can create conditions and promote behavioural patterns that allow the virus of instability to grow and spread. The challenge for monetary and financial authorities therefore is not to roll back globalization but to influence those conditions and patterns in order to exploit the benefits of globalization without fuelling the fire of crises.

It is a challenge that must be accepted because the cost of financial crises for the real economy and the well-being of companies and households has been very high. Reliable estimates of such cost are available mostly for the debt crises of developing and emerging countries (IMF 1998a, pp. 74–97; World Bank 2001b, pp. 78–85). A more comprehensive analysis was conducted by Bordo et al. (2001) covering currency and banking crises over a period of 120 years from 1880 to 1997. Reviewing all available evidence Eichengreen (2004, pp. 254–5) notes that the loss of output from the average crisis over the entire period 'approaches 9 per cent of GDP' but adds that 'some financial crises produce relatively limited output losses, while others, such as those of Indonesia in 1997–98 and of Argentina in 2001–02, precipitate a full-scale economic collapse in which output falls by upwards of 20 per cent and living standards, further eroded by the collapse of the country's exchange rate and the terms of trade, fall by even more'. Similar estimates of the cost of other types of financial crises are not available, but the impact of asset price bubbles, for example, on the growth rate of real output in Japan or the United States is quite significant (see Table 5.1).

NOTES

1. Cassese (2006, p. 36), an Italian Constitutional Court judge, has ascertained that the word 'globalization' appeared in *The Economist* for the first time in 1959 and was included in *Webster's New International Dictionary* for the first time in 1961. Visco (2001) has checked that the 1996 edition of the *Palgrave Dictionary of Economics* did not have an entry on globalization.
2. For a comprehensive historical analysis of financial crises see Kindleberger (1978), from which the examples quoted here are drawn. See also Galbraith (1993).
3. Mortimer (2006, pp. 209–20), a British historian, questions whether the royal default was the sole cause of the failure of the two Florentine banks, arguing that the amount of money owed by the king was a mere £13000, much smaller than claimed by contemporary chroniclers of Florence. Therefore: 'Edward's failure to repay this amount would have dented the companies' profitability, but it would not by itself have proved disastrous'.
4. The interconnections between the South Sea bubble and the Mississippi bubble and the similarity of these episodes with the financial turbulences of the late twentieth century are well analysed by Dale (2004).
5. Among the many valuable contributions, I would single out: IMF (1998a) which has a chapter on 'Financial crises. Causes and indicators'; IMF (1999a) where 'International

financial contagion' is analysed; and the works of Lamfalussy (2000), Summers (2000), Eichengreen (2002), Tirole (2002), Desai (2003); Fischer (2004), which provide a broad range of views on the causes and remedies of financial crises.

6. Again, among the many interesting works my personal preference goes to Calverley (2004) and Shiller (2005) for analysis, and to Stiglitz (2003) and Krugman (2003) for policy implications.

7. See de Brouwer (2001) and Garbaravicius and Dierick (2005). However, on the issue of whether hedge funds' activity is destabilizing, the IMF's view up to 2004 was that 'we still do not know what we do not know' (IMF 2004a, pp. 57–8).

8. As Crockett noted (1997), in the Minsky–Kindleberger model the determinants of the crises are generically associated with irrational exuberance and the destabilizing behaviour of economic agents. Later analyses attributing such dynamics to information asymmetries, herd behaviour and moral hazard (mentioned in Chapters 2 and 3) added to and reinforced the model's validity. Kindleberger (2000, pp. 21–2) himself, in the fourth edition of his book, notes that: 'One place where the model surely applies today is foreign exchange markets . . . Other . . . examples can be found in the Japanese stock and real-estate markets in 1998 to 1990 and in mutual fund investments in emerging markets in 1993'.

9. This was the significant difference with the Mexican crisis of 1982–83 (also involving other Latin American countries) when the triggering factor was the outflow of capital originated by domestic residents. The indebtedness was mostly vis-à-vis international banks, which were late in realizing the unsustainability of their debtors' position, reacting only when the increase in US official interest rates made the rollover of short-term credit lines unsustainable (Lamfalussy 2000, pp. 5–6).

10. A detailed description of the fall-out of the Asian crisis is provided by Desai (2003, pp. 87–135).

11. In the period October 1997–October 1998 there were three phases in which the international bond market was de facto 'closed' for emerging countries' issuers: October–December 1997, May–June 1998 and August–September 1998 (IMF 2001a, p. 19).

12. Among the economists that have taken this position, the most severe critic of the IMF is Stiglitz (2002); Desai (2003, p. 6) instead identifies the 'inequitable relationship' between developed and developing countries as the cause of the 'premature opening up' of markets to the free flow of capital. Mishkin (2006), more recently, argued that the international community did not provide incentives for emerging countries to introduce reforms and establish institutions to enable them to benefit from financial globalization.

13. Empirical works (Eichengreen and Mody 1998) have confirmed that US interest rate variations have a negative impact on the volume of international bonds issued by emerging countries; analyses carried out by the International Monetary Fund (IMF 2001a) and the World Bank (2001a) underscore the strong positive correlation between the performance of US interest rates and the emerging market bond spread.

14. This results in a 'currency mismatch' which is now seen as a major element of vulnerability of the financial position of emerging countries (see Goldstein and Turner 2004). The constraints faced by emerging countries when borrowing in their own currency, in order to limit the currency mismatch, have been referred to by economists as the 'original sin' of these countries (see Goldstein and Turner 2004, pp. 5–9).

15. The IMF (2004b, p. 157) addresses the question 'Are credit booms in emerging countries a concern?' and finds that 'credit booms pose significant risks for emerging market countries because they are typically followed by sharp economic downturns and financial crises'.

16. See Lowenstein (2001) for a full account of how LTCM, a company managed by an extraordinary group of financial experts, including a couple of Nobel Prize laureates and former Fed officials, ran into trouble.

17. See for example IMF (2006e). The concept has recently reappeared in the new Decision on surveillance over members' policies which was approved by the IMF Executive Board on 15 June 2007 (see Chapter 6, Section 4, for a detailed examination).

18. At a technical level, the negotiations were conducted by the Committee of the G10 Deputies (deputy finance ministers and deputy governors of central banks in the G10 countries), with the institutional participation of representatives of the IMF, BIS and OECD.
19. The adventures of the French franc in the EMS are narrated in Chapter 8.
20. The United States/Japan monetary and trade conflict is analysed in Chapter 9.
21. In 1999 euro-denominated bonds accounted for about 45 per cent of the total share of international bonds, as against a share of 43 per cent of dollar bonds (OECD 2000, p. 66), remaining on average a little below these levels in 2000 and in the first half of 2001 (Galati and Tsatsaronis 2001).
22. The issue has been debated at the Institute for International Economics: see Bergsten and Williamson (2003 and 2004). See also Obstfeld and Rogoff (2005) and Blanchard et al. (2005).
23. Among the many contributions to the general euphoria, Shiller quotes David Elias's book entitled *Dow 40 000*: the title alone fully captures the spirit of the times (see Elias 1999).

6.   In search of international monetary and financial stability

> However compelling the argument that global financial markets require a global financial regulator, global bankruptcy court, global money and a global central bank, realism requires acknowledging that national governments are not prepared to turn over significant additional powers to a super-IMF.
>
> Barry Eichengreen (1999b, p. 3)

> Reforming the international financial architecture without reforming the currency regime is like watching *Hamlet* without the Prince [of Denmark]. The international monetary system will continue to be ineffective and crisis prone until that crucial centrepiece of its operation is thoroughly revamped.
>
> Goldstein Report (1999, p. 129)[1]

> The perception that the IMF is asleep at the wheel on its most fundamental responsibility – exchange rate surveillance – is very unhealthy for the institution and the international monetary system.
>
> Timothy D. Adams (2006, p. 135)

> The IMF is in eclipse as the pre-eminent institution of international financial cooperation. Consequently, the world is worse off. Despite the considerable reforms during the past decade, more should be done.
>
> Edwin Truman (2006, p. 119)

6.1   COPING WITH CRISES

The reaction of the international community to the various episodes of instability that have periodically shaken the international monetary and financial system has on the whole been characterized by partial responses and ad hoc interventions, at least until the 1990s. Towards the end of the second millennium, the need for a more systematic and comprehensive approach to global financial instability was increasingly recognized due to the growing number of crises and turbulences and the mounting size of international payments imbalances. Only after the debt crisis in Mexico did leading countries begin to pay serious attention to instability in the global monetary and financial system. Even then, the need to understand fully the systemic causes of sovereign debt crises was generally not appreciated until after the Asian and Russian episodes and their repercussions. A G7-led initiative to reform the international financial architecture (IFA) got underway in 1998 and concluded with the launch of a broad set of initiatives approved by the G7 Summit of heads of state and government in Cologne in 1999. A less visible and highly technical debate, mostly among central banks, on how to cope with asset price inflation took off following the equity and housing bubbles at the turn of the century and centred essentially on the role that could be played by monetary policies in preventing the formation of unsustainable asset price trends. Finally, after a long period of benign (and not so benign) neglect, the issue of the IMF's role in dealing with global payments imbalances and misalignments between the exchange rates of key currencies was addressed by the G7 and the IMF itself in the strategic review of the institution initiated in 2004 in connection with the sixtieth anniversary of the Bretton Woods agreement.

In order to arrive at a thorough understanding of the timeframes, working procedures, and scope of the reforms introduced or proposed in these areas, it is useful to recall earlier efforts made by the international community to re-establish monetary order following the collapse of the Bretton Woods system in 1971, and to analyse the underlying political factors that guided the attitude of the principal countries in the complex bargaining game of international cooperation. What transpires is that, 30 years on, these underlying motivations have remained largely unchanged (Solomon R. 1982; James 1996).

The key aspect that merits detailed analysis is the attitude of the United States. At Bretton Woods the United States stood shoulder to shoulder with Great Britain in promoting a monetary system that, while assigning a central role to the dollar and gold, imposed constraints on the autonomy of America's economic policy, obliging it to maintain exchange rate stability. Economic developments in the post-war era made these constraints increasingly unacceptable to the United States: both its politicians and businessmen became convinced that the exchange rate tie was detrimental to US interests and left it vulnerable to trade competition from the principal European countries and Japan. The decision to adopt a floating exchange rate regime and subsequently devalue the dollar, announced by President Nixon in August 1971, was presented to American public opinion as a liberation from iniquitous ties. The then Treasury Secretary John Connolly, an influential Democrat in a Republican administration, declared that the United States had grown tired of 'fighting with one hand tied behind its back', confirming the bipartisan nature of the political consensus surrounding Nixon's action.

In this climate, the US government, in close coordination with Congress, shaped the stance to be taken in negotiations for the reform of the international monetary system that began in late 1971. Following a series of unsuccessful attempts to agree on the re-establishment of a fixed exchange rate regime with symmetrical obligations to adjust imbalances for countries running a deficit (the United States) or a surplus (Europe and Japan), the United States proposed to legalize floating exchange rates by amending the statute of the IMF. European countries, and to a certain extent Japan, claimed on the contrary that fixed exchange rate regimes should remain the rule and floating currency regimes the exception; moreover, floating regimes should be considered as being of a temporary nature, accompanied by the presumption of a return to the 'normal' fixed parity regime in the future. When a compromise between the United States and Europe seemed possible ahead of the G7 Summit in Rambouillet, the US Congress imposed a series of limits on the government's freedom to negotiate. A report approved by the Joint Economic Committee of the Senate and the House of Representatives in August 1975, entitled *Exchange Rate Policy and International Monetary Reform*, recommended that: floating currency regimes be permitted without prior authorization from the IMF; that such a regime be considered a fully acceptable option, on an equal footing with fixed exchange rate regimes; that the IMF introduce rules to prevent member countries from manipulating exchange rates in order to dump their domestic economic problems elsewhere; that US monetary authorities intervene in currency markets only to prevent the emergence of disorderly market conditions and that they abstain from intervening to influence the trend of exchange rate movements; and finally, that the American central bank should not accumulate further foreign currency reserves.[2] In essence, the United States insisted on the right to devalue the dollar without having to ask anyone's permission and without being obliged to take special measures to control foreign exchange rate movements. They also wanted to be protected from unfair 'exchange rate manipulation' by countries wishing to export their own stagnation and unemployment to the United States.[3] Henry Kissinger (1979) recalled in his memoirs how in that period 'the frustrations of the Vietnam War were inciting xenophobia'. This could perhaps explain why the US Congress and government, having devalued the dollar in 1971 and 1973, felt it was essential to the country's interests that this might be recognized as inalienable, unconditional and not subject to any limits of international origin, in a document, like the IMF charter, having constitutional value for the world monetary system. But it was precisely this attitude that was among the causes of the perpetuation and acceleration on a global scale of the inflationary tensions ignited by the devaluations of the dollar and the subsequent quadrupling of oil prices in 1974. In a floating exchange rate regime, if the highest authorities of a country want to devalue their national currency, the market will not hesitate to grant their wish. And it was no coincidence that the compromise on the reform of the international monetary system reached in Jamaica in 1976 coincided with the beginning of a further extended spell of dollar depreciation. A contribution to the growing distrust in the most important reserve currency in the world was certainly provided by the constitutional crisis that led to the fall of the Nixon administration and the beleaguered presidency of Ford, who filled Nixon's mandate until 1976. But even under President Jimmy Carter, the fortunes of the greenback continued to decline, and went on declining until monetary authorities unequivocally signalled a change of attitude with respect to the exchange rate of the dollar and a willingness to take the measures needed to ensure its stability.

The change in US economic policy came about gradually. The Carter administration first addressed the international front, voicing concern over the weak dollar that was fuelling an inflationary spiral without precedent in an economy like that of the United States, which was relatively 'closed' in terms of foreign trade. A series of large-scale interventions bolstered the dollar on foreign exchange markets at the end of 1978 and US monetary authorities actively committed themselves to raising the necessary foreign exchange holdings, both by drawing on the IMF and by issuing foreign currency denominated bonds in the market (the Carter bonds). For the first time ever in the post-war era, the United States financed its own balance of payments deficit at least partially through reserve assets (asset settlement), rather than entirely through an increase in dollar liabilities (liability financing). Moreover, the United States was simultaneously encouraging the IMF to undertake a radical overhaul of the international monetary system by establishing a 'substitution account' that would absorb what was considered to be excessive dollar liquidity. This would be substituted with liquidity denominated in Special Drawing Rights (SDRs), the international reserve asset created by the IMF in 1970. Were the plan to succeed, a genuine mechanism for the stabilization of exchange rates would have been created and the IMF would absorb excess dollars without triggering the currency's depreciation. If, instead, there was a shortage of dollars, the IMF could repurchase SDRs from member countries and put the previously acquired dollars back into circulation, halting any future appreciation. When the moment came to conclude the negotiations, strongly supported by both the Managing Director of the IMF, Jacques de Larosière, and the Chairman of the IMF's policy-making Interim Committee, Italian Treasury Minister Filippo Maria Pandolfi, the United States withdrew its support. In April 1980 the United States claimed that the mechanism had not been adequately examined from a technical-financial perspective (which was only partially true). In reality it held back because it became belatedly concerned about the prospect of the dollar losing its role as the key currency in the international monetary system. The proposal's demise was hastened by the hostile attitude of emerging and developing countries that were deriving benefits from the dollar's weakness and feared the substitution account might unduly restrict the growth of international liquidity and therefore the flow of capital towards the third world (Micossi and Saccomanni 1981).

In the midst of general uncertainty over the outcome of the negotiations, two decisions were nonetheless taken: in 1979, leading European countries agreed to establish the EMS to shield their currencies from the effects of dollar fluctuations and US monetary authorities resolved to combat the weak dollar by taking appropriate economic measures at home. Between August of 1979 and February of 1980 a strategy of severe monetary restriction was adopted by the Chairman of the Fed, Paul Volcker. With inflation levels in the United States running at 13 per cent, the discount rate was gradually increased from 9.5 to 13 per cent. Volcker, a Democrat who had served in the Nixon administration when the dollar's gold convertibility was terminated, was a man of strong convictions and independent spirit, firmly opposed to the traditional American position of 'benign neglect' towards the fortunes of the dollar often summed up by US monetary officials in the phrase 'the dollar is our currency, but it's your problem'. On the contrary, and as Volcker later recalled in his memoirs, he was convinced that the performance of the exchange rate was an important indicator for guiding monetary policy and that 'the depreciation of a currency, especially if repeated, is typically a signal that something is wrong' (Volcker and Gyohten 1992, p. xiv). Volcker's monetary squeeze probably cost Carter the White House, but it stabilized the dollar and cleared the way for Reagan's policy of fiscal expansion, which did so much to re-establish the trust of consumers and investors in the American economy.

Following the failure of the proposed substitution account, there were no further attempts to initiate institutional reforms of the international monetary system until 2006;[4] reforms, that is, made within the institutional context of the IMF and applicable to all its members, be they big or small, industrialized or developing countries.[5] Indeed, with the advent to power of Thatcher and Reagan, doubt was cast on the very notion of an international monetary system. In line with their conservative and free market ideology, the two leaders argued in international arenas that the problems of the global economy derived from internal imbalances of individual nations and erroneous national economic policies. If each state worked to 'put their house in order', limiting public intervention in the economy, cutting taxes, abolishing regulations and eliminating obstacles to the working of market forces, then problems in the international economy would simply melt away, as would the need to manage 'systemic' crises with multilateral instruments and interventions. In this scenario, international institutions such as the IMF or the World Bank would limit themselves to teaching countries (mostly emerging market countries) how to keep their affairs in order and providing industrialized countries with a forum for discussing their respective economic policy strategies and for exerting 'peer pressure', which they believed was the only available instrument for promoting cooperation between leading sovereign nations. This marked the beginning of the 'house in order' ideology, which is still widely practised today (see Padoa-Schioppa 2005). However, since even well-kept houses can catch fire and endanger neighbouring buildings, the ideology conceded that the need could arise for ad hoc interventions by a team of international firefighters. Indeed, it was precisely this kind of ad hoc joint initiative that was adopted to manage misalignments of exchange rates or the debt crises of emerging countries in the 1980s. In the following decade, the gravity and increasing frequency of these episodes persuaded President Bill Clinton to call for a sweeping review of global financial structures to manage what, in a speech he made at the Council on Foreign Relations in September 1998, he claimed was 'the greatest financial challenge facing the world in the last half century'. The emphasis placed by the US government on the seriousness of the global financial crisis at the close of the century could not have sent a more timely message to the markets. It confirmed that the management of international financial instability and the risks of contagion among emerging and even industrial countries was considered a political priority of the highest order and that leading world powers would not tolerate the implosion of the international economy. The message was well received, but it also raised expectations that proved difficult to satisfy.

Great emphasis on the need for a more effective financial regulation was placed following a series of corporate scandals in the United States (Enron, WorldCom, Tyco). New legislation was approved by the US Congress, known as the Sarbanes–Oxley Act of 2002.[6] The Act significantly strengthened the regulation of financial activity, particularly as regards internal controls, accounting practices, risk management procedures and so on. These new regulatory principles have quickly become 'best practices' throughout the global financial system and the pressure has grown on market participants worldwide to adopt them, although they are increasingly seen as an impediment to normal activity and are not always regarded as 'market friendly'.[7]

6.2   THE REFORM OF THE INTERNATIONAL FINANCIAL ARCHITECTURE

The concept of IFA made its official debut on the world stage in the summer of 1995 at the G7 Summit in Halifax, Nova Scotia, convened immediately after the outbreak of the Mexican crisis and its aftermath (Kenen 1996). But it was only after the Clinton initiative of 1998 that the reform of the IFA began. The process was essentially led by finance ministers and governors of central banks in the G7 countries and was translated into the detailed plan later approved by heads of state and government at the G7 Summit in Cologne in June 1999 (G7 Finance Ministers 1999). The G7 proposals were subsequently adopted by the deliberative bodies of the IMF and the World Bank, charged with promoting the implementation of the reforms. The term 'IFA' is often considered to be a synonym of 'international monetary system' but there are fundamental differences between the two concepts. The international monetary system is a macroeconomic concept encompassing, as has been said earlier, the exchange rate regime, the regime for capital movements, the mechanism for international liquidity creation and distribution, and all the 'rules of the game' for the adjustment of international payments imbalances. The IFA, by contrast, is a microeconomic concept referring to the set of principles and practices that influence the behaviour of individual participants in the global financial market, that is, borrowers, investors, intermediaries and regulators.

6.2.1   Main Features of the G7 Proposals

The fundamental idea behind the reform of the IFA was that the functioning of global financial markets generates tensions and instability – and occasionally crises – because of the existence of various obstacles hindering accurate risk assessment by intermediaries, the adequate protection of creditors' and debtors' rights, and an orderly management of situations of illiquidity. These obstacles may create the conditions for the kind of excessive capital flows and sharp credit contractions that are at the root of turbulence and international financial crises. The objectives of the reform were therefore to identify and remove obstacles to the correct functioning of markets that have an impact across a broad range of activities important for international financial stability. Countless papers have been produced on the specific contents of the IFA, analysing its operational characteristics and systemic implications (Eichengreen 1999a; Saccomanni 2000; Kenen 2001; Goldstein 2005 and Truman 2006). Here it will be sufficient to recall that the G7 proposals to consolidate the IFA implied taking action to: (1) strengthen financial systems in emerging market countries;

(2) enhance financial regulatory frameworks in industrial countries; (3) improve instruments and procedures for debt crisis prevention and management; and (4) adapt the institutions of international cooperation to the realities of global finance.

1.   The plan drew up several rules for emerging market countries wishing to strengthen their financial systems. These essentially consisted in the advice to adopt a series of standards and codes of best practices drawn up by institutions and international working groups, in line with the commitments made at the G7 Summit in Halifax in 1995. The principal codes of best practice agreed by the international community can be grouped into three main areas: policy transparency, covering disclosure requirements for data and statistics on economic performance and information on the conduct of monetary, financial and fiscal policies; financial sector regulation and supervision; and market integrity, including codes for corporate governance, bankruptcy procedures, and accounting and auditing.

2.   The rules that the G7 devised for industrial countries, including its own members, were more succinct but equally important. It was acknowledged that situations of financial instability at an international level can derive from an inadequate assessment of risks and creditworthiness by intermediaries. The monetary authorities of industrial countries were therefore urged to supervise international financial flows, correct inadequacies and close loopholes in the regulatory framework. In particular, they were urged to:

     ● improve risk assessment and management, through increased supervision of risk management practices and enhanced capital adequacy;
     ● assess the implications of the activity of 'highly leveraged institutions' (HLIs), such as hedge funds, for financial market dynamics;
     ● evaluate the implications of the activity of 'off-shore financial centres' (OFCs), tax and regulatory 'havens' often based in exotic locations as potential sources of financial instability, and encourage these entities to comply with international supervisory standards.

     Finally, industrial countries were urged to set a good example for the rest of the world and to allow their banking and financial systems to be scrutinized by international bodies charged with assessing their solidity and ensuring compliance with the codes of best practices.

3.   In respect of crisis management, the G7 Report distinguished between the phases of crisis prevention and resolution. It was recognized that

recourse to official financial assistance from the IMF could play an important role in preventing crises and limiting the risk of contagion. However, the G7 urged emerging countries to seek out innovative market-based tools aimed at preventing contagion and facilitating adjustment to shocks such as private contingent credit lines and debt instruments with rollover options. Moreover, emerging countries were encouraged to insert collective action clauses (CACs) in bond issues, along with other provisions that facilitate renegotiation of the terms of the bonds (such as interest rates and redemption periods) and discourage recourse to disruptive legal action by individual bond-holders. More generally, debtor countries were urged to maintain an open dialogue with their principal creditors and work in a spirit of mutual cooperation. For the resolution of crises the G7 proposed a framework for their orderly management based on two key principles: (a) crisis resolution must not undermine the commitment of countries to meet their obligations; and (b) market discipline works only if creditors bear the consequences of the risk they take, that is, if there is some 'private sector involvement' (PSI) in the process of sharing the cost of the crises. Within these 'goalposts', the framework linked the granting of official financial assistance by the IMF to countries in crisis with an undertaking by its lenders to provide further credit, to maintain current exposure levels, or to restructure outstanding obligations. Where the crisis resulted in debt service arrears, debtor countries were urged to seek a cooperative debt restructuring agreement under the supervision of the IMF; if the policies to deal with the crisis were judged appropriate, the IMF could then decide to grant financial assistance, applying its 'lending into arrears' (LIA) policy and/or authorizing the introduction of capital or exchange controls.

4. In the institutional sphere, the reform of the IFA did not aim to make a radical overhaul of pre-existing structures. The G7 Report did not seriously entertain the revolutionary proposals originating in political quarters to abolish the IMF, merge it with the World Bank or establish a new 'overarching' institution set above existing ones for coordination purposes. Other proposals, this time mainly from academics, were given equally short shrift, such as those suggesting the creation of a deposit insurance agency, a global bankruptcy court or a body for the supervision of markets and financial intermediaries.[8] The G7 proposed instead to expand the number of active participants in the implementation of the IFA's reform in two ways: by inviting other international institutions, such as the BIS, OECD, IOSCO and IAIS, to work alongside the IMF and the World Bank to strengthen the IFA; and by involv-

ing the leading emerging countries of Latin America, Asia and Africa in a newly established consultative group, the Group of Twenty (G20) (the G7 countries plus the 13 main emerging countries). Within the G7 itself, perhaps the most significant innovation was the creation proposed by the then President of the Bundesbank, Hans Tietmeyer, of a new international consultative body, the Financial Stability Forum (FSF). Its role was to enhance coordination among monetary authorities (treasuries and central banks) and financial regulatory agencies of G7 countries with a view to supervising the global financial system and identifying potential vulnerabilities. The IMF was invited to support these initiatives by enhancing its own research into the working of global capital markets and the determinants of market dynamics and by establishing appropriate forms of consultation with key global players.

6.2.2   Where Do We Stand on IFA Reform?

Standards and codes
The pillar of the IFA where progress has been most consistent and visible is the one dealing with international standards and codes of best practices. This is an area in which international cooperation has assumed innovative guises (Padoa-Schioppa 2006). The *political impulse* emanating from the G7 has mobilized the *rule-making* capacities of specialized agencies and bodies operating in the various segments of financial markets, while the global financial institutions – the IMF and World Bank – have been charged with *monitoring* the implementation of internationally recognized standards and codes (listed in Table 6.1) by their member countries, both developing and developed. The IMF monitors the standards on policy transparency. The IMF and World Bank monitor the standards on financial sector regulation and supervision, as part of their joint Financial Sector Assessment Program (FSAP). The World Bank monitors the standards on market integrity.

The extension of the activity of the Bretton Woods institutions into the area of monitoring compliance has given rise to an impressive number of evaluation missions and assessment reports. Since 1999 the Fund and the Bank have undertaken to write for each member country a Report on Observance of Standards and Codes (ROSC) covering the 12 policy areas indicated above. At the last review of the Standards and Codes Initiative in July 2005 by the IMF Executive Board, the Fund and the Bank staffs reported that 'through 30 April 2005, 593 initial assessments and 130 updates had been completed in 122 countries or two-thirds of the Fund membership' (IMF 2005g, p. 1).[9] Participation in the initiative, which is

Table 6.1   Basic standards for the solidity of financial systems

Area	Standard	Issuing body
Macroeconomic policy and data transparency		
Monetary and financial policy transparency	Code of Good Practices on Transparency in Monetary and Financial Policies	IMF
Fiscal policy transparency	Code of Good Practices on Fiscal Transparency	IMF
Data dissemination	Special Data Dissemination Standard / General Data Dissemination System[a]	IMF
Institutional and market infrastructure		
Insolvency[b]		World Bank
Corporate governance	Principles of Corporate Governance	OECD
Accounting	International Accounting Standards (IAS)[c]	IASB[d]
Auditing	International Standards on Auditing (ISA)	IFAC[d]
Payment and settlement	Core Principles for Systemically Important Payment Systems	CPSS
	Recommendations for Securities Settlement Systems	CPSS/ IOSCO
Market integrity	The Forty Recommendations of the Financial Action Task Force / 9 Special Recommendations Against Terrorist Financing	FATF
Financial regulation and supervision		
Banking supervision	Core Principles for Effective Banking Supervision	BCBS
Securities regulation	Objectives and Principles of Securities Regulation	IOSCO
Insurance supervision	Insurance Core Principles	IAIS

Notes:
a. Economies with access to international capital markets are encouraged to subscribe to the more stringent SDDS and all other economies are encouraged to adopt the GDDs.
b. The World Bank is co-ordinating a broad-based effort to develop a set of principles and guidelines on insolvency regimes. The United Nations Commission on International Trade Law (UNCITRAL), which adopted the Model Law on Cross-Border Insolvency in 1997, will help facilitate implementation.
c. Relevant IAS are currently being reviewed by the IAIS and IOSCO.
d. The International Accounting Standards Board (IASB) and the International Federation of Accountants (IFAC) are distinct from other standard-setting bodies in that they are private sector bodies.

Source: Financial Stability Forum, www.fsforum.org.

voluntary, was very high for emerging market countries, high for advanced economies and lower for developing countries.

Have all these efforts been crowned by success? The results are mixed. On the key objective of helping countries to strengthen their financial systems, the Fund and the Bank report notes that 'the initiative has delivered substantial results . . ., notably identifying vulnerabilities and establishing priorities for strengthening domestic institutions. The impact on actual implementation of reforms may not have been as substantial, but neither has it been insignificant'. On the other main objective of the initiative, that is to provide financial intermediaries with an instrument to guide and strengthen market discipline, the report recognizes that 'the initiative has significantly fallen short of its objectives of informing market participants' and that 'expectations on its attainment should be lowered' (IMF and World Bank 2005, p. 27).

A combination of factors has been responsible for this disappointing outcome. On the one hand, the initiative did not envisage a set of incentives to induce countries to embark on comprehensive and often unpopular structural reforms. Goldstein (2005, p. 390), for instance, had suggested that 'complying countries could obtain preferred access to IMF resources; they could receive more favourable risk weightings . . . in the context of international capital standards' but these proposals 'never really made it on the official agenda'. On the other hand, in response to a survey conducted by the Fund and the Bank market participants expressed the view that ROSCs were not quite suitable for operational purposes, although the information of ROSCs may indirectly influence them via the assessment made by rating agencies. Moreover the empirical evidence is still too limited to conclude that complying countries did indeed benefit from their enhanced creditworthiness by obtaining lower risk premia on their market borrowing (Goldstein 2005). In the event, the IMF itself recognized that the standards and codes initiative would, somehow, have to be scaled down. Outlining the Fund's medium-term strategy, the Managing Director indicated 'it should be possible to focus our work more, with fewer reviews and selectivity in initiating new reports based on macro-criticality. This would free up resources for higher priorities' (IMF 2005e, p. 6).

The involvement of the Fund in this kind of work has been regarded by some observers as 'problematic' and indicative of a 'mission creep', which may have distracted it from devoting more attention to its core activity in the macroeconomic area, especially in the field of monetary, fiscal and exchange rate policies (Truman 2006). However, the fact that the initiative has not had a major impact on promoting structural reforms in emerging market countries is hardly surprising. The sheer breadth and depth of the reforms suggested by the G7 for emerging market countries through the

adoption of best practices and standards necessarily imply a radical institutional overhaul and a thorough revision of the working of the economic
system that can only take place gradually and over a substantial period of
time. Consider, for example, the inadequacy of bankruptcy legislation,
which made the management of the debt crisis particularly painful in a
country like Indonesia, where insolvency principally hit the private corporate sector. The international community's success in persuading the
Indonesian authorities to adopt a modern, comprehensive, bankruptcy law
proved a useful and necessary step, to which the authorities responded
promptly, but was hardly sufficient. What Indonesia also needed was a competent magistracy able both to evaluate international financial transactions
and to apply the relevant bankruptcy procedures in a way that protected
creditors and debtors alike. Bankruptcy judges must also enjoy decision-
making autonomy enabling them, for example, to declare a company owned
by relations or friends of the country's president bankrupt without fearing
for their personal safety. All of this may require, in some cases, the introduction or effective implementation of fundamental principles of democratic systems such as the separation of powers, the independence of the
judiciary, and the respect of civil liberties. These are slow and difficult
processes that often meet with strong resistance in political and economic
quarters. Indeed, according to Olson (2000), efforts to strengthen financial
systems in emerging countries must be seen as part of a broader strategy
aimed at putting in place a 'market augmenting government': a government
that is, which guarantees the individual rights of citizens, including economic rights, and protects them from all forms of 'depredation'.

Promoting transparency is also not as easy as it might first appear. It
involves the publication and reporting of exhaustive, truthful, and timely
data on a vast range of economic factors that influence the decisions of
foreign investors and the global market. Again, the Asian crisis of 1997
revealed that there were grave shortcomings in the data published by some
central banks. Official reserves were overestimated in Thailand because the
statistics neglected to mention that they had been acquired through short-
term swap operations. In Korea it turned out the central bank had
deposited its official reserves in Korean banks overseas and when these
same banks were implicated in the country's liquidity crisis, the reserves
became actually unavailable. These deficiencies in reporting practices are
easy to correct, but it is much less easy to obtain accurate, detailed and up-
to-date statistics on foreign currency debts run up by public sector agencies
that do not have to answer to monetary authorities when it comes to managing their financial activities. Worse still are debts accrued by private companies and households, which, even in the most advanced countries slip
through the data-gathering nets cast by authorities. What the global market

ideally would like to see is a 'national balance sheet' with statistics on all foreign assets and liabilities – divided into the state and public sector, banking and financial systems, and private sector (companies and households) – with a clear indication of the maturity of each asset and liability. It is obvious that such a complex system of data collection and processing, even if all reporting entities were fully willing to collaborate, would entail gaps in the information provided due to the inevitably considerable time lapse between the date of publication and the dates to which the information refer. It is within these gaps that information asymmetries, based on personal relations and subjective assessments, flourish, leading to the kind of underestimation of financial risks which, fuelled by competitive pressures, sets the 'herd' of global operators in motion. For these reasons, the role that transparency can effectively play in guiding global market choices and staving off financial crises has been deemed by academic economists, from the very beginning of the reform process, to be relatively modest. For example, Eichengreen (1999a, p. 84) noted that 'not much can be expected from these initiatives. Data asymmetries will inevitably remain'; and Blinder (1999, p. 58) argued that 'although transparency – which is the current rage – is all to the good, no one should expect it to accomplish very much in the way of crisis prevention. Bubbles form and burst even in extremely transparent markets like the New York Stock Exchange'.

Enhancing capital adequacy and closing regulatory loopholes
Efforts by the major industrial countries to strengthen their banking and financial systems began in the early 1970s, well before the G7 initiative to reform the IFA. The most important work took place in the context of the Basel Committee on Banking Supervision, where the seminal Capital Accord was negotiated in 1988 (see Padoa-Schioppa 2004a, pp. 4–5 and p. 52), introducing a general requirement for internationally active banks to hold total capital equivalent to at least 8 per cent of their risk-weighted assets. In June 2004 a revised framework was agreed (Basel II), which will enter into force over 2007–08 and will introduce more risk-sensitive capital requirements, emphasizing the measurement and management of key banking risks (credit, market, operational risks) and their potential future impact on the banks' activity.[10] From the very beginning the activity of the Basel Committee was guided by three main objectives: ensuring that no bank escape effective supervision; ensuring that banks have adequate capital; and enhancing market discipline (see Padoa-Schioppa 2005, Chapter 1). Similar objectives, with the necessary changes, have been adopted by the other rule-making bodies active in the non-banking sector of the global market and are the guiding principles of the FSF in its activity to promote financial stability on a global scale. The FSF has given itself

a rather broad agenda, regularly reviewing the main global risks and vulnerabilities in the international financial system and overseeing the implementation by participating countries and institutions of measures to strengthen its resilience. At its meeting in March 2006, the FSF identified as 'developments with the potential to cause strains in financial systems': growing external imbalances, high levels of household sector indebtedness, and low risk premia reflecting an abundance of liquidity. It also discussed 'areas of ongoing concern, including issues relating to counterparty risk management, hedge funds, operational risks and valuation practice for complex financial instruments'.[11] In the vast agenda that the FSF has developed since its establishment, the two specific issues singled out by the G7, namely the risks posed by the activity of OFCs and of hedge funds, have indeed received special attention.

Concerns about the activity of OFCs were raised in 1999 in the IMF policy-making Interim Committee as there was anecdotal evidence that they had played a role in the Asian financial crisis and related turbulences (indeed LTCM, the hedge fund whose insolvency caused major tensions in global financial markets in 1998, was established offshore). Moreover, the total amount of bank and financial claims on 44 identified OFCs,[12] estimated by the IMF at around $2 trillion in 2001, was considered to be of a systemically relevant magnitude. At the same time, detailed information on the activity of financial institutions operating in OFCs was very limited and not easily available. Furthermore, concerns had been raised in various organizations: in the FSF about impediments to effective banking and financial supervision; in the OECD about 'harmful tax practices'; and in the Financial Action Task Force of the G7 about money laundering and other financial crimes. Given the sensitive nature of these claims and the sovereign status of OFCs, the technique adopted by the international institutions to obtain compliance and convergence was essentially a 'name and shame' approach or, put more diplomatically, 'blacklisting to spur reforms'. Eventually, the FSF proposed that the IMF be given the responsibility to devise and manage an 'Assessment Program on Offshore Financial Centers', linking it to its ongoing activity in the field of standards and codes. At the first review of the programme in 2003, the IMF noted that:

> The OFC assessment program has had an important effect in improving supervision standards. Concerned about reputation risks, most of the major centres have strengthened their laws, regulations and supervisory arrangements to meet international standards either ahead of or as a result of the assessments. Some smaller jurisdictions with weak supervisory capacity have reduced their offshore activity and requested technical assistance to improve their regulatory and supervisory arrangements. (IMF 2003d, p. 2)

Based on this positive evaluation, the IMF approved the continuation of a second phase of the programme, focused on monitoring activities, technical assistance to OFCs and increased cooperation between onshore and offshore supervisors. The results of this second phase were judged positively in March 2006 by the FSF which stressed, however, how urgent it was 'to address remaining problems in several OFCs, notably in the areas of effective cross-border cooperation, information exchange and adequacy of supervisory resources'.[13] All in all, the programme seems to have strayed from its original premise and has turned from a 'name and shame' process into a more bureaucratic exercise of 'box ticking' and technical cooperation. It will no doubt be continued and will inevitably produce over time some improvements in procedures and practices. Whether it will also contribute to greater financial stability on a global scale remains to be seen.

Efforts to improve the supervision of hedge funds, the most famous members of the category of highly leveraged institutions, have been ongoing for quite some time. Immediately following the near collapse of the LTCM hedge fund in September 1998 in the United States, the issue of whether or not hedge funds should be subject to the direct supervision of a specific regulatory authority was addressed in a number of official and private bodies.[14] The most important were: the Working Group on Financial Markets established by President Clinton, which submitted a report on 'Hedge funds, leverage and the lessons of long-term capital management'; the work conducted by the BSBC focusing on the relationships of banks with HLIs; and the Counterparty Risk Management Policy Group set up by major private capital market participants. These early reports were examined by a Working Group on Highly Leveraged Institutions set up by the FSF (see FSF 2000). The conclusion of this review was basically to reject the option of direct supervision of hedge funds, but to recommend a number of measures to strengthen the supervision of risk taken by banks and other regulated financial institutions dealing with hedge fund counterparties (prime broker dealers). Measures in this direction have been taken by various national financial authorities in the United States and several EU countries with the aim of improving the risk management procedures and techniques adopted by intermediaries dealing with hedge funds. The question of the appropriate regulatory regime for hedge funds has, however, received renewed attention since 2005 from both national and international financial authorities as well as from major market participants.[15] There are several reasons for this revival of interest: the continuing growth of the hedge fund industry and the growing use of complex derivative instruments, like credit default swaps; the increasing 'retailization' of its products to an ever larger range of investors – including pension funds – mostly through the network of 'funds of hedge funds'; and the increased correlation among hedge funds' strategies, which in late 2005 exceeded levels prevailing at the time of the LTCM crisis, thereby increasing the risk of disorderly exits from 'crowded trades' at a time of decreasing market liquidity (ECB 2006a, p. 142). However, the response of regulators in major financial countries to these concerns has not been uniform. In the United States and the United Kingdom, where hedge funds have been created and developed, regulators have been concerned with the issue of investor protection, mostly against fraudulent practices by hedge fund managers, rather than with the risks posed to systemic stability by hedge funds. In the United Kingdom, the FSA, following extended consultation with the industry, concluded that the activity of hedge funds does not pose a threat to financial stability or to market confidence (see *FSA Feedback Statements*, 2006, www.fsa.gov.uk). In general, Anglo-American regulators view the development of hedge funds favourably, seeing them as instruments that enhance the efficiency and liquidity of financial markets. Consequently, they see their role as confined to monitoring rather than regulating the industry. Typical of this attitude was a speech made by Ben Bernanke, the new Chairman of the Fed, on 'hedge funds and systemic risk' at a conference organized by the Federal Reserve Bank of Atlanta in May 2006 (Bernanke 2006, p. 4). While acknowledging concerns about 'hedge fund opacity and possible liquidity risks', Bernanke dismissed as impractical, proposals to create a database of hedge fund positions as an instrument for financial authorities 'to monitor this possible source of systemic risk and to address the build-up of risk as it occurs'. In continental Europe, financial authorities have expressed much greater concern over systemic risks connected to the activity of hedge and equity funds and a proposal has been made in the European Parliament to introduce a light regulatory regime for 'sophisticated alternative investment vehicles', with the aim of bringing onshore funds that are presently offshore. So far the EU Commission and the EU Council have not taken up the Parliament's proposal and have indicated that the issues posed by the activity of the hedge funds require further analysis and consultation with market participants (Garbaravicius and Dierick 2005, pp. 52–53; ECB 2006a). However, there is anecdotal evidence that the role of hedge funds has increased recently and has to some extent affected the balance of roles among financial intermediaries on the global market. In substance, hedge funds are no longer relatively small players that limit their activity to highly leveraged transactions on behalf of a few 'adult' investors with big shoulders and a strong risk appetite. The IMF (2007c, p. 30) estimates that 'hedge funds now account for a third of trading volume and, therefore, the liquidity provided in several markets'; they also perform a number of important functions that were traditionally the domain of commercial and investments banks.[16] This development may weaken the argument that hedge funds need not be regulated as they are in fact indirectly controlled by the banks or prime brokers (mostly investment banks) that extend credit to them. In fact it may well happen that banks would be under competitive pressure to finance hedge funds without much attention as to whether this entails excessive credit or systemic risks. Hedge funds may in the end gain access to sources of liquidity without the need for bank financing. The outlook for the ongoing debate on these issues is reviewed in Chapter 14.

Crisis prevention and resolution
The implementation of the G7 proposals to strengthen the mechanisms and procedures for crisis prevention and resolution turned out to be much more difficult and controversial than initially expected. In fact, strong differences of view on the best approach to crisis management quickly emerged even among the G7 countries themselves and in the position taken by academic economists and market participants.

Crisis prevention A first area of contention concerns the role of international financial assistance in the prevention of financial crises. Here, two contrasting views are widely held: the first, that in a global financial system there is a need for an international lender of last resort, which can provide countries the financial resources to counter sudden capital outflows and speculative attacks thereby forestalling the spread of financial contagion; the second, that the very existence of a lender of last resort, real or perceived, in itself can represent a moral hazard liable to encourage reckless borrowing in the expectation of a bail-out should a crisis occur.

During the 1990s, the international community's initial response to debt crises was to bolster the scope of financial intervention by the IMF by creating, alongside its traditional instruments,[17] new and broader lending facilities and by making it easier and faster to grant assistance. This was the reasoning behind the creation of the Emergency Financing Mechanism (EFM) in 1994 after the Mexican crisis. In 1997 (after the Korean crisis) the IMF incorporated the EFM in a new fast-track but more costly Supplemental Reserve Facility (SRF) to encourage early debt repayment once the acute phase of a crisis had passed. In 1999, following a series of proposals by the G7, the SRF was amended to include a new instrument, the Contingent Credit Lines (CCL). These were set up to protect countries in good economic and financial shape from the risks of contagion that the globalization of finance entails. Claims that the IMF has over the years increasingly assumed the role and functions of lender of last resort are not, therefore, entirely unfounded. But it is also true that this came about with the consent and by the express wish of the major 'stakeholders' of the IMF itself – in the first instance the G7 countries and the leading emerging countries – and certainly not as a result of the obscure manoeuvrings of faceless bureaucrats, as critics of the Fund sometimes seem to imply. If the IMF has increasingly played the role of lender of last resort, often acting in concert with the World Bank, it is because of the international community's conviction that countries like Mexico, Korea and Brazil were genuinely 'too big to fail', for reasons to do with political or economic stability, or both. It is not surprising, therefore, that a distinguished economist like Fischer (2000), from his vantage point as First Deputy Managing Director of the IMF, justified and defended the role of the Fund as lender of last resort. He emphasized the results achieved in stabilizing the global financial system and avoiding moral hazard, thanks to the conditional nature of financial assistance and its high cost. For the supporters of a strong IMF role in crisis prevention, a more relevant question was whether the IMF had adequate resources to perform the function of lender of last resort. In theory, given that unlike national central banks the IMF has no money-creation powers, it should be able in the current regime of financial globalization to borrow from the international market and raise the resources it needs to carry out the kind of 'unlimited' interventions that characterize lenders of last resort. But when the possibility of granting this 'recycling' power to the IMF was raised in a proposal officially tabled by Italy, it failed to garner the necessary consensus.[18]

Different views were expressed by a task force set up under the aegis of the Council on Foreign Relations, chaired by Morris Goldstein and composed of prominent academics, market participants and members of monetary authorities, which drafted a report on the future of the IFA (Goldstein 1999). The Goldstein Report acknowledged the importance of the IMF's role in managing crises and reducing their macroeconomic costs, but expressed concern at the growing number and size of IMF 'rescue packages'. Accordingly it proposed that assistance granted to countries with balance of payments problems should remain within 'normal limits', except in cases where the crisis put the stability of the entire system at risk or could spread to other emerging countries. In a nutshell, the Goldstein Report maintained that when it came to financial assistance disbursed by international organizations 'less will do more', meaning that a more modest approach will lessen the moral hazard and curtail the excessive lending by the market that is at the heart of crises. To achieve this goal, the report further recommended a return to the strict demarcation of roles between the IMF and the World Bank that was spelt out at Bretton Woods, ending the overlaps and dual interventions of recent years. The report urged the IMF to focus on relatively short-term financing and macroeconomic strategies for balance of payments adjustments, and leave decisions about long-term financing for structural interventions where they belong: back with the World Bank. For its part the World Bank was urged to avoid financial involvement in crisis management and to prioritize the fight against poverty and socially-oriented structural reforms.[19]

Far more radical were the recommendations of the International Financial Institutions Advisory Commission established by the US Congress and chaired by Professor Allan Meltzer of the University of Chicago (Meltzer 2000).[20] The Commission proposed that the IMF finance only those emerging countries which, although solvent, had been temporarily denied access to financial markets. Liquidity loans would have short maturity, be made at a penalty rate and be secured by a clear priority claim on the borrower's assets, who would be provided with strong incentives to resolve problems rapidly in order to return to normal market borrowing conditions. Except in circumstances of systemic crisis, loans would be made only to countries that had met predetermined conditions of financial soundness and the correct functioning of domestic financial systems. Finally, the Commission proposed that the IMF abolish its special Poverty Reduction and Growth Facility (PRGF), given that these objectives should be met exclusively by the World Bank. In short, the IMF should finance a very limited number of its (then) 182 member countries, relinquishing its role as consultant on macroeconomic adjustment policies. The World Bank was similarly urged to review its mandate and abolish all loans to countries that can access the financial market (such as Brazil or Korea) or whose annual per capita income is in excess of $4000. Loans should principally target poorer countries, with per capita income of less than $2500. Finally, the World Bank should never engage in crisis lending; this task should be carried out solely by the IMF.

The decision-making bodies of the IMF and World Bank went no further than taking note of the proposals contained in the Goldstein and Meltzer reports. The US government did not formally follow up on the Meltzer proposals because of the difficulties it would have encountered in securing the necessary majorities in the governing assemblies of the two institutions, given the predictable opposition of developing and emerging countries. Even within the G7, the proposals were unlikely to have been supported by EU member countries or Japan. The debate on the role of the IMF in crisis prevention has continued well into the 2000s and a number of issues are still on the table: the question of the exceptional access to IMF facilities by highly indebted countries; how to shape IMF lending to well-performing countries, since the CCLs had to be cancelled in 2003 because no countries had applied for them; whether the IMF should provide support (policy advice) without lending; and whether and to what extent the IMF (or rather the World Bank) should assist low-income countries.

Reading a comprehensive review of all these issues and the various proposals that have been formulated in official quarters and by academic economists to deal with them, such as the one of Truman (2006), the overwhelming feeling remains one of unfinished business.

Crisis resolution   The second area of contention covers the rules and the institutions that are needed in a global financial system to carry out an orderly resolution of financial crises. It is generally agreed that the IMF should play a central role in this area, to be exercised discretionally and on a case-by-case basis. As demonstrated by Giannini (1999), the notion of the IMF as lender of last resort can be usefully redefined to mean that it should use its financial clout to enhance coordination between borrowers and lenders so as to ensure an orderly management of situations of illiquidity and avoid their degeneration into insolvency crises. Similar views have been expressed within the G7, following proposals by the Bank of Canada and Bank of England (Haldane and Kruger 2001), and within the Eurosystem. Disagreement has surfaced on the issue of whether the role of the IMF should be informal and pragmatic or whether it should be exercised within a strong institutional framework, underpinned by precise rules and procedures. The IMF, building on the broad framework for crisis resolution agreed (in Prague, September 2000) by its International Monetary and Financial Committee (IMFC)[21], proposed the creation of a formal Sovereign Debt Reconstruction Mechanism (SDRM). The proposal, which was made against the background of the disorderly 'denouement' of the debt crisis in Argentina, marked a major change of attitude regarding the role of the IMF in crisis resolution (Krueger 2001, p. 5). By reducing the emphasis on the IMF's role as lender of last resort, the IMFC was opening the way to a possible institutional involvement of the Fund in crisis management in the guise of an authentic 'international bankruptcy court'. Despite the impressive analytical effort by the IMF staff in devising the operational features of the SDRM using a market-friendly approach, the proposal encountered the immediate opposition of major private sector intermediaries. They feared that, in the cooperative framework provided by the IMF, the establishment of the SDRM would offer an irresistible incentive to highly indebted countries to default on their sovereign debts. The major capital market participants, acting through the International Institute of Finance (IIF), lobbied intensively for alternative approaches, and this eventually led the US authorities to withdraw their support for the SDRM, which was unceremoniously shelved at an IMF meeting in April 2003. Since then significant progress has been made in implementing the alternative concepts preferred by the IIF. A first achievement was the more widespread use of CACs in sovereign bond issues by emerging countries, which rose from 31 per cent of the outstanding stock of bonds at the end of 2002 to 53 per cent at the end of June 2005 (IMF 2005d). This has been achieved through the combined efforts of the IMF, the financial authorities in major capital market centres (New York, London and Tokyo), and global financial intermediaries and sovereign issuers in key emerging countries in Latin America, Asia and Eastern Europe. Moreover, in November 2004 the IIF, in consultation with major sovereign borrowers, drew up a set of 'Principles for Stable Capital Flows and Fair Debt Restructuring in Emerging Markets' (IIF 2004). The Principles, which are built upon the framework for crisis resolution devised by the IMF, cover four broad areas: transparency and the timely flow of information; close debtor–creditor dialogue and cooperation to avoid restructuring; good faith actions; and fair treatment. The Principles have been favourably received by a number of emerging countries[22] and the IMF is promoting their adoption by sovereign issuers, as part of its activity in the field of standards and codes. The viability of such voluntary cooperative schemes is, however, still untested, as conditions in the global financial market in 2004–06 have generally been favourable to sovereign borrowers, with abundant liquidity and narrowing spreads.

Institutional reforms
The modest institutional changes proposed by the G7 have indeed been implemented: the G20 and the FSF have become operational in their respective roles of consultative bodies, the G20 among the G7 countries and major emerging economies; the FSF among G7 monetary and financial authorities and the main standard-setting bodies of financial markets. The creation of the G20, although welcomed by emerging countries, has not really addressed the key issue of how to reform the governance of the Bretton Woods institutions, in particular as regards members' quotas and voting power, which no longer reflect the weights of key countries and regions in the world economy. As Truman (2006) noted in his comprehensive review, this is a highly sensitive political issue, which may involve a significant increase in the quotas of emerging countries, especially in Asia, at the expense of industrial countries, especially those in Europe.[23] This is not going to be an easy question to address. While the stature and influence of the IMF in the world economic and financial system would no doubt be enhanced by a more realistic and balanced representation of key countries and regions, the reform should not alter the key features of the Fund as an institution in which member countries have a voting power based on their population, national income, and foreign trade shares. A first step in rearranging the quota structure was agreed by the IMFC at its meeting in Singapore in September 2006: it envisages a selective increase in the quotas

of China, Korea, Mexico and Turkey. Further negotiations will be required to bring about a significant and more realistic distribution of quotas.

As regards the FSF, much has already been said about its activity in monitoring the global financial system and its risks and vulnerabilities. The challenge for the FSF is, however, to maintain the focus on key policy issues, resisting the temptation to oversee an ever expanding agenda which would downgrade the FSF role to a box-ticking bureaucratic activity. To support the FSF, the IMF has expanded its activity in the field of international financial markets. In addition to its ongoing work on macroeconomic policy issues conducted by the research department and reported in the twice-yearly publication of the *World Economic Outlook* (*WEO*), the IMF set up in 2001 a new Department for International Capital Markets, which since 2003 has been responsible for the preparation of the *Global Financial Stability Report* (*GFSR*), also published twice-yearly.[24] The GFSR is based on internal analysis and research as well as on informal consultations with commercial and investment banks, securities firms, asset management companies, hedge funds, institutional investors, stock and futures exchanges, credit rating agencies and also regulating authorities and academic researchers in major financial centres and countries. However, despite these improvements, in 2005 the perception among the G7 was still that 'the IMF needs to integrate more fully capital market and financial sector analysis into the daily life of the Fund'.[25] In response to these pressures, in June 2005, the IMF Managing Director appointed a working group of experts under the chairmanship of former New York Fed President W.J. McDonough to review the IMF financial sector work and provide advice on the effectiveness of the organization and allocation of the work that was 'dispersed among several functional and area departments' (IMF 2005f). Following the recommendations of the McDonough Report, the Managing Director announced in February 2006 the creation of a 'new Department that will be a centre of excellence for all aspects of financial, capital market and monetary work in the IMF' (IMF 2006f). The new department merges the functions and staff of the International Capital Markets Department and the Monetary and Financial Systems Department and is headed by Jaime Caruana, former Governor of the Bank of Spain and former Chairman of the Basle Committee on Banking Supervision. It is to be hoped that as a result of these further adaptations, the IMF will finally be in a better position to analyse and monitor the impact of globalization, some 20 years since its inception, for the working of the international monetary and financial system.

Missing pillars in the architecture?

Despite being billed as a response to the challenges of globalization and financial instability, the reform of the IFA was in fact essentially about managing the debt crises of emerging countries. Indeed, the G7 Report omitted any reference to the interdependence of monetary and exchange rate policies of major countries and to its implications for the operation of global financial markets and their propensity to generate credit booms and busts and unsustainable asset price trends. The second major shortcoming of the IFA reform was its lack of attention to exchange rate policies for the key reserve currencies of the global economy and to their role in correcting payments imbalances and exchange rate misalignments. In the remaining sections of this chapter it will be shown how the issues ignored by the IFA reform project have resurfaced after a time and how they have been addressed.

6.3   THE PREVENTION OF BUBBLES

The prevention of bubbles has not been included in any of the many reform plans elaborated in official or academic circles, essentially because there has been no consensus as to what could usefully be done by monetary and financial authorities with the instruments at their disposal.[26] There is a broad consensus that monetary policy cannot be used to pursue financial stability (that is, to prevent bubbles) as it is already assigned to pursue price stability: if you have two objectives, you need two instruments. This view has received strong support by such an authority in the field as Alan Greenspan (2002), who argued strongly against using interest rate hikes to counter the formation of bubbles. Rather – Greenspan maintained – monetary policy should be relaxed promptly and aggressively to limit the deflationary impact of the bursting of the bubble, after it has occurred. If monetary policy is not available to pursue financial stability, it is also widely recognized that the tools of the regulatory authorities of financial markets are not really suitable to cope with situations of systemic instability such as those generated by excessive credit creation. Typically these authorities are equipped to deal with the instability of individual market participants, be they banks or other financial intermediaries, and their primary concern is to ensure that market participants have an adequate capital base with respect to the risks they incur and that their operations are transparent. The approach followed by supervisory authorities is, in other words, 'micro-prudential' while the problem they have to deal with is of a 'macropruden-tial' nature. In these circumstances, one would have to conclude that there is not much that the authorities can do to prevent systemic financial insta-bility or the emergence of bubbles. To take such a resigned attitude, however, could be seriously counterproductive as it might convince citizens and their elected representatives that the only way to cope with financial instability is to introduce restrictions on capital movements or to 'throw sand in the wheels' of international financial markets as suggested by James Tobin (1978 and 1998). The risk of using protectionist measures to deal with international financial instability has been recognized, mostly within the central banking community, as it would distort the flow of international trade and investment with negative repercussions for growth and employment on a global scale. Analytical and empirical efforts are underway to devise a policy framework that would allow the normal operation of global financial markets while promoting conditions of financial stability.

A first call for a thorough review of the issues financial instability raises for monetary authorities came from Andrew Crockett with his seminal paper for a SUERF Colloquium (Crockett 2000). In it he identified two areas for further research and analysis: the first, how to deal with the systemic risks associated with the financial cycle; the second, the relationship between monetary and financial stability. This second area, Crockett advised, should be explored with a 'critical but open mind'. Not surprisingly, Crockett's suggestion has been heeded primarily within the BIS, where a number of very stimulating papers have been produced in recent years. One such paper (Borio and Lowe 2002) presented empirical evidence that it is possible to identify ex ante financial imbalances and that sustained credit growth, combined with large upward movements in asset prices, increases the probability of an episode of financial instability. The paper also argued that while low inflation promotes financial stability, it also increases the likelihood that excess demand pressures show up first in credit aggregates and asset prices rather than in the prices of goods and services. Subsequent papers analysed the policy implications of these empirical findings. As regards the framework for financial supervision and regulation, it is argued that a macro-prudential approach is required in which the main concern would be 'the disruption of economic life . . . brought about by generalized financial distress' rather than 'the pursuit of narrowly interpreted depositor protection objectives' (Borio 2002, p. 25). As regards the framework for monetary policy, it is argued that no change is required in the objectives of monetary policy, but in the way these are pursued: basically, greater weight should be given 'to signs of the build-up of financial imbalances in deciding when and how far to tighten policy' (Borio et al. 2003, p. 44). In practice, the macro-prudential approach relies to a large extent on cooperation between central banks and supervisory authorities. In a subsequent paper Borio and White (2004) called for 'subtle modifications in current policy frameworks in both the financial and monetary spheres' with the aim of limiting 'the potential excessive procyclicality of the financial system'. In the monetary sphere, in particular, they drew attention to the risk that financial imbalances may also materialize when inflation is low and to the need to lean against those imbalances by lengthening the time horizon and giving greater weight to financial risks in monetary policy formulation. In a more recent paper, White (2006) elaborated on how such a new monetary policy framework could operate with more symmetry over the credit cycle:

> There would be greater resistance to upswings. This, in turn, would obviate the need for asymmetric easing in the subsequent downturn and the problems arising from holding policy rates at very low levels for sustained periods. One important effect of more symmetric policies is that they would also act to prevent financial imbalances from cumulating over time. This, in turn, would free the authorities' hands to respond appropriately to the upward phase of any given credit cycle, since there would be less fear of precipitating a crisis. In this way, a virtuous rather than a vicious circle might be more firmly established. (p. 16)

The issue also received considerable attention within the ECB. Padoa-Schioppa (2002) urged monetary authorities to look for 'the land in between' monetary policy and prudential supervision; that land indeed does exist and contains instruments that can be used to pursue monetary and financial stability at a systemic level. These include: the management of the payments system, emergency liquidity support, crisis management coordination, and public and private comments (sometimes defined by market participants as 'oral interventions'). As these instruments are available to central banks or supervisory authorities or both, it follows that their efficient use depends crucially on the coordination of interventions by the authorities involved. Moreover, Otmar Issing (2004) recognized that central banks can 'fight excessive asset prices developments' through the control of the creation of money or the multiplication of credit. However, empirical analysis conducted by the ECB (Detken and Smets 2004, p. 31) indicated that 'not all asset price booms lead to a bust and not all busts to a financial crisis' and that, therefore, 'monetary policy response depends on the nature of the underlying shock responsible for the asset price increase'. In other words, no predetermined rules for monetary policy can be prudently set and the response should be decided case by case. From a policy framework perspective, the position of the ECB has been clearly described by President Trichet (2005):

> With regard to the optimal monetary policy response to asset price bubbles, I would argue that its informational requirements and its possible – and difficult to assess – side effects are in reality very onerous. Empirical evidence confirms the link between money and credit developments and dismal asset price booms. Thus a comprehensive monetary analysis will detect those risks to medium and long run price stability. The fact that the ECB's monetary policy strategy has this

property is in my view a significant advantage in light of the current challenges facing modern times central banks. (p. 14)

The search for strategies to deal with monetary and financial instability has thus started, but it is still at a preliminary stage. Nevertheless, a few general comments may be in order. Irrespective of the precise content of the strategy, it is quite likely that monetary and financial authorities of the countries involved would have to use some degree of policy activism. In a regime of global finance, there are no 'automatic pilot' devices in the framework for monetary and exchange rate policies or in the prudential regulatory system to which one can safely relinquish the responsibility of ensuring financial stability. Nor is it advisable to adopt a policy of benign neglect and rely solely on market discipline. Policy activism does not necessarily mean adopting new measures or changing policies at every sign of turbulence; it means being ready to broadcast appropriate policy signals whenever there appears to be evidence of unsustainable trends in key financial variables such as credit aggregates, asset prices and exchange rates. The 'signal' should make clear to market participants that the authorities consider current trends unsustainable and likely to lead to severe financial imbalances. The nature of the signal may be appropriately tailored to circumstances: it may take the form of an oral warning, or might involve monetary policy measures, exchange market interventions, tax or regulatory changes. It could be argued that such policy activism may be in itself destabilizing and give rise to greater market volatility. Moreover, if the activism included a pre-emptive monetary tightening by the central bank, without clear evidence of an inflationary threat, this may be criticized as damaging to the economy and the legitimate interests of, say, private investors in the stock market. These arguments are understandable, but are not really convincing. Any policy action is bound to change financial market expectations and the assessment of risk and return by intermediaries and investors. The volatility in financial markets that normally accompanies policy changes reflects precisely the adjustment process carried out by the market as intermediaries rearrange their positions in the light of the new expectations about risk and return on their investment. Inevitably in this process there are winners and losers. But what matters is that the volatility entails an enhanced perception of risk by market participants, which may be the crucial ingredient for deflating a potential financial bubble. Indeed bubbles are generated when markets lose the perception of a two-way risk; it is one-way markets that generate overshootings, bandwagons and bubbles. In the end, investors should be grateful that a bubble has been deflated sooner rather than later.

The key question in any strategy to counter bubbles is whether a poten-tial financial imbalance can be unmistakably identified at an early stage. In a regime of globalization it may be difficult for the monetary authorities of any individual country, large or small, to have all the information needed to assess the impact on financial conditions of international capital flows and of the operation of global financial markets. It is only in the fora of international consultation and cooperation that the full picture of the trends and the vulnerabilities of the international financial system can be pieced together. This issue will be addressed in detail in Chapter 14.

6.4 HOW TO COPE WITH GLOBAL IMBALANCES AND EXCHANGE RATE MISALIGNMENTS

The omission of exchange rate policies in the IFA reform was immediately detected by a minority of the task force's members who drew up the Goldstein Report (1999), including the former Fed Chairman, Paul Volcker, financiers like George Soros and John Heimann, and former members of Democrat and Republican administrations, like Fred Bergsten and John Schlesinger. These members suggested that the IFA reform should also include a proposal to create 'target zones' for the exchange rates of the dollar, euro and yen. A similar proposal had been put forward first by John Williamson (1983) but, despite having had some eminent support-ers in McKinnon (1996) and Mundell (2000), has remained a 'minority view' even in the wider context of academic circles and private research institutes. But aside from these 'lone riders' whose ideas have more often been seen as representing stimulating intellectual provocations rather than concrete proposals, policy-makers in Europe and Asia, the two monetary areas that, together with the dollar, impact on the entire global financial system, have expressed growing concern over the high costs of exchange rate volatility and misalignments. At the time of the IFA proposals, however, in light of the G7's well-advertised preference for a floating exchange rate regime between the major currencies, these concerns were voiced more to encourage debate and test reactions, rather than as official proposals. But they nonetheless confirmed that the question of exchange rate regimes remained open. In France, the only EU country where the functioning of the international monetary system has been traditionally considered one of the main priorities in government programmes, the Conseil d'Analyse Economique (1999), a unit within the Prime Minister's office, drew up a report on the IFA in which it proposed 'a joint manage-ment of flexible exchange rates' to tackle the underlying causes of inter-national financial instability. Asia's steps in this direction have been more cautious – given the complexity of the political relations between the leading countries in the area – but equally meaningful. In 1999 the Association of South-East Asian Nations (ASEAN) together with Japan, China, and South Korea (the ASEAN+3) decided to establish a mechanism for monetary cooperation between the region's central banks with the aim of protecting the exchange rates of their national currencies from the instability generated by speculative capital flows.[27] The purpose of the initiative was very clear: to set up a foreign exchange regime for Asian currencies that would be neither pegged to the dollar nor freely fluctuating.

The need to supplement the work initiated with the IFA to include the management of systemic imbalances has been belatedly recognized by the international community as part of a review exercise initiated in 2004 in connection with the sixtieth anniversary of the Bretton Woods Treaty. Following a call from the G7 to conduct a strategic review of the working of the international monetary and financial system, the Managing Director of the IMF, Rodrigo de Rato, elaborated a Medium-Term Strategy for the Fund which was endorsed by the IMFC in September 2005. In his report de Rato recognized that 'the challenges of the past decade have pulled the Fund in too many new directions – further straining the original vision of an institution devoted to international monetary stability and the financing of temporary balance of payments problems' (de Rato 2005, p. 2). The report contained a number of suggestions to reorient the Fund towards its original mission, essentially by strengthening its surveillance role on the larger, systemically important economies and on the global financial system, focusing on the interaction between macroeconomic developments and financial sector dynamics and vulnerabilities. Coinciding with the presentation of de Rato's proposals, the US Treasury Undersecretary Adams (2006) delivered a very critical speech at a seminar on IMF reform organized by the Institute for International Economics. The key point raised by Adams was that the IMF had neglected its main objective of conducting an effective surveillance on exchange rate developments and policies, accusing it of having been 'asleep at the wheel on its most fundamental responsibility'.

The US position on the role of the IMF on exchange rate matters seemed to mark a significant departure from the traditional American stance that a regime of freely floating exchange rates would work best without any interference from official instances, national or international. In fact, however, the departure was more apparent than substantive. The main concern of the US Treasury was not so much the working of the world exchange rate regime, but rather the 'exchange rate manipulation' carried out by most Asian countries, primarily by China, but also by Japan, which the Fund had been unwilling or unable to prevent and sanction. The strong commitment by China and other Asian countries to peg their currencies to the US dollar (and their refusal to allow an appreciation of their exchange rates vis-à-vis the dollar in the face of a mounting current account surplus) had been a long-standing concern of both the US Administration[28] and Congress, where the possibility of introducing retaliatory protectionist measures against 'currency manipulating' countries had been seriously considered.[29]

Whatever the motivations behind the US move, the call for the Fund to pay more attention to exchange rate issues and therefore to global payments imbalances was well received[30] and endorsed by the IMFC at its meeting in April 2006. As a result, during 2006, the IMF has been able to conduct 'multilateral consultations' with the United States, Japan, the euro area, China and Saudi Arabia to discuss strategies for the orderly adjustment of global payments imbalances. The results of this exercise of multilateral consultations were made public at the end of the IMFC 2007 spring meeting: 'The consultation process has proved a useful initiative, bringing together representatives of relevant economies to discuss how best to make progress in addressing this critical challenge. The discussions have been open and constructive, and have contributed to an improved understanding of the issues and of each other's positions'. Participating countries also noted that the implementation of their policy plans 'would in combination constitute a significant further step towards sustaining solid economic growth and resolving imbalances'. They added: 'We agreed to meet again when developments warrant' (IMF 2007f, p. 1).

In April 2006 the IMFC had also asked the Fund to undertake a review of its 1977 Surveillance Decision, a key legal instrument for the performance of this delicate function, and proposed a new framework for IMF surveillance consisting of four elements:

> First, a new focus of surveillance on multilateral issues, including global financial issues, and especially the spillovers from one economy on others. Second, a restatement of the commitments which member countries and their institutions make to each other under Article IV on which surveillance can focus on monetary, financial, fiscal and exchange rate policies. Third, the Managing Director should implement his proposal for a new procedure, which will involve the IMFC and the Executive Board, for multilateral surveillance. Fourth, the IMFC should set a new annual remit for both bilateral and multilateral surveillance through which the Managing Director, the Executive Board and the staff are accountable for the quality of surveillance. (IMF 2006c, p. 118)

Work on this crucial item of the IMF reform has been more difficult than expected as the main emerging countries fear that any strengthened surveillance authority of the IMF would not be exercised in an even-handed way and will be focused mostly on their exchange rate policies. At its meeting in April 2007, the IMFC, recognizing these difficulties, stated:

> The Committee, with a view to gaining broad support across the membership, agrees that the following principles should guide further work: first, there should be no new obligations, and dialogue and persuasion should remain key pillars of effective surveillance; second, it should pay due regard to country circumstances, and emphasize the need for evenhandedness; and third, it should retain flexibility to allow surveillance to continue evolving. (IMF 2007e, p. 3)

On the basis of these guidelines the IMF Executive Board reached a consensus on 15 June 2007 on a new Decision on 'Bilateral Surveillance over Members' Policies' (IMF 2007d). The analytical framework of the surveillance activity indicates that in order to ensure a stable system of exchange rates (systemic stability), each IMF member should promote its own 'external stability', by achieving a 'balance of payments position that does not, and is not likely to, give rise to disruptive exchange rate movements'. This implies that each country should ensure that there are no 'fundamental misalignments' in the real exchange rate of its currency and that there are no external sector vulnerabilities that could affect the sustainability of capital flows. As the decision does not involve any new obligations of members, the ability of the IMF to influence members' policies depends mostly on 'dialogue and persuasion' and it is therefore important that there is a broad consensus on the analytical framework underlying surveillance. From this point of view, it is regrettable that despite the considerable efforts made to reach a compromise solution acceptable to all, China was the only member that did not endorse the decision. The new surveillance decision has also contributed to revive the debate in the US Congress on the exchange rate policy of the United States. Four senators have recently taken a bipartisan initiative to revise the US exchange rate oversight laws: 'In line with IMF standards, US policy should focus on currencies that are in fundamental misalignment, abandoning the pejorative and accusatory term "manipulation" that was used. In line with WTO standards, US policy should play by the rules of the international economy' (Baucus et al. 2007).

An assessment of the implications of these developments for the working of the international monetary and financial system will be made in Chapter 14. Here it is perhaps appropriate to pause for a moment and review in Part III of the book, episodes in which major countries have succeeded in carrying out strategies designed to adjust payments imbalances with policy strategies designed to influence or resist exchange rate trends in the global financial markets. A brief historical reappraisal of how such strategies have been implemented may be useful in assessing the prospects of the initiatives currently being undertaken by the international community as it sets out to address, once again, the adjustment of global imbalances.

NOTES

1. The quotation is from the *dissenting view* subscribed to, among others, by C. Fred Bergsten, John Heimann, James Schlesinger, George Soros and Paul Volcker.
2. See Joint Economic Committee (1975, p. 2). For more information on these aspects of the American position, see Saccomanni (1988).
3. The concept of exchange rate manipulation has been used by the US Congress several times since then as an instrument of foreign economic policy, lastly in 2005–06 in the negotiations with China on the exchange rate of the renminbi (see Chapter 12).
4. This is when the IMF Managing Director presented his proposals for reforming the Fund (see paragraph 4 in this chapter and Chapter 14).
5. The reasons for the disappearance of reforming impulses were analysed at an international conference organized by the Bank of Italy (Kenen et al. 1994).
6. After the name of the two sponsoring members of Congress: Senator Paul Sarbanes and Representative Michael Oxley. Formally entitled Public Company Accounting Reform and Investor Protection Act of 2002 (30 July 2002).
7. A survey conducted among market participants of the city of London ranks 'regulation' as the number one in a list of problems confronting intermediaries and which includes (ranking in brackets): credit risk (2), derivatives (3), hedge funds (7), fraud (11), merger mania (19) and rogue traders (27) (CSFI 2006).
8. See Rogoff (1999) and Eichengreen (1999a) for detailed assessments of these proposals.
9. Progress on the implementation of FSAPs and ROSCs is regularly reported by the IMF on its website (www.imf.org).
10. On the implications of Basel II, see Himino (2004) and Caruana (2005). Jaime Caruana was at the time Chairman of the Basel Committee and Governor of the Bank of Spain.
11. See FSF (2006). The FSF also regularly publishes reports on 'Ongoing and recent work relevant to sound financial systems', providing a full account of progress achieved in the numerous initiatives monitored by the FSF.
12. The OFCs group includes exotic locations such as Aruba, the Bahamas, the British Virgin Islands, Samoa, the Seychelles, but also industrial countries such as Ireland, Luxembourg and Switzerland; see IMF (2006a, p. 12).
13. See FSF 2006. The FSF is expected to review the OFC Initiative in September 2007 (FSF 2007).
14. See Garbaravicius and Dierick (2005) for the references to various reports and studies.
15. See, among the most recent reviews: FSA (2005a); Counterparty Risk Management Policy Group II (2005); ECB (2005c) and ECB (2006a).
16. In a front page article in the *Financial Times* (2007), Ben Steil of the Council for Foreign Relations was quoted as saying: 'Once hedge funds start accounting for this much of the market . . . they are not really bank customers anymore'.
17. The normal facilities of the IMF are the Stand-By Arrangements (SBA) designed to provide financing to members facing short-term balance of payments problems; the Extended Fund Facility (EFF) deals with longer-term and structural balance of payments financing problems; the Compensatory Financing Facility (CFF) helps members cope with temporary declines in commodity prices and with financing needs arising from natural disasters; the Poverty Reduction and Growth Facility (PRGF) grants longer-term loans at low interest rates to low-income countries with structural balance of payments problems.
18. The proposal was tabled by the Italian Treasury Minister, Lamberto Dini, during the preparatory work for the G7 Summit in Halifax. See Padoa-Schioppa and Saccomanni

(1996).

19. The gradual blurring of the distinction between the roles of the IMF and the World Bank has been a subject of debate for at least a quarter of a century and is rooted in the growing demand for international financial assistance from developing countries. The major stakeholders of the two institutions, namely the leading industrial countries, responded by allowing a proliferation of 'facilities' and 'windows' whose scope and purpose is often vaguely defined. With the debt crisis of the developing countries in the 1980s, the problems posed by the overlapping of roles of the Bretton Woods institutions could initially be described as incompatible treatments or pharmacological overdoses being administered to the same patient together with a surfeit of check-ups; in 1989 the problem of better coordination of the activities of the two institutions was examined by the G10 in a report (G10 Deputies 1989) containing proposals similar to those advanced in the Goldstein Report. The matter was taken up again in 2006 by an ad hoc committee of experts chaired by Pedro Malan, a former finance minister of Brazil. The Group's report was delivered to the IMF on 23 February 2007 (www.imf.org).

20. The decision to review the activity and organization of a certain number of international bodies was taken in November 1998 by the Republican majority in Congress, in a compromise brokered with the Democrat government. This involved the approval of the US contribution, corresponding to approximately 18 billion dollars, to the coffers of the IMF, World Bank and the regional development banks. There is a strong conservative and bipartisan faction in Congress that traditionally opposes the institutions created under Bretton Woods, which it believes are an emanation of the East Coast liberal financial establishment, accused of using taxpayers' money to save the major banks of Manhattan from bankruptcy. Every time the American government requests authorization from Congress to take part in the periodic capital increases of the IMF and the World Bank, the conservative faction introduces special conditions and requirements into the budgetary allocations.

21. This is the new name given in 1999 to the Interim Committee, the ministerial policy-making body of the IMF.

22. On the involvement of private creditors in crisis management, see ECB (2005b).

23. Currently the quota of China (2.98 per cent) in the IMF and the World Bank is not much higher than that of Belgium (2.16 per cent).

24. The GFSR replaces the annual *International Capital Markets* report and the electronic quarterly *Emerging Market Financing* report.

25. Statement by US Undersecretary of the Treasury, Randal Quarles before the US Senate, as reported by Truman (2006).

26. What follows draws heavily from Saccomanni (2005).

27. This was the Chiang Mai Initiative, agreed on the margin of the annual meeting of the ADB in Chiang Mai in May 1999. The member countries of the ASEAN are: Brunei, Cambodia, Indonesia, Laos, Malaysia, Myanmar (Burma), the Philippines, Singapore, Thailand and Vietnam.

28. See *Economic Report of the President* (Chapter 6, 'The US Capital Account Surplus') transmitted to Congress, February 2006 (US Administration 2006).

29. The question of exchange rate policy of China will be examined in detail in Chapter 12.

30. Surprisingly, this initiative by the IMF was greeted at the time as a major innovation in international cooperation. In fact the very concept of multilateral surveillance was already introduced in the second Amendment in the IMF Articles of Agreement in 1976. The 1985 report on the international monetary system by the G10 included detailed proposals for a revamping of multilateral surveillance. Even outside official circles, there has been no shortage of concrete proposals indicating how a strengthened cooperation on exchange rate policies could be organized within the IMF; see in particular, Artus and Crockett (1978), Saccomanni (1988), Goldstein (1995), Volcker (1995), Coeuré and Pisani-Ferry (2000), Cecchetti et al. (2000).

PART III

Challenging the tigers

7.   A cage for the dollar: the Plaza and Louvre Accords (1985–87)*

> At the beginning of the 1980s, a number of economies – most notably the United States – had believed, not only that they need not listen to the IMF, but that they could ignore the market. They needed a shock of the kind that occurred in 1985 for the United States to shake them from their illusions. But now the disciplining mechanism was rather different to that of the 'classical' Bretton Woods system. It turned out that an ability to adjust to what the market might do would best be secured through a measure of international cooperation. The result would be the creation of a more stable framework of expectations that might diminish the impact of the shocks in financial markets caused by abrupt policy changes.
>
> Harold James (1996, p. 466)

In the period from 1985 to 1987 the G7 devised and implemented an elaborate strategy for the international coordination of economic policies aimed at stabilizing the exchange rate of the dollar and adjusting the internal and external disequilibria that were hindering non-inflationary growth in the G7 countries. This strategy comprised two distinct phases: the first, during 1985 (Plaza Accord), ended the excessive appreciation of the dollar and cleared the way for a period of significant depreciation; the second, during 1987 (Louvre Accord), involved a concerted effort first to halt the dollar's decline and then to stabilize it at a sustainable level.

The birth of the policy coordination strategy, its implementation and subsequent gradual abandonment makes it one of the most eventful and instructive pages in contemporary monetary history – the subject of numerous accounts and analyses by economists, journalists and the protagonists of the day (see Funabashi 1988; Volcker and Gyohten 1992; Solomon S. 1995; Solomon R. 1999; Clarida 2000). The antecedents of the strategy have been described in detail in Chapter 5, together with the chronicle of the failed efforts by all other members of the G7 to convince the United States of the need to correct the misalignment. As indicated earlier, the Reagan Administration had, until 1984, refused to acknowledge the existence of a dollar misalignment. But something changed at the end of the year, after the electoral victory confirming Reagan for a second term. The President seized the opportunity afforded him by the cabinet 'reshuffle' to change both the Treasury Secretary and the US dollar policy. Stubborn champions of laissez-faire were replaced with a more pragmatic team of people willing to take account of pressures from Congress and business, which bemoaned the loss of competitiveness caused by the excessive appreciation of the dollar. The new Treasury Secretary, James Baker – a lawyer devoid of any dogmatic preconceptions, capable of acting decisively but also diplomatically – immediately reopened talks with the main G7 partners to signal the reversal of American policy.[1] At a meeting of the G5 held in London on 17 January 1985, it was decided also to signal this changed attitude to the market, and the press communiqué issued at its conclusion expressed the group's intention to work towards achieving greater stability of exchange rates and reaffirmed the 'commitment made at the Williamsburg Summit to undertake coordinated intervention in the markets as necessary'. In reality, as already mentioned, no precise undertaking had been made at Williamsburg and the market paid little attention to the G5 declaration. The dollar continued to appreciate in a process that increasingly looked like a speculative bubble. It was obvious that market participants, after four years of daily bombardment with the rhetoric of non-intervention, were unwilling to alter their expectations unless official pronouncements were backed up by action. Clearly, the market perceived that despite its concern for the overvaluation dollar, the United States was not yet ready to correct it by significantly altering the main thrust of its domestic economic policies. It predicted instead that for reasons of political opportunism a strategic shift could only come about gradually, and would not mark a major departure from the fundamental principles of the Reaganite philosophy.

It was against this backdrop that some European countries took the initiative to halt the dollar's appreciation for fear it would ignite an inflationary spiral on the Old Continent. The intervention was coordinated by the Bundesbank and involved the Banque de France, the Banca d'Italia and other European central banks: it started in the morning of 26 February 1985, when all the participating central banks simultaneously intervened in the respective currency markets selling dollars against their respective national currencies (the Bank of Japan also intervened selling dollars against yen). The move took the market by surprise because at that hour of the morning 'America was closed' and the likelihood of a dollar intervention taking place without the participation of the Fed was considered remote. Indeed, most market participants had forecast that the dollar would continue to appreciate. When the markets opened on 26 February, currency traders at the major banks were quoting 3.40 German marks to the US dollar and indicating the level of four marks in a few days' time as the likely target of the bullish trend. At the beginning of the intervention the dollar was quoted at 3.47 marks, but the exchange rate declined rapidly as the central banks of Europe continued to sell dollars throughout 26 and 27 February. After some initial resistance and hesitation, the market trend was inverted and the dollar began to fall (see Figure 7.1). One month later, at the end of March, the dollar was being quoted at around 3 marks representing a depreciation of over 10 per cent.

The intervention, which was only partially sterilized, was successful not so much because of the volume of dollars sold (which in any event was in the order of several billion), but rather due to the European countries'

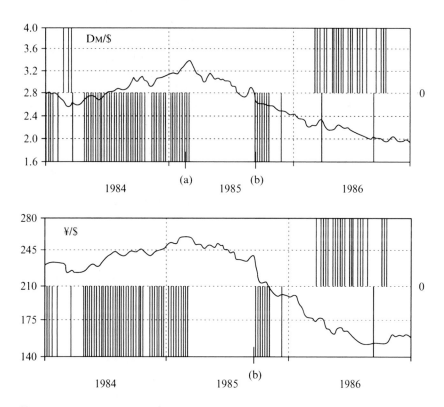

Notes:
* Nominal exchange rates of the US dollar (left scale) against DM and yen. The vertical bars indicate (right scale) periods in which dollar purchases (positive bars) or dollar sales (negative bars) have taken place.
  (a) = Intervention by European central banks.
  (b) = Plaza Accord.

Source: Catte et al. (1994).

Figure 7.1   *The Plaza Accord: performance of the dollar and G7 interventions**

display of a strong common will to act and effective operational coordination. What was also striking was the fact that the interventions had achieved the objective of halting the appreciation of the dollar without changing official interest rates in Europe or America. The market was nonetheless perplexed by the discordant signals emanating from the United States, where the monetary authorities hinted that they were satisfied with the fall in the dollar but hesitated to take any active position on the matter. These perplexities increased when a report by the G10 on the working of the international monetary system was released in June (G10 Deputies 1985). The report confirmed the conventional scepticism towards the effectiveness of interventions and proposed only to strengthen surveillance by the IMF on economic policies of leading countries in order to ensure their convergence and compatibility, seen as prerequisites for lasting stability of exchange rates. Although, from an analytical perspective, the broad consensus regarding the need for convergence and compatibility of policies represented a step forward with respect to the 'house in order' philosophy, the market interpreted the report as a substantial acceptance of the status quo and during the summer the volatility of the dollar market increased, signalling uncertainty about future movements. In reality, international monetary diplomacy was quietly moving towards the formulation of an agreement that would see the full involvement of the United States in the stabilization of currencies as just one element in a much bigger picture of economic policy coordination aimed at achieving sustainable growth of output and employment levels as well as monetary stability.

The finance ministers and central bank governors of the G5 countries finalized the agreement on the evening of Sunday 22 September 1985, during a meeting held at the Plaza Hotel in New York. Each country agreed to take specific economic policy measures designed to reduce America's public debt and to foster recovery of the Japanese and European economies, thereby adjusting balance of payments disequilibria. In addition to a long and detailed description of the procedures for policy coordination, the agreement contained provisions of more immediate operational relevance. It was acknowledged that exchange rates must play a role in adjusting external imbalances and that in order to do so they must better reflect fundamental economic conditions than had been the case. It was agreed that policy coordination would strengthen the fundamentals and that in view of this 'some further orderly appreciation of the main non-dollar [*sic*] currencies against the dollar is desirable'. Finally, the parties involved declared themselves ready to cooperate more closely to achieve this goal 'when to do so would be helpful' (see IMF 1985, p. 297). In reality, one other important decision was made at the Plaza Hotel: to carry out a coordinated intervention on foreign exchange markets in Asia, Europe and the United States on the following Monday. The coordination was entrusted to the G5 central banks, with the understanding to associate in the action other central banks in the G7 and G10 countries. The intervention cleared the way for a further depreciation of the dollar, which continued to fall until March 1986, and for a gradual reduction in interest rates carried out in a coordinated manner in America, Asia and Europe. In all, approximately $17 billion were sold by the G7 in the period between September 1985 and March 1986. Although the intervention could basically be described as sterilized, it nonetheless proved very effective in bursting the speculative bubble. Some authoritative observers downplayed the impact of the interventions, claiming that the central banks of the G5 and G7 had acted when the trend was already in decline (see Feldstein 1988), but forgetting that the inversion in the trend at the 'peak' of the previous February had been brought about by a concerted foreign exchange market intervention – of a unilateral nature – by European central banks.

Despite the success on exchange markets, the United States continued to be dissatisfied with the track record of policy coordination by the G5 and G7. With rapidly decelerating growth rates in 1986 and a growing trade gap, the US government judged the efforts of the European countries and Japan to revive economic activity to be inadequate. For their part, these countries saw attempts to foster economic recovery frustrated by the sharp appreciation of their currencies against the dollar and wanted the phase of devaluation of the dollar to reach a conclusion. In contrast, the United States pressed its G7 partners to take more aggressive reflation measures using the threat of a further depreciation of the dollar: to this end America pushed for a greater formalization of the policy coordination process through the introduction of 'objective indicators' of economic performance by the G7 countries, which would serve as guidelines for members' fiscal and monetary policies. This was the key issue at stake at the G7 Summit held in Tokyo in May 1986, where agreement was reached on a set of economic indicators to be subject to multilateral surveillance by the deputy finance ministers of the G7. But differences of opinion persisted over what should be done, and by whom, should the indicators signal the need for a corrective action.

It was in these circumstances, whose conflicting nature the market was well aware of, that the dollar continued to depreciate, and its descent was only partially braked by interventions by the Bank of Japan and the European central banks; throughout the whole of 1986 the United States refrained from making any intervention in support of its currency. The dollar's descent appeared to stall briefly at the end of October, after a widely publicized meeting between Treasury Secretary Baker and Japan's Minister of Finance Miyazawa, in which the United States made a commitment to arrest the fall of the dollar if Japan cut its taxes and discount rate. But the meeting, immediately hailed by the press as signalling the dawning of a G2 apparently better able to produce results than the quarrelsome G7, did not succeed in halting the dollar's progressive depreciation. Despite the Bank of Japan's prompt reduction of official rates, the markets did not perceive a desire to act in a coordinated fashion, also because the Bundesbank was reluctant to relax monetary conditions. However, fear that the United States–Japan agreement could marginalize Europe's role on the international monetary stage put talks on the objectives and instruments for economic policy coordination in the G7 back on the agenda at the beginning of 1987. The result was the Louvre Accord of 22 February 1987, in which the finance ministers and central bank governors acknowledged that from the Plaza onwards, the dollar had fallen significantly and 'agreed to cooperate closely to foster stability of exchange rates around current levels' (see IMF 1987, p. 75).

The agreement envisaged the fixing of 'reference zones' for the three main currencies and of flexible limits of fluctuation around the central rate: this implied a strong presumption – but not a formal obligation – that central banks would intervene to maintain the market rate within the fluctuation band. This commitment did not imply unlimited interventions, however, and a relatively modest limit was fixed ($4 billion). Immediately after the agreement had been signed, the market tested the solidity of the commitments and, despite further interventions, the dollar continued to depreciate throughout 1987, departing significantly from the 'current levels' contemplated under the agreement (see Figure 7.2).

In 1987, however, significant steps forward were taken in policy coordination by the G7, testified to by the reduction of fiscal deficits in the United States and other countries, the correction of trade imbalances, and the adoption of policies to support demand by countries running a balance of payments surplus. But the coordination process was also beset by what were sometimes very public misunderstandings and controversies regarding the conduct of monetary policies by the Bundesbank and the Bank of Japan, which the United States felt were insufficiently accommodating and on occasions, like in September 1987, even contrary to the Louvre commitments. The growing feeling among market participants was that policy coordination was not working and that the United States would be obliged to correct its imbalances by itself, through the adoption of restrictive monetary and fiscal policies.

This was the setting for the Wall Street crash of 19 October 1987 that saw stock prices plummet by over 20 per cent. The crash, however, did not have the feared recessionary consequences for the American economy thanks in no small measure to the now legendary two-line statement issued by the

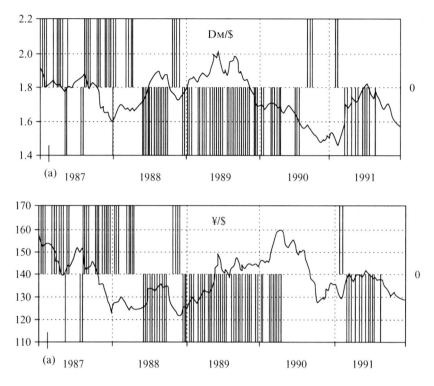

Notes:
* Nominal exchange rates of the US dollar (left scale) against DM and yen. The vertical bars
  indicate (right scale) periods in which dollar purchases (positive bars) or dollar sales
  (negative bars) have taken place.
  (a) = Louvre Accord.

Source: Catte et al. (1994).

Figure 7.2   *The Louvre Accord: performance of the dollar and G7
intervention*

President of the Fed, Alan Greenspan, which reassured markets worldwide.[2] This, however, implied a de facto suspension of the commitments to
policy coordination and a generalized loosening of monetary conditions in
the United States and the other G7 countries. Again, the dollar resumed its
downward course and it was only thanks to a renewed agreement within the
G7, communicated to the market in a detailed statement issued on 22
December 1987 (see IMF 1988, pp. 8–10), and a wave of unusually aggressive interventions that the dollar finally stabilized at the beginning of 1988.
The exchange rate of the US currency would largely remain at these levels,

despite ups and downs, until 1990, when it once again began to depreciate as a result of the strong cyclical slowdown of the US economy. In all, the coordinated interventions in support of the dollar conducted by the G7 between February 1987 and June 1988 amounted to over $80 billion. Subsequently, the interventions became increasingly sporadic and were conducted on a more ad hoc basis; the emphasis on exchange rate objectives in the coordination process also lessened.

Any assessment of the effectiveness of the strategies adopted by the G7 in the period 1985–87 must necessarily be made on several levels. As regards the effectiveness of foreign exchange interventions, the developments in 1985 were certainly positive, while those following the Louvre Accord were more questionable, except for the final phase towards the end of 1987 and in early 1988. Overall, between February 1985 (the peak) and February 1987, the trade-weighted exchange rate of the dollar depreciated by 30 per cent, which was more or less in line with the G7 objectives. But this should come as no surprise: it is not difficult for monetary authorities to burst a speculative exchange rate bubble when they succeed in convincing the market that the rising trend is exactly that – a bubble; it is less easy to stop a downward trend of a currency if the latter is perceived as being desired and promoted by the authorities of the issuing country, particularly if the market is fully aware of the persistence of payments imbalances. In the end, the aim of ensuring a 'soft landing' for the dollar was achieved, by setting up a 'cage' with a ceiling and a floor that were relatively close to one another.

From a macroeconomic point of view, the G7 strategy was seen as less effective. One of the criticisms formulated at the time was that, by preventing the devaluation of the dollar, interventions in the exchange markets had shifted the imbalance onto the financial market, ultimately provoking the US stock market crash of October 1987. But the charge (made by Feldstein, (1987, 1988)[3], a well-known opponent of interventions and policy coordination) is questionable, both because the crash lasted just one day and because subsequent analyses conducted by a specially appointed fact-finding committee attributed the temporary decline of the quotations to the functioning of automatic broking mechanisms that amplified the initial drop, generating a wave of selling orders.

A second criticism, formulated several years later, claimed that the international liquidity created by the interventions in support of the dollar was the cause of the increase of inflation within the G7 countries, and in particular of the speculative bubble that triggered the explosion of stock and property markets in Japan between 1986 and 1989. The loosening of monetary conditions in the two years from 1986 to 1987 undoubtedly put pressure on prices in the G7 countries, but this in itself cannot explain the widely varying price performances from country to country. In fact, the highest increase in inflation was in Germany, where it rose from 0.2 per cent in 1987 to a high of 5.1 per cent in 1992, but this was essentially due to the aftershock of German reunification. The consumer price index in Japan rose from 0.1 per cent in 1987 to 3.3 per cent in 1991 and the increase was effectively offset by a tighter monetary policy. In any event, the expansionary effect on the Japanese economy of interventions in support of the dollar partly compensated the deflationary effect of the exceptional appreciation of the yen after the Plaza Accord. The expansion of liquidity needed to brake the appreciation of the yen might be among the causes of the Japanese asset price bubble but it was certainly not the only, or principal, one. As described in Chapter 5, the bubble had its origins in structural factors of the Japanese economy and it was for political considerations of a domestic nature that the necessary monetary restriction was delayed. In any event, even without the external pressures for policy coordination coming from the G7, it would have been difficult for the Japanese authorities to pursue a completely different monetary policy, given the appreciation of the yen and the rigidity of fiscal policy as a short-term anti-cyclical instrument (see McKinnon and Ohno 1997; Cecchetti et al. 2000).

In general, the verdict of impartial observers was largely positive as regards the effectiveness of policy coordination (Dobson 1991; Goldstein 1994): it was acknowledged that the process had benefited the world economy and that it had produced better macroeconomic and financial policies than there would have been without it. In particular, the exercise was praised for having curbed the protectionist trends that the overvaluation of the dollar had generated in the United States. It was also applauded for promoting the adjustment of current account imbalances through the adoption of policies respectively to revive or dampen demand in countries running a surplus or a deficit; and finally, for signalling the need to dismantle structural rigidities in the leading industrial countries. Moreover, with the Plaza and the Louvre Accords, the market received a clear message from monetary authorities that they were paying attention to the exchange rates of the major currencies, a message that contrasted strongly with the 'benign neglect' doctrine that had been practised above all else in Reagan's first term.

Despite these positive results, it was recognized that the policy coordination process, based on a system of 'soft' target zones for exchange rates, had not been able to function in a balanced fashion. This opinion was shared by both protagonists of the operation, such as Volcker and Gyohten (1992) and Dobson (1991), and historians such as James (1996). The announcement to the markets of exchange rate objectives, even if soft and non-binding, accompanied by the pursuit of a wide spectrum of fiscal, monetary and structural measures, ended by generating destabilizing expectations precisely because of the different dynamics that govern the functioning of financial markets and the processes for the formulation and conduct of economic policy in the G7 countries. While the market reacted positively to the commitment to maintain stable exchange rates, it monitored the implementation of economic policy measures needed to achieve the targets with great attention, ready to change its attitude at the first sign of inconsistency. By contrast, in the democracies of the G7, the decision-making mechanisms for fiscal policy eluded the control of the governments that had agreed to the exchange rate objectives but depended on their parliaments for ratification. The parliaments in turn could always raise objections to the imposition of limits on their sovereignty implicit in the exchange rate objectives. This is what happened in the United States, where the government and Congress disagreed over the timeframe and modalities for the reduction of the federal deficit, and since the debate was held in public every analyst and market participant could assess its implications for currency quotations and interest rates. In short, the market was only too well aware, as James said (1996, p. 440), that the United States wanted to use the policy coordination initiative 'primarily to change the policies of other countries' and only marginally to alter its own. On the other hand, the Japanese and European governments also experienced difficulties in producing the kind of expansionary fiscal policies envisaged by the accords and were forced, not always very successfully, to put pressure on their respective central banks to obtain a loosening of monetary policies.

The market also perceived the gradual disengagement of the G7 from the Louvre Accord that was plain for all to see in the statements made at the end of the subsequent meetings, where the emphasis on exchange rate objectives was replaced by more generic commitments to convergence of economic policies towards objectives of non-inflationary growth and financial stability. This rather sad demise of the policy coordination initiative was hastened by the widespread awareness that the interventions had achieved all that could be reasonably expected: the bursting of the speculative bubble of the dollar and its relative stabilization on a course of modest depreciation. This was seen as being more than enough by the new Bush administration that took over after Reagan in 1989 and did not subscribe to the internationalist activism of Baker and Volcker. The shift from a binding form of coordination to a more flexible and pragmatic approach was also looked on favourably by the other G7 partners, each one struggling with its own set of domestic structural problems that were no less challenging, such as the unification of Germany and the creation of monetary union in Europe, or the management of the burgeoning economic-financial crisis in Japan. There was, in essence, a consensual separation from policy coordination. It would be wrong to conclude that the G7 was obliged to drop it due to the hostility of the market.

NOTES

* This chapter draws heavily from a paper by Catte et al. (1994). The authors, at the time all working at the Bank of Italy's Research Department, analysed G7 foreign exchange policies as a contribution to a conference sponsored by the Bank of Italy in 1992 which I organized together with Peter Kenen and Francesco Papadia (Kenen et al. 1994).

1. The United States initially maintained contacts with the four leading G7 countries (Japan, Germany, France and the United Kingdom), essentially for practical reasons that, however, were never explained publicly to avoid embarrassing the other excluded members of the G7, Italy and Canada. But France and the United Kingdom insisted in keeping a 'Group of Five' format (G5) for political reasons as they wanted to reassert their role as 'major powers' and participants in an exclusive directorate. In the end, the exclusion of Italy and Canada became a political issue within the G7 and the United States agreed to discontinue the meetings of the 'five' at the G7 Summit in Tokyo in 1986.

2. The statement read: 'The Federal Reserve, consistent with its responsibilities as the nation's central bank, affirmed today its readiness to serve as a source of liquidity to support the economic and financial system'. The text of the statement and the unfolding of events that led to its formulation can be found in Woodward (2000, pp. 24–47).

3. For a divergent view, see Volcker (Volcker and Gyohten 1992, ch. 8, p. 285).

8. The seven-year war of the French franc (1991–98)*

Je donnerai à la France un franc modèle, dont la parité ne changera pas aussi longtemps que je serai là.**

Charles de Gaulle (1970, p. 143)

A conceited German . . . imagines that he possesses the truth in science – a thing of his own invention but which for him is absolute truth.

Leo Tolstoy (*War and Peace*, p. 757)

The EMS crisis of 1992 to 1993 is usually regarded as a prime example of the impossibility of achieving a fixed exchange rate regime in the context of financial globalization and, in particular, of the futility of interventions on the exchange market. It is a generalization that has been widely subscribed to, but one which is not based on a balanced reading of European monetary developments during that time. Analysts have tended to focus on the unsuccessful defence of the parities of the Italian lira and pound sterling and their abandonment of the ERM, without adequately taking account of France's success in maintaining the parity of its currency unchanged against the German mark over the period that began on 12 January 1987 – the date of the last realignment of the French franc in the EMS – and ended on 1 January 1999 – the date of France's entry into EMU.

Anchoring the franc to the mark with a fixed parity was not a priority objective for France in the EMS, which the French President Valéry Giscard d'Estaing had sponsored together with the German Chancellor Helmut Schmidt in 1978. Nevertheless, exchange rate stability had been a traditional linchpin of the strategy of politicians close to President Charles de Gaulle ever since the currency reform he himself promoted in 1958. In the early years of the EMS, the parity of the franc was in fact devalued in the context of periodic realignments made to compensate for the inflation rate differential vis-à-vis Germany and other EMS member countries. With the advent to power in 1981 of the Socialist Party, influential members of the French government openly advocated abandoning the ERM, seen as an unacceptable constraint on national policies for reviving the economy and boosting employment. It was only in March 1983, in the wake of a serious currency crisis, that President Mitterrand began orienting government policy towards monetary and exchange rate stability, supporting the line taken by Finance Minister Jacques Delors and distancing himself from the traditional socialist strategy of supporting growth by increasing public deficits and devaluing of the national currency. Initially, this rigorous line was lent a flexible interpretation and the central rate of the franc was devalued – even if only marginally – with respect to the mark on two further occasions, in April 1986 and January 1987. Throughout this period inflation in France remained high, and the rate of interest on government bonds was consistently above that in Germany for all maturities of the yield curve. This led to growing consensus among monetary authorities that France could not credibly reduce its interest rates so long as the markets continued to expect further periodic devaluations of the franc against the mark. In this context, a strategy for maintaining a fixed parity between the franc and the mark in the EMS gradually emerged; a plan that France placed in the broader context of the project for European monetary unification which it had traditionally championed. As it turned out, the realignment of the franc in the EMS on 12 January 1987 was the last change of its parity, and from that date France committed to taking any economic or monetary policy measure, or political measure *tout court*, necessary to defend the exchange rate at 3.35 francs against the mark.

The market was not given an opportunity to test the resolve of the French monetary authorities for several years, due to a set of favourable economic circumstances that included: the relative stability of the US dollar, which limited upward pressure on the mark in the EMS; the fall of the Berlin Wall and the prospect of German reunification from 1989 onwards, which weakened the mark on currency markets; the EMU project, which was making rapid progress following the approval of the Delors Report which was released in June 1989; the intergovernmental conference launched to draft the treaty on EMU in Rome in December 1990; and, finally, the signing of the Maastricht Treaty in February 1992. Indeed, the period from 1987 to 1991 was entirely devoid of any episodes of tension or realignments of parities in the EMS.

But when the Danish people voted against ratifying the Maastricht Treaty in the referendum of June 1992, the market began to doubt the determination of the French government. Market participants could no longer exclude the possibility that the entire process of monetary union in Europe could yet be derailed. Meanwhile, within France the political debate registered growing resistance to the 'strong franc' policy supported by the government, in the run-up to the crucial political tests of the referendum on the Treaty of Maastricht in September 1992 and the March 1993 parliamentary election. The monetary policy adopted by Germany to combat inflationary pressures deriving from reunification had prevented France, like other countries in the EMS, from lowering interest rates in line with the progress made in containing inflation during the long period of stable exchange rates. In 1991, inflation in France had been lower than in Germany, but French interest rates were higher: the result was a compression of the growth rate of economic activity in France, with inevitable negative repercussions for output and employment and a deterioration of the political and social climate.

The market's attitude was also influenced by the apparent unwillingness of Germany to take account of the situations of its partner countries in the EMS in the formulation of its economic and monetary policies. In particular, the Bundesbank's decision to increase the discount rate from 8 to 8.75 per cent in July 1992, when tensions were running high on exchange markets, was seen as a further demonstration of the impossibility of maintaining central rates within the multilateral parity grid of the EMS. This interpretation was reinforced by the failed meeting of the finance ministers and central bank governors of the European countries held in Bath in the United Kingdom on 5 September 1992, where the Bundesbank rejected all pressures by its partners to make even a symbolic interest rate cut (Eichengreen 2000). In the following days, France's position was made more difficult after market pressures began to take their toll. The first victims were the Finnish markka, the Swedish krona and the Norwegian krone, which severed their unilateral pegging to the 'basket' of currencies in the EMS known as the ECU (European Currency Unit). On 12 September, following an unsuccessful attempt to promote a broad realignment of EMS parities, the Italian authorities were granted a 7 per cent depreciation of the lira, accompanied by a token reduction of official interest rates by the Bundesbank from 8.75 to 8.50 per cent. On 17 September the pound sterling abandoned the ERM, obliging the lira to float as well. Spain, which five days earlier had believed it could maintain the central rate of the peseta, devalued its currency by 5 per cent. The crisis spread despite exchange market interventions of unprecedented dimensions, often financed by wide recourse to international capital markets, and record increases in interest rates. The total bill for interventions on exchange markets carried out in the four-month period ending September 1992 was estimated at $160 billion; short-term interest rates on the money market reached peaks of 25 per cent in the first half of September in France and 500 per cent in Sweden.

The defence of the franc's exchange rate was initially conducted through massive currency intervention aimed at keeping market levels very close to the official central rate without breaching the permitted fluctuation band of ±2.25 per cent. The interventions were conducted in secret in an attempt to hide the very existence of tension from the market. This was no longer possible when the EMS crisis erupted in September and relations between the European countries began to deteriorate. Market participants became increasingly convinced that France would be forced to devalue because its economy could no longer sustain the loss of competitiveness generated by the devaluations of its major trading partners. It was widely believed that in a stagnant economy, monetary authorities would be unable to impose further increases in interest rates to support the franc, and could not count on a softening of monetary policy in Germany.

The pressures on the franc sharpened after the result of the referendum of 21 September 1992 for the ratification of the Treaty of Maastricht. The extremely narrow 'yes' majority revealed a country that was deeply divided over the strategy of the monetary authorities. The government's determination in its defence of the franc, however, was unshakable. In political and diplomatic circles, France categorically refused to admit to the very existence of a systemic problem within the EMS and took all the measures at its disposal to prevent a 'general realignment' of the EMS currencies, which could have involved the franc. More importantly, France obtained a solemn promise from Germany to maintain the parity of the franc that was announced publicly to the markets on 23 September in a joint statement by the governments and central banks of the two countries. As regards monetary policies, official interest rates in France were increased to 13 per cent and short-term liquidity was tightly rationed; the Banque de France continued its interventions on exchange markets, financed both by the Bundesbank and through currency swap operations. The market was impressed by the strength of the political and monetary signals sent and became convinced of the futility and expensiveness of continuing to attack the franc. Already from 28 September onwards significant reflows of funds enabled the Banque de France to rebuild its own reserves profitably, and at the end of October these had risen to levels higher than at the beginning of the crisis.

Monetary tensions reverberated within the EMS throughout the following months and gradually involved all the other currencies that had resisted devaluation, ultimately resulting in the broad realignment that Italy had unsuccessfully proposed the previous September. Between November 1992 and May 1993 the peseta and escudo were each devalued twice and the Irish punt was depreciated once by 10 per cent. Initially, the franc benefited from the sharp reduction of interest rates in Germany,[1] but the deterioration of the overall economic climate, with deepening recession and rising unemployment, reawakened doubts in the market regarding the staying power of the franc. Tensions began to run even higher with the defeat of the Socialist government in the parliamentary election of March 1993, which brought to power a centre-right coalition that had repeatedly criticized the strong franc policy claiming that it was contrary to the interests of France. The fact that Mitterrand remained as President went some way towards reassuring the market, which, however, could no longer exclude changes of strategy by the new government. But the abandonment of the strong franc policy could have entailed grave risks of financial instability and inflation, and despite some initial hesitation, the new government rejected this option. It was decided, however, to exploit every possible opportunity to reduce interest rates, banking on the fact that after the 'lesson' of September 1992 the market would not dare launch new attacks on the French exchange rate. In June 1993 the Banque de France took advantage of the more relaxed climate in the market following the 'yes' vote of the second Danish referendum on the Treaty of Maastricht to let interest rates fall below German levels. However, the announcement of a further rise in unemployment in France at the end of the same month revived market tensions, highlighting the limits of monetary policy in support of economic activity.

At the same time, rumours began to circulate in the markets that French officials were considering, more or less in secret, an alternative strategy to loosen the exchange rate tie of the franc by suggesting that Germany abandon the EMS and let the mark float upwards. The proposal (which would have allowed France to 'stay put' by accepting the 'divergence' of the mark and its inability to continue to play the role of 'anchor' in the EMS), turned out to be unviable, not only because of the predictable unwillingness of Germany to become a scapegoat for the crisis of the EMS, but also because of the less obvious desire of countries like the Netherlands and Belgium to preserve the existing peg to the mark. The market perceived the existence of insoluble policy dilemmas both in France (the need to revive the economy and to maintain the stability of the franc) and in the other EMS countries (the need to avoid recurrent crises and to preserve the European framework of economic and monetary cooperation). The catalyst for the crisis was the publication on 7 July of the official forecasts for the French economy predicting a drop in GDP in 1993 of 1.2 per cent. Tensions were further fuelled by rumours of profound splits within the new government over the conduct of economic strategy, with the Prime Minister Edouard Balladur in favour of a stable exchange rate and the Gaullist leader Jacques Chirac reportedly willing to take the franc out of the EMS. Despite various denials, every possible option was in fact explored during a bilateral meeting of the French and German monetary authorities on 22 July. France agreed to tighten its monetary policy but called on Germany to demonstrate a firm commitment to reducing its own interest rates – being aware that the Bundesbank would be unlikely to make more than a token gesture in this direction. Both countries nonetheless publicly reaffirmed their commitment to maintaining the parity of the franc with the mark, a position that had been essential in stabilizing market expectations in September 1992.

The market did not react favourably to the decision to raise interest rates in France, which were considered, correctly, to be sustainable only for the time needed for Germany to decide a cut in its own interest rates. When, on 29 July, the Bundesbank decided to leave its discount rate unchanged at 6.75 per cent, the markets reacted by selling huge volumes of francs, which the Banque de France attempted to counter with increasing difficulty. On the next day, Friday 30 July, the franc was allowed to depreciate until it reached the level of obligatory intervention with respect to the mark: in this way the Banque de France could activate the unlimited credit lines of the EMS and the Bundesbank would be obliged to intervene in support of the franc on the Frankfurt market. Market participants read this change of strategy as a signal that French authorities had exhausted their official reserves and that the devaluation of the franc was now imminent. The sale of marks on the market to defend the rate totalled approximately DM 25 billion, and was entirely financed, directly or indirectly, by the Bundesbank. That same evening the German monetary authorities requested the activation of procedures for the realignment of the EMS, convinced that their financial commitment to maintaining the parity of the franc would prove incompatible with the maintenance of monetary stability in Germany. During the negotiations that followed in Brussels on the weekend of 1 and 2 August, two opposite strategies clashed: the first advocated by France, which resolutely opposed any devaluation of the franc and was determined to shift the responsibility for the origins of the crisis and its solution onto Germany; the second, that of Germany, which refused to cut domestic interest rates or let the mark fluctuate, but was willing to consider widening the fluctuation bands of the ERM. In the end a proposal elaborated by Banque de France Governor Jacques de Larosière was endorsed: it implied the maintenance of the central rates, accompanied by a substantial widening of the oscillation bands, which France succeeded in increasing from 2.25 per cent to 15 per cent around the central rates. France believed that this strategy would prove sufficient to discourage speculation and enable a flexible defence of the currency without requiring further hikes in interest rates.

Many observers described the decision of 2 August 1993 as the 'death of the EMS' or used similar lugubrious expressions. It was claimed that a monetary system in which currencies could fluctuate up to a maximum of 30 per cent was no longer a fixed exchange regime and that what had happened with the French franc merely reconfirmed the impossibility of maintaining stable exchange rates in a financially globalized context. A reading of these events some years on allows less drastic conclusions to be drawn.

Following the broadening of the fluctuation bands, the franc was immediately allowed to drop by up to a maximum of 6 per cent against the rate of 3.35 francs to the mark, enabling speculators to gain from shorting the currency (see Figure 8.1). Subsequently, the market no longer believed that it was wise to test the new band limits of the franc, in view of the cautious monetary policy pursued by the Banque de France, which seemed designed to deflate the speculative bubble surrounding the franc rather than promote any rapid and significant depreciation. Moreover, the maintenance of the old central rate sent a strong signal of continuity in France's economic policies, which were implemented with flexibility to manage the external implications of the German reunification shock; the idea was to guide the expectations of market participants towards the gradual return to narrow bands of fluctuation around the central parity as soon as the European economic climate would allow it. As it turned out, the monetary and fiscal policies of France were coherent with the aim of a stable exchange rate, and except for a temporary downward fluctuation during 1995 (reaching a maximum depreciation of 7 per cent from the central rate) due to uncertainties related to the Mexican debt crisis and the presidential elec-

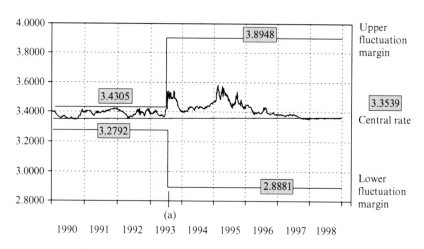

Note: (a) = 3 August 1993.

Source: Bank of Italy.

Figure 8.1   Exchange rate French franc/German mark and the EMS fluctuation band

tions in France, the movements of the franc were largely convergent to the fixed central rate and remained at these levels without difficulty until the introduction of the euro on 1 January 1999.

There was no doubt, however, that the crisis of July 1993 represented a defeat for those in the French monetary authorities who believed they could control the currency market and speculation through a combination of energetic foreign exchange interventions, moderate monetary tightening and emphatic political declarations, as had proved possible in 1992. At the same time, it would be unfair to use the 'defeat' of 1993 to void the 'victory' of 1992, almost as though that victory had merely postponed the inevitable 'day of judgement' for the parity of the franc. In reality, the two episodes should be assessed separately because of the quite different circumstances of the evolution of each, in particular as regards the interaction between the monetary authorities and market forces. In 1992 the franc had been involved in the final phase of the EMS crisis, after the tensions had shifted essentially onto the currencies of countries like Italy and the United Kingdom that were not part of the 'hard core' of the EMS and that suffered from both internal and external financial disequilibria. The market believed that France had lost competitiveness as a result of the devaluations of important trading partners, and positioned itself to benefit from an eventual devaluation of the franc; but overall the market deemed that France was in good economic shape. Moreover, the response of the monetary authorities, in both France and Germany, was such as to disperse all doubt about political support for the stability of the exchange rate, and the signals sent in terms of policy declarations and actions were strong and coherent with this objective.

In 1993 the economic situation of France was quite different. There was a marked recession and rising unemployment, both due primarily to the evolution of the global economic cycle rather than to errors in the government's economic policy. But what had changed even more was the domestic political situation, with a new centre-right government anxious to translate the promises it had made on the campaign trail to revive the French economy. In these circumstances the market could not but note the poorly disguised divergences of opinion within the government and the continuous criticism of the strong franc policy pursued by the previous socialist government, accused rather unjustly of being the primary cause of the French recession. The turning point in the market's attitude came about in June, when the Banque de France allowed short-term interest rates to fall below those in Germany. Even though it was a move that was technically justified by the fact that inflation was lower in France than in Germany, the decision appeared to the market as a move dictated by political considerations. First of all, Germany's higher rate of inflation was believed to be a temporary phenomenon, due to reunification. Market participants were also puzzled by the fact that the loosening of monetary policy in France was accompanied by repeated official declarations that hailed the 'overtaking' of German inflation and interest rates as an indicator that the role of anchor for monetary stability in Europe had switched from the mark to the franc. Such declarations merely alerted the market to the possibility that monetary policy in France would risk being more expansionary than necessary to preserve exchange rate stability; thus maximum attention was paid to French economic data, and the publication of each negative report was an opportunity to open speculative positions against the franc or hedge against the risks of its devaluation.

By July of 1993, the position of the exchange markets had also changed. The franc was the only important currency in the EMS not to have been devalued, while the Italian lira, pound sterling and Scandinavian currencies floated, denying market participants any foothold for speculation. In the circumstances, the market could not but focus its attention on the franc, a factor that the monetary authorities should have taken into account when making declarations on monetary and exchange rate policies.

The last change concerned the attitude of the German monetary authorities, which had given France unprecedented political and financial support in 1992. By 1993 they had become persuaded that the franc must be depreciated and that there was a fundamental inconsistency in the French desire, on the one hand, to achieve exchange rate stability and, on the other, to promote growth of output and employment. In late July, the Bundesbank became increasingly concerned by the volume of sales of marks needed to support the franc and the possible inflationary consequences of such interventions. While available empirical evidence does not suggest that internal monetary conditions in Germany were ever affected as a result of interventions by the Bundesbank in support of other currencies during the EMS crisis, including that of September 1992, the sheer scale of intervention for amounts of tens of billions of marks in just a few days undoubtedly posed a problem for monetary management that no country could ignore. Moreover, it had been well known since the inception of the EMS that the Bundesbank believed it had undertaken the obligation to carry out 'unlimited' intervention *only* to the extent that this was compatible with the maintenance of domestic monetary stability objectives, and that the existence of this compatibility should be left to the independent assessment of the Bundesbank itself. This had been the condition imposed by the President of the Bundesbank Otmar Emminger on Chancellor Schmidt in return for the central bank's support for Germany's participation in the EMS.[2] Technical and monetary factors aside, the attitude of the German government was also influenced by political factors. Even though the Franco-German alliance had never been seriously challenged, Bonn was unimpressed by the way in which the new Balladur government managed its relations with Germany. Paris's insistence that the fundamentals of the French economy were sound and that the EMS crisis was a German problem, and the audacity of its proposal that in order to solve it the mark should exit the EMS, was a source of further irritation that contributed to the hardening of the German position at the end of July.

With the benefit of hindsight, it can be said that France's position was not without some justification. The strategy of strengthening its competitiveness through 'competitive disinflation' (by keeping inflation lower than that of its trading partners), rather than through the devaluation of the franc, proved to be a winning one in the long term, and France was able to boost the growth of output and employment and run significant surpluses on its balance of trade. In the medium term, France performed better than Germany and Italy, despite the fact that Italy had acquired a significant competitive advantage following the devaluation of the lira in 1992 and 1995 (see Table 8.1).

There can be no doubt, however, that the management of the crisis was ultimately a coordination failure, and that the signals sent to the market were misleading and likely to induce precautionary and speculative responses. At the root of this failed coordination were fundamental questions of a political and economic nature that were impossible to ignore. German reunification turned out to be a longer, as well as a more complex and costly, process than was originally foreseen, and these internal issues were accorded priority over questions of European integration and cooperation. In France, the political turning point initiated with the victory of Balladur in the March 1993 general election was fully achieved only in May 1995 with the election of Jacques Chirac as President of the Republic. The review by the new ruling majority of the key options of economic policy, including that of exchange rate management, was therefore also a longer and more complex one than had originally been envisaged, and it was not until his keynote speech of 26 October 1995 that President Chirac announced his full support for the policy of the strong franc and the project of European monetary unification. In the end, the vicissitudes of the franc prove that in times of financial globalization, the longer it takes for political choices to filter through the system, the greater the probability of incoherent actions and signals being sent to the market and the higher the risks of financial instability.

Table 8.1 France, Germany, Italy: performance indicators

	1991	1992	1993	1994	1995	1996	1997	1998	1999	2000
France										
Growth[a]	1.0	1.3	-0.9	1.8	1.9	1.0	1.9	3.3	3.2	3.2
Inflation[b]	3.2	2.4	2.1	1.7	1.8	2.0	1.2	0.8	0.5	1.7
Balance of payments[c]	-5.7	4.8	9.6	7.4	11.0	20.8	37.8	38.2	37.5	24.7
Germany										
Growth[a]	5.7	2.2	-1.1	2.3	1.7	0.8	1.4	2.1	1.6	3.0
Inflation[b]	3.6	5.1	4.4	2.8	1.7	1.4	1.9	0.9	0.6	1.9
Balance of payments[c]	-18.4	-14.5	-9.7	-24.3	-20.7	-7.9	-3.1	-6.7	-18.0	-20.5
Italy										
Growth[a]	1.4	0.8	-0.9	2.2	2.9	1.1	2.0	1.8	1.6	2.9
Inflation[b]	6.3	5.3	4.6	4.1	5.2	4.0	2.0	2.0	1.6	2.6
Balance of payments[c]	-24.0	-29.3	7.7	12.8	24.9	39.4	32.4	21.8	8.6	-3.9

Notes:
a. Percentage growth rates of real GDP.
b. Percentage increase of the CPI.
c. Balance of current account transactions in billions of US dollars.

Source: OECD, *Economic Outlook*, June 2001.

NOTES

* The title of this chapter draws its inspiration from the book by Aeschimann and Riché (1996), which provides a detailed account of the political context that gave rise to the 'strong franc' strategy.
** 'I will give France a model franc, the parity of which will not change as long as I am around' (this author's translation).
1. Between August 1992 and July 1993 the discount rate was reduced by 2 percentage points, to 6.75 per cent.
2. On the content and implications of the notorious 'Emminger letter' to the German government, see Eichengreen and Wyplosz (1993).

9.   The resistible rise of the yen (1995)

The experience and still-strong memory of wartime defeat and total subordination to United States policy during the occupation period greatly discouraged Japan from taking an active and visible role in international affairs. In that sense, international relations for Japan consisted to a great extent simply of our bilateral relationship with the United States. In those days the Japanese delegations to international conferences were ridiculed as the 'triple S' delegations: smiling, silent, sometimes sleeping.

Toyoo Gyohten (Volcker and Gyohten 1992, ch. 2, p. 57)

Mercantile disputes between Japan and the United States eventually led to the 'syndrome of the ever-higher yen'. Incessant pressure – implicit and explicit – from the United States to make the yen appreciate from 360 to the dollar in 1971 to just 80 in 1995 is the historical origin of Japan's deflationary psychology today.

Ronald McKinnon (1999, p. 77)

In 1995 the dollar fell to an all-time low against both the Japanese yen and the German mark. The record slump was the result of a number of concomitant causes, but the unsettled state of economic and trade relations between Japan and the United States was undoubtedly a key factor, against a background of highly volatile exchange rate relations between the dollar and the yen (Noland 1995; Lincoln 1999). The trend was finally reversed in mid-1995 thanks to a series of concerted actions by the G7 and following a trade agreement between the United States and Japan that put an end to a dispute that had lasted for at least a decade, reaching one of its most acute phases during the first Clinton administration.

It was not until it was identified as being among the primary causes of American unemployment in the 1970s that the question of Japanese commercial penetration in the United States began to assume political significance. Protectionist pressures made themselves felt in Congress and among trade unions and the US government in turn pressured Japan to increase its openness to imports from abroad or else face retaliatory measures. Japanese companies had increased their presence in the US market through direct investments in the areas where they were most competitive, like the automobile or large-scale electronic goods sectors. When a group of Japanese investors acquired such a profoundly symbolic property as the Rockefeller Center in New York, the feeling that Japan was assuming a dominant position in the American economy turned to certainty, refuelling the protectionist sentiment of the general public and Congress. But in Japan too, US pressures were provoking indignant reactions on the part of industrialists and politicians, as testified to by the appearance in 1991 of a book, rather tellingly titled *The Japan that Can Say No*, written by the influential politician, Shintaro Ishihara, and the Chairman of Sony, Akio Morita. So strong and persistent were the US pressures on Japan that they even found their way into the political and economic language of the two countries: 'Japan bashing' in English and '*gaiatsu*' in Japanese.

A first protectionist initiative was taken by the US government under Reagan, but Congress's democratic majority judged the proposed measures to be inadequate. In 1988 Congress approved the Trade Act, authorizing the President to designate as 'unfair competitors' countries that adopted restrictive policies on American imports and to apply specific measures of commercial retaliation (under the super 301 clause) if they refused to open their markets. Pressures intensified under the Bush Sr. administration, both due to the enforcement of super 301 on a limited number of products and the launch in 1990 of the 'structural impediments initiative', involving a series of wide-ranging talks with the Japanese government aimed at removing structural obstacles to opening markets in goods and services. The modest results of these negotiations induced President Clinton to take an even harder line in his trade talks with Japan (Lee 1998). The new American administration announced that its objective was to reach a framework agreement setting specific growth targets for American exports to Japan, and incorporating an effective supervisory mechanism to verify the achievement of targets for the reduction of the Japanese trade surplus. The new strategy was announced during a bilateral summit held in April 1993, at the conclusion of which President Clinton told the press that the most efficient way to accelerate the decline of the Japanese surplus would be through the appreciation of the yen, or in other words, the depreciation of the dollar. The news was immediately transmitted to the financial markets, which interpreted it as a sign of America's willingness to use the dollar's exchange rate as a bargaining tool to extract trade concessions from Japan. The dollar depreciated against the yen, but picked up again in July when the agreement was signed. Immediately afterwards negotiations began for the application of the agreement in each specific sector. Washington had hoped to achieve concrete results during another bilateral summit, to be held in February 1994, but the strength of Japanese resistance precluded any such *entente* and instead provoked renewed American threats of recourse to the exchange rate weapon. The dollar depreciated in February and March, and again in June, in response to the resignation of the Japanese government, which raised fears of a breakdown in trade talks.

Following a number of other stormy episodes, partial agreement on some sectors was reached in October and relative stability was restored to the exchange market. Overall, in the two years from 1993 to 1994 the yen appreciated by 15 per cent against the dollar. During the same period and on some five occasions (two in 1993, three in 1994), the American and Japanese monetary authorities conducted coordinated interventions on the exchange market with the stated intention of slowing the rise of the yen with respect to the dollar. The majority of these interventions proved ineffective, given that the market interpreted them as attempts to counter the short-term volatility of the currency market, rather than as a strategy aimed at moving exchange rates in a particular direction. Nor was any clarification given to the market through the traditional channel of G7 statements, which merely reiterated the willingness of the Seven to cooperate on exchange markets. Moreover, the market remained sceptical as to how sincere the United States was about supporting the dollar in a period in which the US trade gap continued to widen, especially with respect to Japan. The apparent contradiction between the position of the White House (willing to weaken the dollar for negotiation purposes) and that of the Fed (committed to stabilizing it for monetary purposes) was resolved by the market by attributing a strong strategic value to political signals and only a tactical value to intervention by monetary authorities.

Washington's support for a weak dollar remained unchanged even after the Mexican debt crisis of 1994, when the dollar fell sharply due to market fears that Mexico's insolvency could involve some major US banks. By contrast, the international repercussions of the financial crisis in emerging market economies and in Europe induced the G7 countries to intervene to stabilize the dollar and restore a minimum amount of investor confidence on capital and exchange markets. The interventions began on 17 February 1995 and involved to varying degrees the Bank of Japan, the Fed and the Bundesbank. The market noted immediately, however, that the three central banks were pursuing different strategies and probably acted under different political 'instructions'. The Bank of Japan demonstrated the strongest commitment to intervention, especially when the yen exceeded the psychologically significant thresholds of 100 yen and 90 yen against the dollar. For its part the Fed, despite the declarations by the Treasury in support of the coordinated action, was authorized to intervene on just five occasions over a total of 33 days (from 17 February to 18 April). The Bundesbank intervened just twice and made no attempt to conceal its belief that the weak dollar was a pre-eminently American problem and that it was up to the Fed to intervene decisively to support its currency, even if this meant raising official interest rates (Levy and Pericoli 1999). In these circumstances the interventions proved unable to influence the market, which had expected, perhaps somewhat naively, that the initial declarations would be followed by massive interventions conducted with an equal level of commitment and intensity by the three main central banks involved and accompanied by coherent interest rate policies: a rise in America, a cut in Germany and Japan. In reality, the Fed kept monetary policy unchanged for the entire period, while the Bundesbank reduced official rates only on 30 March (by 50 basis points, to 4 per cent), with the Bank of Japan following on 14 April (by 75 basis points, to 1 per cent). During the same period the trade talks between the United States and Japan had reached a critical stage, running aground over the sensitive automobile and spare parts sectors. Against this backdrop the dollar reached its record low against the yen on 18 April 1995, dropping momentarily under the threshold of 80 yen, with a depreciation of 22 per cent with respect to the 1994 average. On the same day, the dollar also reached an all-time low against the German mark, down by 16 per cent against the 1994 average.

It was not until the traditional spring meeting of the G7 on 25 April 1995 that any concrete steps were taken to reverse the trend. A statement was issued declaring that the recent exchange movements had 'gone beyond the levels justified by underlying economic conditions' and that an 'orderly reversal of those movements is desirable' (see IMF 1995a, p. 138). On the market (where the inadequacy of G7 coordination was among the factors inducing speculators to accelerate the dollar's depreciation) the statement was interpreted as a signal of imminent concerted action by the major industrialized countries. Market participants adopted suitable hedging strategies and closed their short positions on the dollar, thereby stimulating the depreciation of the mark and the yen. Surprisingly, however, the announcement was not followed by any new monetary policy measure or G7 intervention. The market did not see this as an indication of disagreement within the G7 as to how to proceed, but rather as a tactical play for time until a more propitious moment arrived for coordinated action. In reality, the market had perceived that internal relations within the G7 had changed. Concern over the spread of financial instability in Europe had persuaded Germany to increase its commitment to support the dollar. The devastating effects of the yen's appreciation on Japan's industrial sector, already suffering the negative repercussions of the bursting of the speculative bubble on stock and property markets, had induced the government to soften its stance in the trade dispute with the United States. These were the circumstances in which the dollar began to appreciate on the exchange market and when, on 31 May, the central banks of the G7 countries took concerted action to purchase dollars, with the active and visible participation of the Bundesbank, market participants were taken by surprise (see Figure 9.1). The intervention was all the more unexpected as it went against

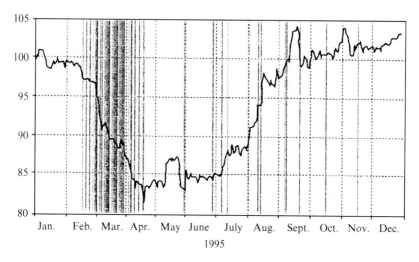

Note: Nominal yen/dollar exchange rate (left scale). The vertical bars indicate the periods of dollar purchases.

Source: Bank of Italy.

Figure 9.1   *Performance of the yen/dollar exchange rate and G7
              interventions*

the prevailing convention both on the markets and among economists that advised against 'aggressive' interventions, aimed at accelerating a market trend that dealers would have wanted to let run its natural course.

At the G7 Summit in Halifax, Nova Scotia, on 17 June, the heads of state and government reiterated their support for the operation in a declaration that seemed designed to contradict the conventional wisdom on intervention: 'continued cooperation in the exchange markets can be a useful and effective means for moderating exchange rate movements that are not driven by fundamental changes in economic conditions or policies'. Another concerted intervention, this time involving the Bank of Japan and the Fed, was carried out on 28 June, the same day on which an agreement was finally reached that ended the serious trade dispute between the two countries. In this way the United States signalled to the market that it would no longer use the exchange rate devaluation weapon for trade policy purposes. The dollar continued on its course of modest appreciation for the whole of July until in early August there was a further intervention that accelerated its rise. The intervention was then repeated on 16 August at a time of low market liquidity that amplified its effect. Between 2 and 24 August the dollar rose 7.5 per cent against the yen and the mark. Subsequently, the upward trend of the dollar was supported by cuts in official interest rates in Germany and in Japan, and by further interventions conducted by the Bank of Japan alone in September. At a meeting of G7 ministers and central bank governors on 7 October, the monetary authorities welcomed 'the orderly reversal in the movements of the major currencies that began following their April meeting' and expressed their desire that these trends continue 'consistent with underlying economic fundamentals'. During the period between the April and October meetings, the dollar appreciated with respect to the yen by 27 per cent, signalling the start of a trend that continued well into the third millennium; net dollar acquisitions by the central banks of the G7 and of other industrial countries totalled approximately $40 billion, an amount equal to roughly half the purchases made in the period between February 1987 and June 1988 when the previous intervention in support of the dollar was made.

The episode offers fertile ground for an analysis of the relations between monetary authorities and financial markets. It confirmed that when monetary authorities express a strong preference for the devaluation of the national currency, the market adapts rapidly. In practice, dealers fear that this desire will be followed by an excessively expansionary monetary policy, with aggressive cuts in short-term interest rates and the creation of substantial liquidity, and they hedge against the risk of losses on their investments in that currency by getting rid of it through the exchange market. The wish of monetary authorities is thus transformed into reality very quickly and in conditions that maximize the risk of overshooting. In actual fact, there is no doubt that the depreciation of the dollar in the two-year period 1994–95 went well beyond the levels justified by the need to adjust the US balance of payments disequilibrium with Japan and Germany, and that this created conditions of instability for the entire international monetary and financial system. Ex post, the temporary depreciation of the dollar had no effect on the US trade deficit, which continued to increase from $166 billion in 1994 to approximately $200 billion in 1996 and 1997. Moreover, while it is true that the appreciation of the German mark helped weaken the residual inflationary tensions following the reunification shock, in Japan the appreciation of the yen put a further brake on economic growth, aggravating existing structural imbalances. A second lesson regards the efficacy of currency intervention: it will be ineffective if the market perceives that the action, even when coordinated, conceals a fundamental incoherence between the objectives pursued by any of the participating countries, as happened in this case with the United States. By contrast, if the authorities signal through declarations and clear monetary and exchange policy measures that the coherence of the objectives has been restored and is being faithfully pursued, the market will react in accordance with the aim of the intervention. Finally, a third lesson concerns the procedures and communication of intervention to the market. The market assigns greater value to acts of intervention whose objectives have first been made known to the public. Intervention made without this advance communication can be misunderstood or generate adverse reactions based on technical considerations regarding the volume, method and timing of the interventions. In the case of Japan and the United States, interventions were conducted up to the start of 1995 in relatively large amounts but in a sporadic fashion, often leaving market participants uncertain as to whether the move was part of a coordinated strategy aimed at pursuing specific exchange rate objectives or whether they were aimed at reducing the volatility in the market. It was only with the G7 statement of April 1995 that the objectives of concerted action were made explicit, followed by the aggressive intervention of 31 May, which signalled to the market the strong determination of the G7 to continue its strategy of supporting the dollar.

Any overall assessment of the G7 intervention must ultimately be positive. The objective was to halt the freefall of the dollar and enable a substantial devaluation of the yen that would help revive Japanese economic growth – and this objective was delivered, with a clear reversal of the trend. It is legitimate to ask whether this result is entirely due to the resolution of the trade dispute between the United States and Japan, and if the monetary and exchange policy strategies adopted by the G7 were truly necessary and useful. These questions will inevitably divide analysts. What is clear is that the evolution of the trade talks played a major role in influencing market sentiment; but the market was also aware that the agreement could not of itself eliminate the US trade deficit with Japan, and neither would it end the ongoing debate over the opening of Japan to US imports, not only to goods but also, and above all, to financial services. It is therefore likely that without the G7 intervention the reversal of the downward trend of the dollar would not have happened. The market would have slowed or temporarily halted the fall of the dollar, but it would have done so in conditions of heightened volatility, caused by persistent uncertainty over the possible future course of US foreign economic policy and that of the other G7 countries.

10.   Double play in Hong Kong (1998)

> It was a contrived game with clearly destructive goals in mind – drive up interest rates, drive down share prices, make the local population panic and exert enough pressure on our linked exchange rate until it breaks.
>
> Donald Tsang (1998, p. 4)[1]

In the midst of the Asian financial panic and the Russian debt crisis of August 1998, extreme downward pressure was exerted simultaneously on the fixed exchange rate of the Hong Kong dollar and the local stock exchange, the Hang Seng. The Hong Kong Monetary Authority (HKMA) established that the pressures were being fuelled by hedge fund transactions conducted jointly on the currency and equity markets and moved to reinforce its support of the exchange rate through massive intervention purchases in the stock market. The decision to intervene, viewed by many as being in breach of orthodox practices and the professional code of conduct of central banks, was severely criticized both within Hong Kong and abroad, but nonetheless proved effective in withstanding market pressures. Indeed, Goodhart and Dai (2003, p. 4) consider the event 'a rare example of waging a successful battle against speculators'.

In 1983 Hong Kong adopted a currency board regime that involved setting a fixed rate of exchange of 7.80 Hong Kong dollars per US dollar. The HKMA maintained currency stability by increasing or restricting domestic liquidity in equal proportion to the inflows or outflows of capital from and to other countries. International financial players were reassured of the regime's credibility by the substantial holdings of dollar reserves by the HKMA. The currency board commenced operations without problems, and the authorities of China and Hong Kong announced their intention to retain the regime after the return of the British 'colony' to the People's Republic of China on 1 July 1997. Under the terms of the handover, Hong Kong would maintain economic and financial autonomy and be accorded the status of Special Administrative Region (SAR) of China under the 'one country, two systems' principle. The agreement was entirely in line with the exchange rate policy pursued by the Beijing government, which, following the devaluation of the renminbi in 1994, had itself made a firm commitment to maintaining currency stability, albeit without the institutional support of a currency board (see Chapter 12).

When the Asian financial crisis exploded in May 1997, the market scrutinized the behaviour of the Chinese and Hong Kong authorities, looking for possible signs of a change in exchange rate policy triggered by the turbulent economic climate. It also tried to ascertain if, and to what extent, Beijing would support the Hong Kong regime should the crisis spread to the new SAR. In fact, like the other Asian countries, Hong Kong had experienced strong growth in its stock and property markets, and a downward readjustment was deemed both likely and necessary. Hong Kong emerged unscathed as the crisis slowly engulfed the Philippines, Malaysia and Indonesia between June and September, but it suffered the consequences of Taiwan's unexpected decision of 20 October to float the Taiwanese dollar, which depreciated by 3 per cent. The market was caught completely unawares by the move, which was made without any particular pressure having been exerted on the Taiwanese currency, already well-insulated by Taiwan's vast volume of official reserves and benign economic conditions. Analysts interpreted the decision as a precautionary gambit, reflecting fears of further contagion or possible changes in exchange rate policy by the authorities of Beijing or of the SAR. Suddenly, however, the Hong Kong dollar was perceived as vulnerable and a tidal wave of selling orders buffeted the Hang Seng. In four trading days, from 20 to 23 October, the Hong Kong stock exchange lost 23 per cent of its value and overnight interest rates were allowed to climb from 7 to over 250 per cent to combat exchange rate pressures. But the storm soon subsided, as other and much more worrying flashpoints were attracting the attention of market participants: the Wall Street crash of 27 October; the abrupt decline of European and Latin American stock exchanges in the days that followed; and the build-up of pressure on the Korean won. By the end of October, short-term interest rates in Hong Kong had dropped back to under 10 per cent, a sign that pressures on the currency had evaporated.

Conditions began to improve on Asian markets at the beginning of 1998 following the IMF's approval of a substantial financial aid package for Korea. But tensions reignited in the second quarter, when it became apparent that the financial crisis of the emerging Asian countries would have negative repercussions for output and employment growth prospects across the continent, already beleaguered by the Japanese recession. The crisis spread to countries like Hong Kong and Singapore, whose economies relied on trading and financial relationships with the region. Hong Kong in particular appeared vulnerable, as the Hong Kong dollar had appreciated against all the major Asian currencies, including the yen, and was seen as a likely target for a downward correction. During the summer, Hong Kong's monetary authorities became convinced that, while justifiable in the context of the Asian crisis, currency pressures were being artificially inflated by the speculative strategies of hedge funds operating simultaneously on the foreign exchange and stock markets in a prearranged 'double play' strategy (IMF 1999b, pp. 92–115; Yam 1999). The hedge funds first purchased Hong Kong dollars against US dollars on the international market through swap deals with counterparts that had previously funded themselves by issuing one- or two-year bonds on the Hong Kong market; in a second phase, the speculative strategy involved the sale of Hong Kong dollars on the currency market and the simultaneous short-selling of shares or futures contracts on the Hang Seng stock market index. The idea was that pressure on the currency market would force a rise in interest rates by the currency board; this in turn would trigger a fall in the stock market, allowing speculators to close the futures contracts on the index profitably. The HKMA was alerted to the double play by the rising amount of Hong Kong dollar-denominated bond issues by non-resident intermediaries and the extraordinary growth in Hang Seng futures contracts. Further proof of the double play came from the fact that the speculative pressure on the exchange rate, contrary to what had happened a year earlier, appeared impervious to rising interest rates, which had climbed from 5 to 20 per cent. This meant that the speculators had raised Hong Kong dollars in advance and were therefore immune to the increased costs of short-term financing. Based on this evidence, and on contacts with market participants, the HKMA concluded that the only way to deter the speculation effectively was to use official currency reserves to carry out a massive share purchasing intervention on the local stock market. In this way the drop in share prices on which the speculators depended in order to make a profit would be prevented. Moreover, the sale of dollar reserves to purchase shares would simultaneously bolster the Hong Kong dollar. Between 14 and 28 August 1998 the HKMA carried out stock market interventions on spot and futures contracts for a total of $15 billion, equal to over 15 per cent of its official reserves. At the beginning of September, measures were taken to improve the functioning of the currency board and to enhance oversight of share and future contracts. The market was completely unprepared for such a non-conventional move and reacted by allowing share prices to rise rapidly (see Figure 10.1). The Hang Seng index rose by 18 per cent during the intervention period, then fell by 10 per cent in the two days following its conclusion, before stabilizing in line with the upward trend of other Asian stock exchanges and Wall Street. In the period between 1 September 1998 and 30 June 1999, the value of the HKMA's share portfolio rose from $15 to $26.7 billion, thanks to the Hang Seng's performance, which outstripped all the other Asian stock exchanges.

The HKMA's highly unorthodox intervention was strongly criticized by market participants and economists (Lynch 1999). In a speech delivered at

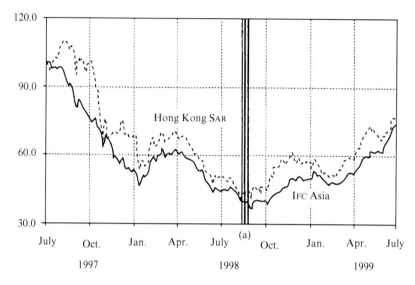

Note: (a) = Period of HKMA stock market interventions.

Source: Thomson Financial-Datastream.

Figure 10.1   Performance of the Hong Kong stock market and Asian share index

the end of 1998 the Chief Executive of the HKMA, Joseph Yam (1999), recalled how the intervention had been considered by some observers a 'criminal violation of the principles of the free market' and how Milton Friedman described the government's stock purchases as 'insane' or part of a plan to nationalize the Hong Kong economy. Setting aside these extremist positions, the majority of market participants stressed the implications of the intervention for the functioning of Hong Kong's financial markets. On the one hand, participants thought it possible that the lack of advance warning of the intervention by the monetary authorities could trigger a retreat of international investors from the SAR; on the other, it was felt that the authorities' desire to limit stock market losses could create moral hazard conditions, favouring excessively risky behaviour by investors who relied on the safety net provided by the monetary authorities. Observers also wondered how the stock market would react to the existence of a vast equity portfolio held by the government, presumably eager to sell at the first favourable opportunity. Similar considerations may have contributed to the decision by the credit rating agency Standard & Poor's to downgrade Hong Kong's credit rating from A+ to A.

In the event, the political and monetary authorities of Hong Kong decided to communicate clearly to the market the means and ends of the strategy, underscoring the exceptional nature of the intervention required to withstand an emergency situation which, if left to run its course, could have had disastrous consequences for the economy and the financial system. It firmly denied that there was any intention of tilting the balance of economic power within the SAR towards nationalization, and made it known in no uncertain terms that the HKMA strategy enjoyed the full support of the Chinese government, which was aware that a collapse of the Hong Kong dollar would have inevitably left its own renminbi vulnerable to speculation. A specially created autonomous body was charged with managing the share portfolio and to devise a transparent strategy for its gradual liquidation: over a third of the portfolio was sold off by 2000, earning substantial profits. These initiatives changed the negative attitude prevailing among global players regarding the intervention, who gradually began to align themselves with the strongly favourable stance expressed from the outset by market participants in Hong Kong. The change of sentiment was helped by the perception that the international financial system was experiencing a crisis of exceptional gravity, made even more acute by the Russian declaration of insolvency on 17 August and the collapse of LTCM, a New York based hedge fund, on 23 September. In light of these tensions the market interpreted the extraordinary intervention of the HKMA, which was necessary in order to defuse a flashpoint of potentially systemic proportions, as a sign of the capacity of monetary authorities to react to international financial instability. Further, albeit indirect, support of the Hong Kong dollar came on 4 October from the Interim Committee of the IMF. In the press communiqué issued in Washington at the meeting's conclusion, the Committee noted that 'many countries in Asia and in other regions are dealing effectively with the spillover effects from the crisis' while welcoming 'the reaffirmation of China's commitment not to devalue its currency, which has provided an important anchor to the region' (see IMF 1998b, p. 318). The tone of the statement was unusually forthcoming and its content unconventional, evidently motivated by the need to provide the markets with a strong signal in favour of monetary and financial stability at a time of grave risks and tensions.

The HKMA response to the double play must be assessed in the context of the technical characteristics of the fixed exchange rate regime in the SAR and the primary importance of the share market in Hong Kong's economy. From this perspective, the intervention was not dissimilar to initiatives taken by the Fed in situations of grave stock market instability, such as the Black Monday Wall Street crash of 19 October 1987 or the LTCM crisis. In all these cases, in Hong Kong and Washington, the monetary authorities' decision to intervene was based on a necessarily subjective evaluation that pointed to the existence of disorderly market conditions and risks of economic contraction justifying intervention by the lender of last resort. The action was therefore held to be coherent with the institutional mandate conferred on the competent monetary authority. This is not to underestimate the economic, legal and institutional issues raised in the case of Hong Kong by the HKMA's holdings in the share capital of some of the largest companies and financial institutions in the private sector. There can be no doubt, however, that the unconventional strategy pursued by the monetary authorities represented the turning point for Hong Kong in a crisis situation and laid the foundations for relaunching the SAR's economy (Gobat 2001).

NOTE

1. The then Finance Minister of Hong Kong.

11.   A safety net for the euro (2000)

> The circumstances in which the major countries would want to use intervention to attempt to influence exchange rates are relatively rare, but they do arise from time to time, and one would need to ask, 'if not now, when?'
>
> Michael Mussa (IMF 2000b, p. 336)

During 2000 the downward trend of the euro exchange rate, already apparent in the new European currency's first year of life, became even more pronounced. In addition to the economic factors already mentioned in Chapter 5, the euro's performance began to be affected by the scepticism of market participants about the ability of the European monetary authority, the ECB, to counteract the declining exchange rate through monetary policy alone. Despite the fact that as early as November 1999 the ECB had begun to pursue a more restrictive monetary policy to prevent inflation from rising above 2 per cent, gradually increasing the main refinancing rate from 2.50 to 4.75 per cent in October 2000, the market believed that further monetary tightening aimed at supporting the exchange rate was unlikely. Inflationary tensions appeared to derive essentially from factors external to the euro area and were blamed primarily on a rise in oil prices. Yet the weakening of the euro exchange rate was itself a factor, as it induced capital outflows from Europe to the United States where investors were attracted by better profit prospects in the stock market and private sector. On this last point, there was broad consensus among market participants that monetary policy could do precious little to reverse the outflows: only structural reforms capable of revitalizing productivity and boosting the growth potential of European economies could attract investor capital back towards the euro.

The market believed it was even less likely that the ECB could support the euro through interventions on the currency market. First, it noted the absence of the requisite unanimity in the euro area on the objective of strengthening the euro, as confirmed by the numerous statements of leading politicians, underscoring the contribution that a weak euro could make to Europe's economic recovery. Secondly, there was a perception among market participants that the ECB's own statute prevented it from intervening by obliging it to pursue the objective of price stability, without making any reference to exchange rate stability. These perceptions were unjustified because the ECB can take exchange rate performance into consideration when it comes to making a 'discretionary' assessment of the potential risks of inflation signalled by a broad set of economic and financial indicators. Nor is there any provision in its statute preventing the ECB from carrying out exchange market interventions, which in any event are part of the operational 'arsenal' of any central bank. The fact, however, that in over a year and a half of existence the ECB had refrained from making any currency intervention led the market to extrapolate a similar stance in the future, notwithstanding a track record of numerous currency interventions in support of national monetary policy by all of the central banks belonging to the Eurosystem, including the Bundesbank.

The market believed, finally, that even if the ECB were to decide to support the exchange rate through intervention, this would prove ineffective unless the Fed also participated in what would then be a coordinated action to sell dollars against euros on the currency market. The likelihood of such a move was considered negligible, given the commitment of the second Clinton administration to a strong dollar, constantly reiterated by its Treasury Secretary Robert Rubin (a former Goldman Sachs investment banker with proven experience in the field of international finance). Rubin was well aware that the prospect of a strong dollar was an essential prerequisite for bolstering the capital inflows needed by the United States to finance its growing current account deficit. Accordingly, he masterminded a communication strategy to the market, whose sole message, 'a strong dollar is in the interest of the United States', was faithfully adopted by every American official, from the US President downwards.[1] That declaration led market participants and economic analysts, irrespective of the strategy's merits, to reach a unanimous conclusion: American monetary authorities would not participate in a coordinated intervention to support the euro at the expense of the strong dollar. This conviction grew from 2000 onwards when the upward trend of the American stock markets went into reverse, particularly in the technology sector shares trading on NASDAQ. At that point even a slight drop in the dollar could have significantly impacted investors' expectations, persuading them to sell their shares and precipitate a sharper decline. With presidential elections looming in November, analysts agreed that the Clinton administration would be highly reluctant to take any step that risked triggering a politically dangerous trend. In these circumstances, as investors continued to predict stronger output growth in the United States than in the European Union and an interest rate differential in favour of the US dollar, a one-way market was created in which the supply of the European currency greatly exceeded demand and the short-selling of euros proved consistently profitable.

In May 2000 the euro dropped against the dollar to just under the 90 cents threshold, prompting the first ever public statement, made on 8 May, by the informal 'Eurogroup' comprising the finance ministers of the euro area countries and the ECB President. The statement expressed the group's common concern about the level of the euro, which they said did not reflect the economic fundamentals of the euro area; the exchange rate then rallied in June, returning to over 95 cents against the dollar, essentially on the basis of expectations of a US economic slowdown and a narrowing of the growth rate gap between Europe and the United States (see Figure 11.1).

During the summer months these predictions were proven incorrect – albeit partially – and the euro weakened again, dropping to 85 cents in September 2000. When data on the performance of the United States and European economies were released the market began to exhibit signs of asymmetric behaviour, reacting positively to favourable statistics on the dollar and negatively or indifferently to favourable statistics on the euro (ECB 2000; BIS 2001). A survey of the analyses conducted by major financial intermediaries at the end of the summer provides some interesting

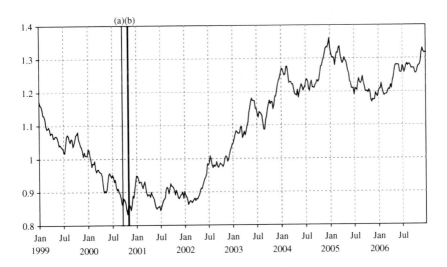

Notes:
*   Nominal bilateral exchange rate, dollar per euro.
(a)   Intervention by the G7 in support of the euro.
(b)   Intervention by the Eurosystem in support of the euro.

Source: Bank of Italy.

Figure 11.1   *The dollar–euro exchange rate* and foreign exchange market intervention by the G7 and the Eurosystem*

clues as to the prevailing market sentiment. First, analysts anticipated a decline of the euro in the short run, even though the great majority of them continued to forecast a sharp rise in the European currency within six to 12 months; second, market observers noted the increased frequency of market 'decoupling' from economic fundamentals, characterized by episodes of herd behaviour; third, it was acknowledged that the weakness of the euro risked undermining the stability of the international monetary system; and finally it was emphasized that in these cases intervention by central banks would be useful and necessary, but doubts persisted over the willingness of the United States to work alongside the ECB in a coordinated action to support the euro (Goldman Sachs 2000a; Merrill Lynch 2000; Lehman Brothers 2000a).

In official circles, in addition to numerous individual declarations (not all of which helped support the euro),[2] a new common position was communicated to the market in a second statement issued jointly by the Eurogroup and the ECB on 8 September. In the communiqué, the finance ministers and ECB President repeated their shared concern already expressed in May about the euro exchange rate and resolved to monitor carefully the evolution of the situation, declaring (in a formula that deliberately mimicked the US monetary authorities in respect of the dollar) that 'a strong euro is in the interest of the euro area'. In the days that followed the euro continued to weaken, in part because expectations of concrete follow-up measures after the statement were not fulfilled. The announcement by the ECB on 14 September that, in line with a new risk management procedure for official reserves, interest income (equal to approximately €2.5 billion) accrued on its dollar reserves would be gradually sold against euros on the market, initially led market participants to believe that this was a kind of 'dress rehearsal' for intervention. But once the ECB had clarified the aims of the procedure, the impact on the exchange rate proved short-lived. As the countdown began to the G7 Summit of ministers and central bank governors in Prague on 23 September, the public debate on what was needed to support the euro intensified. *The Economist* (2000, p. 105), in the article 'Intervention: divine or comic?' of 23 September, reported that 'the clamour for the ECB to intervene to save the ailing euro is getting louder by the day'. Among the most authoritative voices calling for intervention were those of two American economists not generally known for their pro-interventionist stance. At a press conference held on the previous 19 September 2000 in Prague to present a report on the world economic outlook, the IMF's Chief Economist, Michael Mussa, had claimed that the conditions for intervening to support the euro existed given that its weakness was only partially due to economic factors and its depreciation was at least half due to the 'manic depressive nature of the market'. According to

Mussa, the market had pushed the euro below levels justified by the fundamentals (IMF 2000b). Two days later, on 21 September, in an article published in the *New York Times*, Paul Krugman (2000) confirmed that the weak euro was not the result of fundamental economic factors but of the 'herd mentality' that prevailed on the market; what was needed was a 'slap in the face' to make the market regain its senses. Krugman added that it would be in the interest of America to participate in a concerted intervention to support the euro, whose weakness had begun to damage US exports.

In the early afternoon of 22 September, on the eve of the long-awaited IMF meeting in Prague, the central banks of the G7 and the ECB began taking coordinated action to support the euro, catching the market off-guard. The euro, which in previous days had fallen to a low of 0.8480 against the dollar before climbing to 0.86 on the day of the intervention (buoyed by expectations of possible decisions by the G7), rose to 0.88 cents to the dollar before settling just below these levels. The immediate reaction of observers and market participants, who emphasized the sound technical handling of the intervention, was very positive in respect of the coordination and timing of actions by the central banks (JPMorgan 2000; Goldman Sachs 2000b; Lehman Brothers 2000b). The total cost of the intervention was not made public but was deemed to be substantial by market participants and estimated by the OECD to be at least 6 billion euros (OECD 2001). The monetary effects of the intervention were sterilized only by the non-European central banks. The intervention was formally approved by the ministers and central bank governors of the G7 in a press release that confirmed the group's interest in a 'strong and stable international monetary system' and explained that the action had been undertaken, at the ECB's request, in the context of common concern 'about the potential implications of the recent movements of the euro for the world economy' (see IMF 2000b, p. 328).

Despite these signs of unity of purpose and operational coordination, the markets began to wonder whether the G7 intervention should be interpreted as a reversal of the US strong dollar policy, or less ambitiously as a once-off cooperative initiative that the Americans had been unable to avoid but which would not be repeated at least until after the American presidential elections the following November. Statements made to the *Wall Street Journal* by the American Treasury Secretary Summers immediately following the intervention (see Phillips and Sims 2000) seemed to validate this second interpretation, while European officials stressed the objective of systemic stability and the benefits for the United States of a more competitive dollar. These different views induced the market to test official resistance to any further weakening of the euro. The currency fell again to the minimum levels reached in September as the market attempted to find out whether this threshold would trigger a further coordinated intervention.

The lack of any reaction by the G7 monetary authorities fuelled the downward trend, and despite an increase in the ECB official rate (from 4.5 to 4.75 on 5 October), the euro exchange rate reached a new historic low of 0.8250 at the end of October. The market understood that the Fed would not support moves to intervene more heavily on the currency market (this was later confirmed by the minutes of the Federal Open Market Committee of 3 October 2000, released in November) and believed that the ECB would never intervene alone, in line with the prevailing convention which regards unilateral interventions as ineffective. The ECB was thus confronted with a predicament. Had this market sentiment spread, the conditions for a one-way trend in the euro would have been recreated – the same conditions that the intervention of 22 September were designed to counter. Moreover, for a 'young' institution such as the ECB, whose credibility on the market had not yet been fully tested, it would have been very damaging indeed to confirm the impression that it could defend its own currency only with the consent of the United States, which in this case had a conflicting interest. These were the circumstances that prompted the decision by the Eurosystem to make a unilateral intervention to support the euro at the beginning of November, with sales of dollars and yen spread over three trading days. The market was again taken by surprise and the operation proved effective in guiding expectations: the euro appreciated rapidly, climbing to 0.95 cents (in other words well beyond the level reached after the G7 intervention), where it remained until the end of 2000. Since then, the euro underwent some minor oscillations in 2001, staying constantly above the level of 0.8250, which in November 2000 had triggered the autonomous intervention by the Eurosystem, before embarking on a medium-term rising trend that peaked at 1.36 dollars to the euro in 2005.

The evolution of the dollar/euro exchange rate has again contributed to endless debates among economists and market participants over the determinants of exchange rate movements of the main currencies. But there is broad consensus that the market has finally acknowledged the Eurosystem's determination to limit the depreciation of the euro and its willingness to act to support it with appropriate monetary policy measures, either through coordinated action by the G7 or acting alone when it believes it is necessary to contrast a one-way trend.

NOTES

1. Rubin explained in his memoirs that this 'boring repetition' reflected 'not only my belief in a strong dollar but also my belief in leaving markets to market forces' (see Rubin and Weisberg 2003, p. 184).

2. On 6 September 2000 press agencies reported that the German Chancellor Gerhard
    Schroeder had declared in a public address that a weak euro was useful for supporting
    economic activity and exports. The news, which was later the subject of corrections and
    clarifications, was widely referred to by currency dealers as one of the factors explaining
    the single currency's weakness.

12. The great wall of the Chinese renminbi (1994–2005)

Evidence of currency manipulation has become increasingly obvious during the 2003–05 period. The leading case in point is China.

Morris Goldstein (2006, p. 145)

Some advisors have prescribed the 'shock therapy' to Russia and Eastern European countries, but later on this was described as 'shock with no therapy'. We should be cautious to offer the same prescription again, so as not to have credibility jeopardized. China will only consider to take the gradualist reform approach that wins the trust of the masses of the Chinese people, rather than a 'shock', not to mention that the United States has not taken the lead to use 'shock' to adjust its imbalances.

Zhou Xiaochuan (2006, p. 2)

The exchange rate policy of the People's Republic of China was not the subject of close attention by the international community until the beginning of the third millennium, when it became clear that the extraordinary and sustained growth performance of China was having major repercussions on the world economy, global payments imbalances and exchange rate relationships among key currencies. In fact, until the 1970s China was seen as the gigantic but poor developing country it was, with an annual per capita income of $200 in 1978 (see Bergsten et al. 2006, p. 5). It was also a communist country that had gone through a period of severe political and social instability during the 'cultural revolution' of 1966–69 (with devastating implications for the domestic economy). The gradual political and economic reform strategy introduced by Deng Xiaoping after Mao Zedong's death in 1976 was positively received in the West, but its chances of success were always cautiously assessed because of China's structural domestic imbalances (overpopulation, poverty, income inequalities and so forth), and unresolved political conflicts between hard-line Maoist and reform-minded factions. The brutal repression of the Tiananmen Square protests in Beijing as late as 1989 seemed to confirm that even Deng was not ready to move quickly towards a fully democratic political system and a market-oriented economy. Against this background, China's exchange rate policy seemed hardly to matter on a global scale and was seen as another example of an emerging country attempting to reconcile the need to grow quickly with monetary stability, mostly through exchange rate controls and capital account restrictions. During much of the 1980s China had a fixed exchange rate regime for the renminbi, but the currency was frequently depreciated in line with the ups and downs of the domestic economic and political situation. Between 1988 and 1993 China adopted a dual exchange rate regime with a fixed official rate and a market-determined exchange rate, which accounted for about 80 per cent of current account foreign exchange transactions (see Wang 2004). In 1994, following severe balance of payments problems originated by a rapidly growing domestic economy, the exchange rates were unified at the more depreciated market rate and pegged at 8.28 renminbi to the US dollar with an oscillation band of ±0.3 per cent on either side of the central rate. Although this regime was officially defined as a 'managed floating exchange rate', the peg remained unchanged from 1995 until 21 July 2005 when, bowing to strong and protracted international pressure mostly originating from the United States, China announced it would change its foreign exchange policy. The changes in the exchange regime were modest and consisted of: an immediate revaluation of the renminbi against the dollar; a continuation of the managed float regime with the ±0.3 per cent oscillation band around a daily announced central parity; and the introduction of a reference basket of currencies (although details about weights, parities and band width were not released). No changes on existing restrictions on capital movements were announced (see BIS 2006a, p. 87). As a result of the changes, the renminbi was allowed to appreciate from 8.28 to around 8 to the US dollar by mid-2006, or by about 3 per cent in 12 months. As with many things Chinese, information provided by the monetary authorities on their new exchange rate policy is less than complete and transparent. However, it seems sufficiently clear, from official statements and the research of independent analysts, that China is gradually moving towards a more market-determined foreign exchange rate policy. However, in order to achieve this objective, the priority, after the adjustments announced on 21 July 2005, was not so much a sharp appreciation of the renminbi as the strengthening of the infrastructure of foreign exchange and financial markets in China. Measures to that effect were already taken in early 2006 (see BIS 2006a, p. 88), including the removal of foreign exchange restrictions on companies, banks and individuals so as to allow the market to better reflect the interaction between demand and supply of foreign exchange (see Zhou 2006).

The reform of China's foreign exchange system and policy has to be seen in the context of the evolution of global payments imbalances. As already mentioned, China's foreign exchange policy had been formally praised by the IMF in the aftermath of the Asian financial crisis as providing an anchor of stability that contributed to halting the spread of financial contagion. But the attitude of the international community began to change after 2000 as China recorded an extraordinary GDP growth performance with a 9.4 per cent average annual growth rate, coupled with a rising current account surplus in its balance of payments (up to 9 per cent of GDP in 2006) and with sizeable inflows of foreign direct investment (FDI). To keep the nominal exchange rate stable the monetary authorities conducted massive intervention purchases in the foreign exchange market, leading to a huge accumulation of official reserves, mostly denominated in US dollars. Between 2000 and 2004 China's official foreign exchange reserves rose from $168 to $614 billion; they jumped to $822 billion by the end of 2005 and it is estimated they will have exceeded the $1 trillion level by the end of 2006 (see Goldstein 2006; BIS 2006a).

In parallel with the widening trade surplus and accelerating pace of reserve accumulation, international criticism of China's exchange rate policy became more widespread and explicit. Among professional economists the most vocal critic of China's policies has been Morris Goldstein (2004). In a thorough review of the literature and the empirical evidence he concluded that the renminbi was significantly undervalued (in the order of 15–25 per cent) and that China had been 'manipulating its currency', contrary to the IMF rules of the game. In official circles, the efforts to convince China to adopt a different exchange rate policy were conducted in meetings of the G7 or in trilateral confidential talks among United States, Japanese and German (on behalf of the European Union) officials. As recalled by John Taylor (2007, pp. 284–6), the US Treasury Undersecretary at the time, the strategy involved also convincing Japan to stop its dollar intervention purchases and allow the yen to appreciate. Eventually, the G7 agreed on a language that would convey to the market their policy intentions regarding exchange rates. In their communiqué issued in February 2004 at Boca Raton (and reiterated in October 2004), the G7 finance ministers and central bank governors, without explicitly mentioning China or Japan, called for more flexibility in exchange rates by 'major countries or economic areas that lack such flexibility to promote smooth and widespread adjustments in the international financial system, based on market mechanisms' (see Taylor, J. 2007, p. 298; IMF 2004c, p. 289). At the same time, bilateral negotiations were undertaken by the United States to find ways of reducing the growing deficit in the trade balance with China. The American negotiating position was clear: China should significantly revalue the renminbi or face the prospect of the introduction of a 27.5 per cent tariff on all its exports to the United States. This was the substance of a bipartisan resolution approved by the US Senate with a two-thirds majority in April 2005. As the US government is required, under the Omnibus

Trade and Competitiveness Act of 1988, to report to Congress any countries engaging in 'exchange rate manipulation' in order to obtain an unfair competitive advantage, it was understood that the exchange rate policy of China would be carefully scrutinized by the Treasury. In May 2005, the US Treasury, in its report to Congress on international economic and exchange rate policies, concluded that 'current Chinese policies are highly distortionary and pose a risk to China's economy, its trading partners and global economic growth . . . If current trends continue without substantial alteration, China's policies will likely meet the statute's technical requirements for designation' as a case of currency manipulation (US Treasury 2005, p. 2). With this cautious approach, the Treasury aimed to keep pressure on the Chinese government to adopt a more flexible exchange rate policy, while simultaneously refusing to endorse the protectionist retaliation advocated by large segments of Congress.[1] In the end China agreed in July 2005 to initiate a gradual reform of its exchange rate regime, taking the steps mentioned above. These steps, although seen by some observers as inadequate,[2] allowed the US Treasury to express concern for the limited degree of appreciation of the renminbi since July 2005 whilst refraining once again (in May 2006) from designating China as a currency manipulator (US Treasury 2006).

The 'amicable' confrontation between China and the United States on exchange rate issues is likely to continue for the foreseeable future. Ultimately, both countries have no interest in forcing radical and abrupt changes in their current trade and exchange rate relationship. China's top priority is to prolong as much as possible the stellar growth performance achieved by its economy in the 2000s on which depends the country's ability to deal with its structural economic and social problems, such as poverty in rural areas, widespread unemployment and under-employment, and the fragility of its banking and financial system.[3] China fears that a sharp revaluation of the renminbi may have serious negative repercussions on the export sector, thereby curbing growth in output and employment and exacerbating social tensions. This, in turn, would affect the solidity of the banking system, plagued by a high percentage of non-performing loans, with the risk of setting in motion a financial crisis of systemic dimensions.[4] And although Chinese officials do not like to compare China with Japan, they privately admit that they would like at all costs to avoid following Japan's example when it allowed the yen to appreciate as a result of foreign pressure, a move that led to a banking crisis and a prolonged recession. The Chinese government knows that the international community expects it to do its share in the adjustment of international payments imbalances and that this entails certain responsibilities, which it must accept if China is to play a greater role in multilateral institutions (including the WTO). This implies that China will honour its commitment to a more flexible exchange rate policy in a gradual but meaningful way so as to avoid the risk of protectionist retaliation from the United States, while continuing its strategy of careful macroeconomic management and gradual structural reforms. In fact, since 2006 the Chinese monetary authorities have allowed a further appreciation of the renminbi to 7.61 to the dollar at end June 2007 (that is, an appreciation of 8.0 per cent since July 2005) and have taken a number of monetary and regulatory measures to slow down the growth of domestic demand. The US government, on the other hand, would not necessarily welcome a radical change in China's foreign exchange policy if that entailed the end of any dollar intervention purchases by the People's Bank of China in foreign exchange markets. Such purchases have in fact played an important role in cushioning the decline of the dollar since 2000, and the investment of China's official reserves in US Treasury bills and bonds has been a major source of financing for the US balance of payment deficit (see BIS 2006a). At the same time, the US government will continue to use the threat of the 'currency manipulator' designation to ensure that China allows a gradual appreciation of the renminbi and relaxation of foreign exchange restrictions.

In any event, the exchange rate policy of China is hardly a bilateral trade affair between the United States and China. The policy has to be seen in the broader context of the growing economic and financial strength of the main Asian countries constituting the informal 'ASEAN+3' Group and of their desire to ensure a degree of exchange rate stability in the Asian region. Whether the policies of the ASEAN+3 Group have – with the tacit consent of the United States – collectively given birth to a 'revived Bretton Woods system', as claimed by some observers,[5] and whether such an arrangement is a sustainable one, remains to be seen. What is significant for the purposes of this book is that China has been able to keep its own foreign exchange policy unchanged despite major financial turbulence in the region and an exceptional amount of external pressures. Of course, exchange rate stability has been achieved largely thanks to exchange controls and restrictions on capital movements, but China has been able to influence expectations on global markets that it would not deviate from the established policy of stabilizing the exchange rate while promoting the gradual integration of the Chinese trade and financial system in the global economy. Thus, even after the announcement in July 2005 of the reform of the exchange rate policy, there has been no significant market speculation to push for a sharp revaluation of the renminbi. This is not to say that the Chinese strategy is without risks. The danger is that a stable exchange rate coupled with a large and persistent current account surplus and sizeable FDI inflows will result in excessive money creation and domestic credit expansion, eventually translating into higher inflation, with increased risks of a possible abrupt credit contraction. The challenge for the Chinese monetary authorities would then be to prevent the overheating of the economy with a combination of monetary tightening, gradual appreciation of the renminbi and relaxation of restrictions on capital outflows.

NOTES

1. This strategy was fully backed by the Federal Reserve. In an unusually blunt statement before the Committee on Finance of the US Senate on 23 June 2005, Alan Greenspan stated: 'Some observers mistakenly believe that a marked increase in the exchange value of the Chinese renminbi relative to the US dollar would significantly increase manufacturing activity and jobs in the United States. I am aware of no credible evidence that supports such a conclusion. . . . Any significant elevation on tariffs that substantially reduces our overall imports, by keeping out competitively priced goods, would materially lower our standard of living. A return to protectionism would threaten the continuation of much of the extraordinary growth in living standards worldwide, but especially in the United States, that is due importantly to the post-World War II opening of global markets'. However, Greenspan concluded that 'it is nonetheless the case that a more flexible renminbi would be helpful to China's economic stability and, hence, to world and US economic growth' (Greenspan 2005b, p. 1)
2. See Goldstein and Lardy 'China's revaluation shows size really matters', *Financial Times*, 22 July 2005. Other observers, however, thought the US emphasis on China's exchange rate policy was excessive; see, for example, Samuel Brittan, 'China's currency is its own business', *Financial Times*, 24 June 2005; Joseph Stiglitz, 'America has little to teach China about a Steady Economy', *Financial Times*, 27 July 2005.
3. For an overview of China's structural imbalances, see Prasad (2004).
4. Although China has made significant progress in strengthening the banking system and its supervisory institutions (especially with the establishment of the China Banking Regulatory Commission in April 2003), major banks are still state-controlled and their lending and provisioning policies are still subject to a high degree of government interference. The IMF (Prasad 2004) estimated that in 2002 non-performing loans (NPLs) at the four major state commercial banks were ranging between 15 and 37 per cent of total loans. More recent independent estimates put the ratio of NPLs at 20 to 25 per cent, far exceeding official figures (see the article 'A great big banking gamble. Special report on China's banking industry', *The Economist*, 29 October 2005). The same report indicates that 'since 1998, Beijing has injected more than \$260 billion into its banks' to cover bad loans. Goldstein and Lardy note that foreign exchange reserves of the People's Bank of China were used in December 2003 to support the Bank of China and the China Construction Bank (\$45 billion) and in April 2005 to support the Industrial and Commercial Bank of China (\$15 billion) (see the article in *Financial Times*, 22 July 2005). The perception among foreign observers is that NPLs are indeed increasing in the context of a rapidly growing economy because of the aggressive lending policy of banks: in a recent report by the consultancy firm Ernst & Young, NPLs were estimated to be of the same order of magnitude as China's foreign exchange reserves. The estimate was subsequently withdrawn as incorrect by the firm itself following strong protests from the Chinese authorities, but the incident gives an idea of the sensitivity of the issue (see the article by McGregor, 'China's bad loans outstrip reserves', *Financial Times*, 3 May 2006).
5. See Dooley et al. (2003) and (2004); Dooley and Garber (2005). The latter paper includes comments by Eichengreeen and Frankel plus a general discussion with remarks by Krugman, Rogoff, Milesi-Ferretti and Cooper.

13.   How did they do it?

My sense is that, at the end of the day, we will find success easier than feared by
so many – that the market will more often than not respond constructively to a
firm and intelligent lead by governments and exchange rate stability will reinforce prospects for growth. One thing is for sure: without trying, we will never
know.

Paul Volcker (1995, p. 8)

If monetary authorities have succeeded in exerting significant and lasting
influence over the behaviour of the global foreign exchange market, it is
important to identify clearly the factors in the episodes examined that
induced market participants to modify their risk–return assessments and
their expectations about the evolution of exchange rates. This exercise does
not aim to identify the existence of a clear cause and effect relationship
between a specific policy action (be it a change in interest rates, a foreign
exchange intervention or a declaration) and a specific exchange rate movement. Strategies for influencing the foreign exchange market typically comprise a complex set of policy actions that are rarely predetermined and
whose implementation is decided on an ad hoc basis in relation to market
performance. They may also be modified in the light of the results obtained
and are carried out according to procedures agreed anew on each occasion
with reference to domestic political processes or in the framework of international coordination. Still, the survey conducted provides indications
concerning the conditions that have to be met in devising a strategy to
influence the behaviour of the global foreign exchange market.

(1) Credibility of objectives   This is an essential condition. The market
must be convinced that the objectives pursued by the monetary authorities
are realistic and in keeping with the broader economic interest of a country
or of the international monetary system. The role of communication is
crucial. The authorities must explain why they believe that current trends,
even when supported by the choices of market participants and the desires
of private investors, are neither sustainable over time nor compatible with
economic fundamentals. It is also important for the market to perceive that
the policy enjoys broad political and social consensus, and that it does not
incorporate any risk of policy dilemmas liable to erode support for future
actions. The market will always tend to align itself more rapidly with

policies whose objectives include the achievement of monetary and financial stability while taking due account, for example, of the inflationary risks of a currency devaluation, even when this is needed to regain external competitiveness. Overall, in the cases examined there was a high level of credibility of objectives, with two exceptions. The first concerned the defence of the French franc after the elections of March 1993, when the market began to suspect the existence of a policy dilemma; the second regarded the US intervention to support the dollar in 1995, when it was not clear to the market whether the American authorities truly wanted to stabilize the exchange rate or preferred to let it depreciate further for trade policy purposes.

(2) Policy consistency The market must have the impression that the policies adopted to pursue an exchange rate objective are coherent, both in relation to each other and with the announced strategy. Ideally, the authorities should make judicious use of all the instruments at their disposal. In fact, foreign exchange interventions alone, even when accompanied by 'declarations' of varying degrees of clarity and solemnity, have failed to convince the market. What is called for is the adoption of a coherent set of monetary, fiscal and income policies that at the very least do not contradict exchange rate objectives. At the same time, it has been seen that economic and monetary policies aimed at achieving exchange rate objectives have gained credibility on the market *after* a strong 'signal' has been sent through foreign exchange interventions and declarations setting out the purposes of such a move. The intervention signals the concrete commitment of both 'arms' of the monetary authority and, in particular, the active role of the central bank, whose participation the market interprets as guaranteeing the respect of monetary stability obligations.

(3) Continuity The implementation of exchange rate policies must incorporate an appropriate timeframe to enable the market to assess fully the credibility and consistency of the new initiatives undertaken by the monetary authorities. Experience confirms that the market's initial reaction to an exchange rate intervention is generally one of scepticism or even defiance. It is only by demonstrating determination and continuity in implementing the strategy that the authorities have been able to convince operators that they were indeed dealing with a new *policy stance* which required a reassessment of risk and return. It is impossible to know beforehand how long the market will need to ascertain the *time consistency* of the monetary authorities; this depends in great measure on the circumstances in which the decision to act is made and implemented. If the intervention takes the market completely by surprise and is perceived as a sharp reversal of the monetary

authorities' position, more time will be required, as happened in the case of the move to arrest the depreciation of the dollar against the yen in 1995. If, instead, the policy appears to confirm a strategy that is already underway and of which the market is well aware, the period of time can be shorter, as in the case of the defence of the Hong Kong currency board in 1998.

(4) International coordination   The market tends to assign a higher level of credibility to exchange rate interventions agreed among major countries and implemented through internationally coordinated actions on several foreign exchange markets simultaneously. Experience has proven this assumption (now part of the market's conventional wisdom) to be true both for policies conducted within the G7 and in the context of the EMS. In fact, France was obliged to abandon its exchange rate policy temporarily when the market perceived that it was no longer fully supported by Germany. However, there have been cases of successful interventions even in the absence of explicit coordination or international support, such as the intervention by the Hong Kong currency board or that of the ECB in support of the euro.

(5) An institutional framework   The market tends to grant greater credibility to policies conducted within an institutional framework that makes it easier to predict economic policy measures and lends a higher degree of coherence over time to the action of monetary authorities. This was the case with the strategies adopted by the G7 in relation to the Plaza and Louvre Accords, which provided a 'soft' reference framework by assigning to exchange rates the role of indicator for economic policies in the context of a target zone mechanism. A stronger institutional framework was provided by the EMS in the defence of the French franc (at least for so long as its rules were rigorously applied), by the currency board in Hong Kong, and by the firm commitment of the Chinese authorities to maintain a stable renminbi in China's overall policy strategy.

PART IV

Epilogue

14.   The golden mean

Auream quisquis mediocritatem
diligit, tutus caret obsoleti
sordibus tecti, caret individenda
sobrius aula.*

Horace (Odes, II, 10)

There is a tide in the affairs of men,
Which, taken at the flood, leads on to fortune;
Omitted, all the voyage of their life
is bound in shallows and in miseries.
On such a full sea are we now afloat;
and we must take the current when it serves,
or lose our ventures.

William Shakespeare
(Julius Caesar, Act IV, Scene 3)

14.1   HAVE THE TIGERS BEEN TAMED?

The conclusion I have drawn from the critical rereading of the history of
financial globalization outlined in the previous chapters is that a key factor
in the episodes of monetary and financial instability that have occurred
since the mid-1980s has been the interaction between the monetary policies of the leading countries and the working of global financial markets.
A central role in this interaction has been played by the exchange rate
policies pursued both by the major industrial countries and by emerging
market economies. I have also argued that the responses by governments
and international financial institutions to the challenges posed by globalization have been either too narrowly focused when designed to be quickly
implemented, or effective only in the long-run when conceived on a global
scale. Substantial financial assistance has been granted to countries
affected by crises and, from time to time, concerted strategies have been
adopted to correct exchange rate misalignments. On a macroeconomic
level, countries have been lectured on the need to keep their 'house in
order' and to avoid overly rigid exchange rate regimes. As regards the
global financial architecture, a long-term process has been initiated to
strengthen banking and financial systems in emerging countries and to

monitor financial vulnerabilities and risks on a global scale. Yet very little has been done to address the fundamental causes of international financial instability.

Despite these shortcomings, the global financial system has proved to be resilient and able to withstand severe shocks: acute situations of crisis and instability, such as those described in Chapter 5, have not degenerated into a financial 'meltdown' or an 'implosion', as sometimes feared by analysts and market participants. Moreover, the pressure put on financial markets by very serious political and economic developments like 11 September, the war in Iraq, the tension with Iran and the uncertainties about the price and availability of oil and gas, has been easily absorbed.[1] Since mid-2004 the volatility of short-term and long-term interest rates, stocks, exchange rates and corporate spreads has been generally low relative to the previous five to ten years in both industrial and emerging countries; this is regarded as evidence of improved financial conditions and risk management practices at major financial institutions (see BIS 2006b). The significance of this resilience, however, should not be overrated, as there are indications that underlying factors of financial instability may still be at work. Indeed, at the end of 2006 an observer as eminently qualified as Larry Summers noted that 'financial markets are pricing in an expectation of tranquillity as far as the eye can see'; and yet, markets 'hardly ever predict serious disruptions and historically the moments of greatest complacency have been the moments of greatest danger' (Summers 2006).

Following the Argentinean default of 2001, there have been no new debt crises in emerging markets, but the situation of Argentina and other smaller countries in Latin America and elsewhere continues to be seen as fragile, with persisting external and domestic imbalances. An episode of tension in financial markets in May–June 2006, originating in expectations of higher inflation and monetary tightening, led to a significant, although temporary, increase of risk premia on a number of emerging countries including Argentina, Colombia, Hungary, India, Peru, Poland, Russia and Turkey (IMF 2006d, p. 11). Moreover, many observers continue to consider the exceptional growth performance of the Chinese economy, and the associated 10 per cent of GDP surplus in its 2006 current account balance, to be unsustainable, raising fears that at some point in time the boom in credit expansion fuelled by capital inflows may reach an end, leading to a rapid credit contraction.[2] In general, emerging countries themselves seem to be expecting the worse as they have taken a very cautious approach in their external policies, using balance of payments surpluses to bolster their official reserve positions, ostensibly to be able to withstand future situations of crisis with their own resources rather than by applying for the conditional assistance of the IMF.

At the same time global payments imbalances remain large, with little evidence of adjustment in the balance of payments deficit of the United States or in the surpluses of China and of oil producing countries. Exchange rates among the key countries remain significantly misaligned despite some depreciation of the dollar mostly vis-à-vis the euro and to a lesser extent vis-à-vis Asian currencies. The prospect of a sudden and disorderly unwinding of payments imbalances (involving an abrupt correction of exchange rate misalignments and a 'hard landing' scenario) is still seen as a concrete risk (see IMF 2007b, 2007c). The hardship of the landing may also be influenced by developments in housing and real estate markets, both in the United States and elsewhere, should the slowdown recorded during 2006 lead to the long-feared bursting of the bubble.

That these potentially destabilizing factors have not resulted in events of crisis is probably due to abundant liquidity in the economies of the United States, euro area and Japan (sometimes referred to as the G3) as signalled by rapidly rising monetary and credit aggregates, particularly since the beginning of the third millennium (Figure 14.1).[3] A 'liquidity glut' has emerged despite the move towards tighter monetary policies in the G3 since 2005–06. Although the timing and the intensity of interest rate increases have been different in the three areas, the change in the monetary policy stances has been remarkable as it reflects a broad consensus about the need to nip inflationary pressures in the bud through a gradualist approach, which would be conducive *inter alia* to an orderly deflation of any asset prices bubbles. Strangely enough, despite the monetary tightening, long-term interest rates in the United States and in international capital markets have remained low, in some cases dipping below the level of short-term rates. No clear explanations have been found for this development, labelled a 'conundrum' by an authority in the field such as Greenspan (2005a). Several factors may indeed be at work: expectations of slower GDP growth and low inflation in the United States, against a medium-term prospect of a dampening impact of globalization on costs and prices; failure in the monetary policy transmission mechanism; heavy purchases of dollar-denominated long-term bonds by Asian central banks (mostly China) and by institutional investors (such as pension funds, to cover their long-term liabilities to beneficiaries). As noted by Ferguson et al. (2007, p. 15) 'abundant global liquidity and low interest rates may have encouraged a quest for yield that might have induced investors to underestimate risks, compressing risk premia and volatility and inflating asset prices'.

In these underlying conditions, financial markets have recorded renewed turbulence in February–March 2007 in connection with a number of 'news' items regarding possible curbs on speculative purchases on the Chinese

Money/GDPa

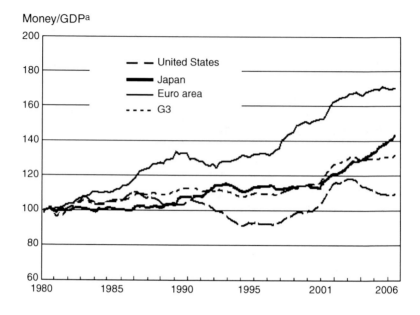

Credit/GDPb

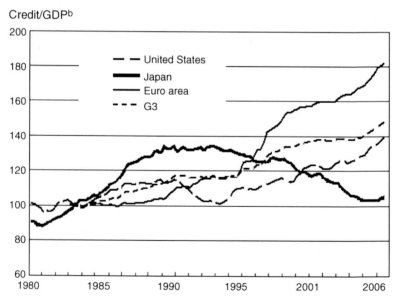

Notes:
a. Index numbers: 1980 = 100.
b. Index numbers: 1983 = 100.

Figure 14.1   Monetary and credit aggregates in the G3

stock market, the unwinding of yen carry trades, problems in the US sub-prime mortgage market, and the likelihood of a recession of the US economy in 2007. The IMF (2007b, pp. 30–31) noted that these 'seemingly minor, unrelated developments across markets quickly led to the unwind-ing of risk positions across a wide range of financial assets'. As in May–June 2006, the impact of the February–March 2007 sell-off on the volatility of asset prices turned out to be temporary. However, renewed ten-sions materialized in June 2007 as the failure of two hedge funds operating in the US sub-prime mortgage market led to a significant widening of spreads on credit markets. Such recurrent episodes of turbulence are worry-ing as they confirm the high degree of correlation between financial markets, and highlight a latent nervousness of market participants in the face of possible changes in the fundamentals of systemically important economies.

14.2   A GLANCE AT THE SYSTEM'S FUTURE

Economic historians are certain that crises will continue to strike the global financial system from time to time. Trying to guess where and how the next crisis will occur is unlikely to prove worthwhile. It may be more useful to attempt to analyse the likely evolutionary pattern of the global financial system and exchange rate regime. In both areas contrasting forces are at play and, although a mainstream may eventually emerge, cross-currents could make the trend non-linear.

The Future of Financial Globalization

Despite its popular name, the global financial system is not really global as it includes essentially all the industrial countries but only a few emerging market economies. It is, however, likely that over time the global system will cover all emerging countries and eventually most of the developing world.

This would imply a consolidation of the main tenets on which financial globalization rests, namely freedom of trade and capital movements, adop-tion of market-friendly regulation, and support for innovative financial instruments and information technologies. The trend will be stimulated by these countries' desire to access the pool of global savings to finance economic and social development programmes and to increase trade flows and foreign direct investment. This process will require the support of inter-national institutions. The IMF will have to ensure through surveillance that the member countries pursue the financial liberalization aim only once they have introduced the necessary structural reforms to strengthen their banking and financial systems. Restrictions on capital movements should be removed gradually and be accompanied by the introduction of the prudential rules and supervisory institutions necessary to manage these countries' accession to the global financial market. The IMF may suggest that restrictions on capital inflows be maintained, favouring the use of tax instruments or other mechanisms that enable market forces to operate freely, and establishing credit lines to help countries that encounter difficulties in the liberalization process. Despite the pressures of social groups hostile to globalization, no worldwide measures are likely to be introduced to halt the processes of international financial intermediation along the lines of the Tobin tax. There is, in fact, a broad consensus at a political, academic and operational level that a tax on cross-border foreign exchange transactions would be extremely difficult to implement, require the participation of every nation the world over, could be easily circumvented, and give rise to rigidity and market dysfunctions that could prove counterproductive.

The process is, however, unlikely to be free from disturbances of various kinds. In Latin America, for example, populist-oriented governments in Argentina, Venezuela, Ecuador and Bolivia are clearly resisting globalization, which is seen as a new form of domination and exploitation by the United States. And there is the risk that Islamic fundamentalism may have a negative influence on the attitude of countries that are already part of the global financial system like Turkey or Indonesia, not to mention the oil-rich, but politically weak, Gulf states. Even among the leading industrial countries contrasting pressures are emerging. On the one hand, supervised intermediaries and listed companies complain about the excessive burden of regulations introduced following the financial turbulences of the 1990s and the corporate scandals of the early 2000s, particularly in the United States and in most other industrial countries. This has led some foreign companies quoted on the New York Stock Exchange to try to 'de-list' themselves in order to avoid compliance with local regulations, raising fears that New York may become less appealing to foreign investors and lose its status of world financial centre to competing venues like London or Tokyo. On the other hand, in several continental European countries there is continuing reluctance to move further along the road of full capital market integration even in the context of the Eurosystem, almost ten years after the introduction of the single currency and creation of the ECB.[4] Behind this attitude is the fear that sub-regional financial centres like Paris, Frankfurt or Milan, may eventually see their role reduced both on a global and EU scale. Moreover, there is concern that a fully integrated European capital market may become an attractive playground for unregulated hedge funds and private equity firms from abroad, with unpredictable implications for the fate of European banks and corporations. Evidence of this attitude is the disappointing text of the EU Takeover Directive which reflects the strong protectionist sentiments expressed by the German and French governments. Specifically, as mentioned in Chapter 6 (see page 153), the activity of hedge funds (or of HLI more generally) has attracted the attention of monetary and financial authorities because of its implications for financial stability, particularly to the extent that HLI have increasingly become the preferred channels of 'alternative investment strategies' pursued by traditional inter-mediaries and institutional investors. Although the global market has been easily able to absorb the failure of a relatively large hedge fund operating in the energy field in late 2006, financial authorities remain concerned about the insufficient transparency of these intermediaries regarding their opera-tional strategies and market exposure and more generally about the possi-ble impact of a hedge fund crisis on the operation of credit derivatives markets (see ECB 2006b, pp. 9–16). It is against this background that the G7 at its meeting in February 2007, under German chairmanship, decided to ask the FSF to review its 2000 report on HLI.[5] This will provide an updated evaluation of the financial stability risks posed by hedge funds' activities as these have evolved since 2000. A good insight into what may be the likely direction of efforts to deal with this problem is provided by the col-lection of articles by regulators, academics and market participants col-lected by the Banque de France (2007). A further indication is given by the Chairman of the FSF (Draghi 2007) in his report to the IMFC meeting:

An issue receiving a lot of attention is the expanding role of highly leveraged institutions, particularly hedge funds, in the financial system. Hedge funds bring substantial benefits to markets, including increased liquidity, additional risk bearing capacity, and innovation. But they can also present potential financial stability risks through their counterparty exposures with core financial intermediaries. The FSF examined these risks in 2000 and produced a set of rec-ommendations for action by supervisors, financial institutions, and the hedge funds themselves. We are now revisiting our earlier conclusions in the light of the changes that have occurred. Supervisory data show that the direct net counter-party exposures of core financial institutions to the hedge fund sector are in the aggregate modest in relation to capital. But these figures are averages and almost certainly underestimate exposures in stress. And it is even more difficult to judge the effect on their indirect exposures to hedge funds were market liquidity to dry up suddenly, with rapid falls in asset prices and herd behaviour by the same hedge funds. Measuring and modelling these exposures is a continuing chal-lenge given the complexity of new products and their continuous and rapid inno-vation. To contain potential financial stability risks, we need to strengthen counterparty discipline and reinforce it through stronger supervisory oversight of credit providers. Here, I want to dispel the notion that this indirect approach is a light approach. Instead, it is an approach that focuses on where the most tan-gible gains can be achieved. (p. 1)

More generally, the ongoing debate about the appropriate approach to regulation in a global financial system is unlikely to deviate significantly from the pattern established in recent years and to hinder the progress of globalization. The distinction between a rule-based and a principles-based approach is likely to become increasingly blurred as major financial centres move towards a market-friendly approach to regulation.[6] This is going to happen first in the banking sectors as the Basel II requirements are adopted, which imply close collaboration between banks and regulators on risk management methods and procedures. More generally, regulators will increasingly rely on consultation with market participants in order to incorporate best practices into regulatory provisions. Monetary and financial authorities, however, will retain the power to shape regulations in a way that takes into account the pursuit of public interest and the prevention of risks to systemic stability as well as the power to take discretionary action to correct market failures.

The outlook for the global exchange rate regime

Exchange rate relationships among the main countries will be the result of two distinct determinants. The first is the pressure arising from the process of globalization to rationalize and simplify currency arrangements among countries that are neighbours and closely integrated in the trade and monetary spheres. The second is the desire of some major countries to 're-peg' their currencies, or reconsider their participation – formal or informal – in monetary arrangements, in relation to changes in the balance of power on the geopolitical stage. The outcomes of these potentially conflicting forces is hard to predict. In principle, the process of consolidation of currency arrangements around a relatively small number of monetary 'poles' should continue.

Europe   The euro area is expanding both in terms of membership to the single currency (following the inclusion of Greece in 2001 and Slovenia in 2007) and of participation in the so-called ERM II exchange rate mechanism, which now links to the euro the currencies of Cyprus, Denmark, Estonia, Latvia, Lithuania, Malta and the Slovak Republic. It remains uncertain whether the United Kingdom and Sweden will ever join the EMU, but it is a safe bet to assume that, economic conditions permitting, most of the EU members of Central and South Eastern Europe, including Romania, Bulgaria and some countries of the former Yugoslavia, will eventually enter the euro area. In any event the euro has clearly acquired the status of a world currency pole and its role in currency trading and reserve holdings is bound to increase gradually over time.

The western hemisphere   Although the United States neither envisages nor encourages exchange rate agreements with other countries, the dollar has been adopted in some Latin American countries either as the national currency or as a base for a currency board. At the outset of the new millennium, it was thought possible that the dollarization trend would continue and become even more pronounced (Alesina and Barro 2001), ultimately including the Mexican peso as Dornbusch (2001) had suggested, or even the Canadian dollar. It is also possible that new formulas will be tested that aim at stabilizing exchange rate expectations while loosening the dollar tie. The recent history of Latin America has shown that this tie is at the root of serious disequilibria, and the financial tensions suffered by Brazil and Argentina in 2001 demonstrate that both types of extreme exchange rate regimes (floating in Brazil, the currency board in Argentina) do not provide total immunity from crises. Regional solutions may also be tested, which take account of the need to maintain the Mercosur, the Latin American common market, whose existence was gravely endangered by the abrupt devaluation of the Brazilian real beginning in 1999 and the reintroduction in Argentina in 2001, of duties on imports and export subsidies. However, recent political developments in Latin America raise doubts about the chances for these regional arrangements to succeed. Indeed, at present there is no currency in Latin America that could play the role of regional monetary pole and replace the dollar.

Asia   There has been lively debate on a regional exchange rate regime in Asia. Historical and political considerations would tend to exclude any form of 'yenization', at least for the major countries in the region. However, as has been previously recalled (see Chapter 6 – page 168), the call for closer monetary cooperation at a regional level was made at the time of the Asian crisis by the countries participating in the Chiang Mai Initiative and the stated objective was to create an 'Asian monetary system' that would try to reconcile the wishes of a region that no longer wants to bear the costs of the dollar tie and yet, for political reasons, does not want to accept the hegemony of the yen. Japanese officials and economists have been among the most active proponents of regional monetary arrangements. Kusukawa (1999) and Ogawa and Ito (2000) proposed that Asian economies peg their currencies to an Asian Currency Unit (ACU), a basket including the dollar, the yen and the euro, in order to stabilize exchange rates in the region and avoid the periodic phases of undervaluation and overvaluation that played an important role in the Asian financial crisis. Kuroda, the President of the Asian Development Bank, proposed a roadmap for regional integration in Asia, based on the Chiang Mai Initiative. This would comprise 'a more solid regional financial facility', a 'more resilient Asian financial system' through the development of an Asian bond market and a 'regional exchange rate arrangement . . . which may lead to a monetary union in the very long run' (see Kuroda 2005, p. 7). The activism of Japan in promoting Asian monetary integration and unification has been greeted with polite but unmistakable scepticism in the region.[7] Indeed it is dubious that countries like China and India, which have recorded exceptional growth performances and are increasingly flexing their economic and financial muscle on a global scale, will want to tie their hands in a monetary arrangement that may be seen as perpetuating Japan's leadership in the monetary and financial sphere.

Africa   Finally, in 2001 Africa also gave itself the objective of creating an African central bank, presumably with the mandate of managing a single currency, in the context of the transformation of the Organization for African Unity (OAU) into an African Union.

The outcome of the process of consolidation in the global currency regime will be heavily influenced by geopolitical considerations regarding the currencies chosen by the major countries to invest their official reserves, peg their exchange rates, and price their exports of key natural resources. It has long been regarded as an oddity, for example, that the EU is the largest importer of oil and gas from Russia and that these imports are paid for in a currency that is neither of the buyer nor that of the seller, namely the US dollar. As political and economic cooperation between the EU and Russia is strengthened these currency arrangements may be revised. Different considerations may apply in the case of oil-producing countries in other regions, such as the Middle East or Latin America, where the link with the dollar may be seen as a key element in the context of strategic alliances, as in the case of Saudi Arabia or Mexico. But even in these regions, different political patterns of investment may be considered in view of the exceptional growth recorded in the stock of international reserves since 2000 and the significant changes in its distribution among the main groups of countries (see Table 4.2). Total reserves at the end of 2006 stood at $5.09 trillion, having more than doubled since 2000, of which $3.3 trillion were held by emerging and developing countries. China alone accounts for over $1.2 trillion, close to the holdings of all industrial countries taken together. As reserves largely exceed the levels required to counter speculative pressures on exchange rates, emerging countries may want to pursue alternative investment strategies both in terms of currency denomination and financial instruments. The euro and the yen, or an Asian Currency Unit if it ever comes to life, may represent viable alternatives to the dollar as a means to reduce the concentration risk on the dollar, which still accounts for over two-thirds of total reserves. In any case, given the size of the amounts involved, even marginal changes in the currency composition of official reserves may have a significant impact on exchange rates. It is therefore likely that any strategy to achieve a greater currency diversification will be implemented gradually. The process could have a greater impact on reserve currencies if it were associated with a move to a floating exchange rate regime or with a 're-pegging' of exchange rates away from the dollar and in favour of a basket or of an alternative currency. Again, changes in this delicate area are likely to be carried out gradually and cautiously. However, the perception by market participants that old practices may be abandoned could accelerate the reallocation of private portfolios and lead to increased volatility in foreign exchange and financial markets. In sum, it is quite likely that the exchange rate regime will continue to be a potential source of instability.

With the consolidation of globalization and the likely polarization of official reserves and exchange rates around a few currency blocs, the international monetary and financial system will become even more dependent on the economic policy choices of the major monetary poles and on the assessment of risk and return by global intermediaries. International liquidity will tend to flow towards countries and investments offering the highest return (and therefore subject to the highest risk), ready to flow back to safer shores at the first hint of divergence and incoherence of underlying economic policies. Boom and bust cycles are likely to remain a recurrent feature on the global financial stage. With floating exchange rates this will entail continuous adjustments of the portfolios' composition to reflect changing expectations of exchange rate levels and interest rates. The result will be greater underlying volatility in exchange rate relations between the major currencies and greater risks of systemic instability. A key question, therefore, will be whether there are realistic alternatives to these prospects or whether the world is condemned to live with a fundamentally unstable monetary and financial system.

14.3 TOWARDS THE GOLDEN MEAN

It is uncertain whether the pursuit of international monetary and financial stability would be easier if the world had a single currency, as long advocated by Cooper (1984) and Mundell (2000) and endorsed, more recently, by Steil and Litan (2006). Were it judged necessary to uphold the rights of citizens to 'flee' from a badly governed currency, then perhaps this would not even be desirable. Setting aside this radical proposal, which in any event does not appear achievable in the foreseeable future, the only conceivable alternative to manage international financial instability is to strengthen international cooperation. This subject has been touched indirectly in countless official reports and academic papers dealing with the more general issue of the reform of the global monetary and financial system.[8] Most of these contributions, which have been reviewed in Chapter 6, assume that reinforced international cooperation will be required to implement reform proposals. Little attention, however, has been devoted to what should be the essential ingredients needed to strengthen existing forms of cooperation and to correct their inadequacies. In what follows I will try to outline a few requirements that should be met to achieve an enhanced international cooperation.

In a financially globalized regime, any form of enhanced cooperation can realistically propose only to follow a middle course, rigorously equidistant from extremes of all kinds. When choosing the institutional framework, it should rely on existing institutions, recoiling from both the dream of new and improbable global institutions and the temptation to do away with them altogether. When suggesting a methodology, it should not hesitate to favour dialogue between the monetary authorities and market forces over sterile diatribes as to the superiority of one or the other. When dealing with exchange rate regimes, it should position itself mid-way along the spectrum of available options, avoiding both the illusory sway of floating rates and the perilous rigidities of fixed rates.

An enhanced cooperation should go beyond the kind of informal arrangements practised in the G7, which tend to be enacted sporadically and only when there is unanimous agreement that the coordinated action is in the individual interest of each participant. The way forward must be through 'institutionalized' cooperation. This, as Padoa-Schioppa (1985) has explained, implies that the participants cooperate in the context of an institution which identifies, on the basis of previously established rules and procedures, the instances where the pursuit of a collective interest requires a cooperative act of intervention. It must then provide for its execution through measures and in ways that have also been previously agreed on within the institution. Institutional cooperation enables agreed objectives to be pursued with greater efficiency and credibility, at least for as long as the member countries respect the institution's rules: this was the case of the Bretton Woods system, until the departure of the United States, and of the EMS (except in the period surrounding the German unification) up until the transition to EMU. The IMF is the only possible institutional forum for enhanced cooperation, in the light of the authority conferred to it by its statute and its broad membership. Although the authority of the IMF has been weakened by the Bretton Woods crisis and the advent of financial globalization and floating exchange rates, it retains sufficient legal powers to formulate and implement a procedure for the multilateral surveillance of the monetary and exchange rate policies pursued by the major countries and their international implications. Ideally, an enhanced surveillance procedure should enable the IMF to operate both as a forum for cooperation between countries whose policies have systemic importance and as a channel of communication with financial market participants.

The objectives of enhanced cooperation could be to influence the creation and distribution of international liquidity so as to avoid creating conditions of excessive financing in favour of particular countries or markets, which may result in unsustainable balance of payments disequilibria and asset price movements. As regards exchange rates, in particular, the objective would be, to use Paul Volcker's words (1995, p. 8), to 'moderate and reverse exchange rate fluctuations among the key currencies before they become extreme, rather than being forced to respond defensively, after substantial risk to the world economy is already evident'.

The IMF has, over time, developed the analytical tools to identify at an early stage monetary or financial developments that may have an impact on systemic stability. The views of the IMF staff, together with those of other financial institutions like the BIS, the OECD and the World Bank, are regularly submitted for consideration to the authorities of the countries concerned and to international policy-making bodies like the IMFC or the FSF. The outcome of these deliberations is normally regarded as confidential and the analysis that these institutions make publicly known is deliberately phrased in terms designed not to interfere with the operation of financial markets, and with the domestic political situations of the countries concerned. The policy advice is thus hidden behind an array of scenarios (including the 'worst case' one, but with no indications as to its likelihood) involving a variety of downside risks and vulnerabilities.

As indicated in Chapter 6, a revised surveillance procedure has been agreed within the IMF. It is encouraging that the stability of the global exchange rate regime has regained a central role in international monetary cooperation. It is also positive that the new procedures were endorsed by all systemically important countries, including the United States, Europe and Japan, but with the notable exception of China. However, the key question is how the new procedures will be implemented in the face of persistent global imbalances. The scope of surveillance is bilateral, that is, it involves the relationships between individual countries and the IMF. It will be essential – as indicated in the revised decision – that the performance of bilateral surveillance 'be informed by, and consistent with, a multilateral framework that incorporates relevant aspects of the global and regional economic environment, including exchange rates, international market conditions, and key linkages among members' (IMF 2007d, p. 8). This is unlikely to occur unless there is a parallel strengthening and institutionalization of a multilateral surveillance function within the IMF, building on the experience of the first, and as yet only, exercise of 'multilateral consultations' conducted in early 2006. In the end, if the new surveillance procedure is to overcome the shortcomings of the old one, it would have to address directly the issue of IMF 'interference'. An effective surveillance procedure must allow the Managing Director of the IMF, when unsustainable trends are emerging in the performance of exchange rates and financial flows, to recommend the adoption of specific corrective policy measures, possibly coordinated among systemically relevant countries. Politically speaking, this is obviously a very delicate cooperative procedure whose success depends on the willingness of participants to act to limit the international repercussions of national economic policies adopted in full autonomy. It is a procedure that requires a balanced assessment on matters that are objectively debatable and that may come to nothing if there is no consensus among the participants as to the nature and gravity of the problems and the strategy to deal with them. In these cases, the IMF must – with all appropriate prudence – nevertheless formulate its own reasoned opinion and make it known to the market. It is possible that this will provoke conflicting reactions among market participants, creating a certain volatility of exchange rates and interest rates. However, it is preferable that the IMF signal to the market that the trends of exchange rates and financial flows are being reviewed and that there is disagreement among major countries on the IMF policy recommendation, rather than signal a position of acquiescence, or worse, of support for current trends. This is likely to strengthen the market perception of a two-way risk, thus curbing unidirectional unsustainable market trends that inevitably lead to bubbles, overshootings and misalignments.

An invasive surveillance procedure of this kind may never be agreed upon, as it may be regarded as destabilizing, incompatible with market economy principles, politically incorrect, and what not. However, it is not obvious why, in a globalized financial system where markets eagerly absorb and process all kinds of information and signals emanating from private market participants and national financial authorities, the only players with no freedom of communication should be the international institutions supposedly entrusted with the crucial function of producing the public good of financial stability.

14.4   CAN SOVEREIGN NATIONS COOPERATE?

In an article on the political economy of the reform of the international monetary system written after the collapse of the Bretton Woods regime,

Harry Johnson (1972) wisely observed that the real problem of the system was ultimately not dissimilar to that which, in one of Aesop's fables, tormented the mice in their attempt to curb the excessive power of the cat of the house. The mice had agreed that the ideal solution would be to tie a bell around the cat's neck so that they could hear it approach and flee in time from the pantry, but they could not find a way either to put the bell on or, even if they succeeded, to ensure that the cat would not remove it. In Johnson's adapted fable, the cat was naturally a metaphor for the United States, which had just disentangled itself from the bell of fixed exchange rates and flatly refused to wear any other kind. The moral of the story is that the major powers are by their very nature contrary to any external attempt to curb their autonomy and therefore also to international cooperation.

Historians and political commentators have closely analysed this issue and one influential school claims that cooperation is only possible if led by a hegemonic but benevolent power (Kindleberger 1988, pp. 123–39). The periods of *pax romana*, *pax britannica* and of the American leadership after the Second World War are cited as examples of 'hegemonic stability' in international relations and of economic and civil progress. This is consistent with Niall Ferguson's (2001) view about the relations between power and currencies from 1700 to 2000, in which the role of international cooperation is seen as entirely incidental. According to this school of thought, in current circumstances the United States, having imposed liberalization (that is, freedom of trade and capital movements and freely floating exchange rates) as a strategic choice to promote its own interests, would not be willing to accept any form of international cooperation aimed at 'governing' globalization, be it through the coordination of economic policies or through global regulations. Another view, well illustrated by Robert Keohane (2005) in his book titled *After Hegemony*, claims that cooperation is possible even in the absence of a leading power (or without its consent) because of the existence of international 'regimes', founded on institutions and rules that have developed over time and which continue to operate in the common interest.[9]

The evidence that can be gleaned from the history of international monetary and financial cooperation in the period of globalization is mixed. Certainly, the United States had already witnessed a gradual erosion of its hegemonic power in the 1960s and 1970s, with the impressive economic recovery in Europe and Japan. Moreover, the Soviet Union was a formidable counterweight in the political-military sphere, which obliged the United States to keep strong cooperative arrangements with the other industrial democracies (hence the establishment of the G7). With the collapse of the Soviet Union, the United States enjoyed a period of hegemony and promoted its role as 'sole superpower', at least until the sudden surge of China in the world economy and the emergence of difficulties in the war in Iraq. But even in this period of hegemonic euphoria, the United States attempted to enlarge the sphere of international cooperation while retaining some sort of right to initiative and leadership in certain areas, in Eastern Europe and the Balkans, together with the European Union, under NATO; in the western hemisphere, together with Canada and Mexico, under NAFTA; and in Asia, together with Japan and China, under the Asian Pacific Economic Cooperation (APEC). It is also true that the management of crises triggered by globalization was conducted in a framework of international cooperation. These actions fully utilized the potential of existing 'regimes' and made the most of both the role of the IMF and the G7, as well as drawing on new instruments such as the FSF and the G20. However, the United States resorted to international cooperation in an institutional framework mostly in order to gather support for the pursuit of American interests, rather than for the sake of multilateralism. This was the case of strategies to deal with international financial crises, where the United States wanted to assist key allies in Latin America or Asia; or, more recently, of the initiatives to strengthen IMF surveillance over exchange rates, where the US objective was to pressure China to revalue the renminbi. In all fairness, it must be noted that the United States was not alone in showing reluctance to join a systemic framework of institutional cooperation. Indeed, most major countries showed a proclivity to operate on an ad hoc basis and in a short-term perspective. The general tendency was to prefer initiatives which produced immediate positive effects and to rule out anything that might prove too painful initially, even if this was a more healthy option in the long term. Due to this short-termism, countries ended up tolerating the development of speculative bubbles, boom and bust cycles and overshooting.

The unsustainability of this approach in a context of globalization has been recognized by political scientists long ago. Even within the United States there is increasing awareness of the emergence of a multi-polar world in which economic power, and therefore potentially political power, is spread among different countries with which it is necessary to cooperate. On this point there appeared to be consensus among political commentators, both in the conservative and liberal schools. Henry Kissinger (1994) advised patience and prudence in pursuing a US foreign policy based on the spread of traditional American values of democracy and free trade, cautioning that even after the victory of the Cold War the United States remained a first among equals. Samuel Huntington (1999) saw a reversal in US policy, from 'unilateral globalism' in the golden period from 1945 to 1950, characterized by a strong commitment to creating the multilateral institutions needed for the consolidation of peace and democracy and economic and social development, to a kind of 'global unilateralism' in which the United States pursues its own national interests with every available instrument, often in conflict with the indications of multilateral institutions. Huntington thus warned the United States against the risk of isolation in the international community and of becoming a kind of rogue superpower.[10] Other scholars took a more positive view: Joseph Nye (2002) emphasized the paradoxical position of the United States as a 'superpower that cannot act alone'; Ferguson (2004b, p. 301), the British historian of empires, having stated that the United States was 'the best candidate for the job' of liberal empire to rule globalization, concluded that 'yet for all its colossal economic, military and cultural power, the United States still looks unlikely to be an *effective* liberal empire without some profound changes in its economic structure, its social make up and its political culture'. Arguing along the same line, Steil and Litan (2006, p. 166) warned that 'America's long-term prosperity and security are intimately bound up with a liberal, rule-based international economic and political order to which people around the globe aspire to be attached'; to meet this challenge – they maintain – the United States would have to change its 'financial statecraft' considerably.

There is a growing concern, however, that the inability of major countries to cooperate may in the end threaten the survival of globalization. Recurrent monetary and financial instability may foster protectionist tendencies always lingering in both industrial and emerging countries, as illustrated by James (2001) in his study of the Great Depression, aptly titled *The End of Globalization*. Financial instability may lead to protectionism even if the financial system proves resilient to shocks and no intermediaries go bankrupt. In fact, to the extent that credit and market risks are transferred outside the financial system, pressure for increased regulation and protectionism may eventually come from households and final investors, who may be called on to shoulder the losses generated by the activity of global financial players. Protectionism, in turn, may hamper growth and as noted by Frieden (2006, p. 472) 'history showed that support for international economic integration depended on prosperity. If global capitalism ceased to deliver growth, its future would be in doubt'. It is thus not in the interest of any country to ignore the costs and risks of international monetary and financial instability, nor to offload the blame for instability on the markets, pretending that they are omnipotent and ungovernable. Nor is it in the interest of the major powers to avoid the scrutiny of multilateral institutions, limiting them to a role of vigilance and of 'fire-fighting' exclusively with respect to emerging economies and developing countries.

In his thought-provoking book titled *Does America Need a Foreign Policy?*, Henry Kissinger (2001, p. 233) wrote: 'The industrial democracies must preserve and extend the extraordinary accomplishments that fostered globalization. But they can do so in the long run only if they endow the economic aspects of globalization with a political construction of comparable sweep and vision'. Wolf (2004, p. 317) believes that the key issue is 'how to reconcile the reality of a world divided into unequal sovereignties with exploitation of the opportunities offered by international economic integration'; to cope with the challenge, Wolf elaborates 'ten commandments of globalization' among which the following: 'it is in the interest of both states and their citizens to participate in international treaty-based regimes and institutions that deliver global public goods' (p. 319). Scholars coming from very different political and cultural backgrounds reach similar conclusions. For a conservative like Fukuyama (2006):

> The world today does not have enough international institutions that can confer legitimacy on collective action, and creating new institutions that will better balance the requirements of legitimacy and effectiveness will be the prime task for the coming generation. As a result of more than two hundred years of political evolution, we have a relatively good understanding of how to create institutions that are rule-bound, accountable, and yet reasonably effective in the vertical silos we call states. What we do not have are adequate institutions of horizontal accountability among states. (p. 155)

For a liberal like Stiglitz (2006, pp. 280–5) 'the most important changes to make globalization work are reforms to reduce the democratic deficit' in international institutions and he advocates 'an international economic regime in which the well-being of the developed and developing countries are better balanced: a new global social contract'.

One can only be encouraged by the emerging consensus that seems to be developing about the need to manage globalization through new international rule-based institutions. Experience, however, shows that this process is going to be slow and that its course is unlikely to be linear. In the sphere of global finance, while law-makers attend to the reform of the 'circus', global tigers may grow restless for fear of protectionism. That will make it all the more necessary for national tamers to get their act together.

NOTES

* Whosoever cherishes the golden mean,
safely avoids the squalor of a hovel,
and discreetly keeps away from a palace,
that excites envy.
Translated by Peter Saint-André
www.saint-andre.com/poems/fire/horace 2_10.html.

1. Central bank cooperation played a crucial role in ensuring the orderly functioning of financial markets worldwide in the aftermath of 11 September. A \$50 billion reciprocal swap agreement was quickly established between the Fed and the ECB to supply dollar liquidity to European counterparts who may have become insolvent as a result of the destruction of the World Trade Center in New York.

2. The turnaround in the credit cycle could be triggered by the end of the construction boom related to the 2008 Olympics or by adverse developments in the area of non-performing loans in the Chinese banking system. In other Asian countries, evidence of the concerns for the destabilizing impact of excessive capital inflows are the attempts by Thailand and South Korea in 2006 to curb such inflows through capital controls and prudential measures.

3. The OECD has developed a measure of excess liquidity defined as deviation from historical norms. According to this measure global bank lending has been growing above long-term trends since 1998, gradually reaching a deviation of 15 per cent in 2006 (OECD 2006, p. 34). Similar conclusions are drawn by the IMF (2007c) using different indicators.

4. Although no restrictions to capital movements are in force among EU countries, a number of administrative, tax and regulatory obstacles persist and are hindering the establishment of a fully integrated European capital market.

5. Statement of G7 Finance Ministers Meeting, Essen, 9-10 February 2007. www.imf.org.

6. On this debate, see McCarthy (2007) and Bernanke (2007).

7. See Shanmugaratnam (2006). In the lecture, the former Managing Director of the Monetary Authority of Singapore, cautions Asian countries not to follow the European example of top-down integration and to be proud of the results achieved by their bottom-up, market-driven approach.

8. Among these, I would single out Kenen et al. (2004), which focuses on how to reorganize the fora and the procedures of international cooperation, and Truman (2006), the most comprehensive survey of reform proposals regarding the role and functions of the IMF.

9. Keohane's book, originally published in 1984, has been republished with a new preface by the author, explaining why the central arguments of his theory have held up well.

10. Huntington uses the provocative term 'rogue', which the United States employs to define states such as Iran and North Korea for their destabilizing role.

Bibliography

Adams, T.D. (2006), 'The IMF: back to basics', in E.M. Truman (ed.), *Reforming the IMF for the 21st Century*, special report 19, April, Washington, DC: Institute for International Economics, pp. 133–8.

Aeschimann, E. and P. Riché (1996), *La Guerre de sept ans*, Paris: Calmann-Lévy.

Alesina, A. and R.J. Barro (2001), 'Dollarization', *American Economic Review*, **91** (2) (May), 381–5.

Artus, J.R. and A.D. Crockett (1978), 'Floating exchange rates and the need for surveillance', in *Essays in International Finance*, 127, May, Princeton, NJ: Department of Economics, Princeton University Press.

Baldwin, R. (2006), 'The Euro's Trade Effects', *Working Paper Series*, 594, March, Frankfurt: European Central Bank.

Bank of England (2001), *Financial Stability Review*, **11** (December).

Banque de France (2007), Special issue on hedge funds, *Financial Stability Review*, April, Paris: Banque de France.

Basel Committee on Banking Supervision, Credit Risk Transfer (BCBS) (2004), *A Report by the Joint Forum*, October, Basle: Bank for International Settlements.

Baucus, M., C. Grassley, C. Schumer and L. Graham (2007), 'We must act when currencies become misaligned', *Financial Times*, 6 July, p. 11.

Bergsten, C.F. (1999), 'America and Europe: clash of the titans', *Foreign Affairs*, **78** (2) (March/April), 20–34.

Bergsten, C.F. and J. Williamson (eds) (2003), *Dollar overvaluation and the world economy*, IIE special report 16, February, Washington, DC: Institute for International Economics.

Bergsten, C.F. and J. Williamson (eds) (2004), *Dollar adjustment: how far? Against what?*, IIE special report 17, November, Washington, DC: Institute for International Economics.

Bergsten, C.F., B. Gill, N.R. Lardy and D. Mitchell (2006), *China: The Balance Sheet*, New York: Public Affairs.

Bernanke, B. (2005), 'The global saving glut and the US current account deficit', remarks presented at the Sandridge Lecture, Virginia Association of Economics, Richmond, VA, 10 March, accessed at www.federalreserve.gov.

Bernanke, B. (2006), 'Hedge funds and systemic risk', speech delivered at the Federal Reserve Bank of Atlanta Financial Markets Conference, 16 May, accessed at www.frbatlanta.org.

Bernanke, B. (2007), 'Financial regulation at the invisible hand', remarks presented at the New York University Law School, New York, 11 April, accessed at www.federalreserve.gov.

Bernstein, P.L. (1996), *Against the Gods. The Remarkable Story of Risk*, New York: J. Wiley and Sons.

Bhagwati, J. (2004), *In Defense of Globalization*, New York: Oxford University Press.

Bank for International Settlements (BIS) (1995), *65th Annual Report*, **V**, Basle: BIS.

Bank for International Settlements (1999), *69th Annual Report*, **V**, Basle: BIS.

Bank for International Settlements (2001), *71st Annual Report*, Basle: BIS.

Bank for International Settlements (2002), *72nd Annual Report*, Basle: BIS.

Bank for International Settlements (2003), *73rd Annual Report*, Basle: BIS.

Bank for International Settlements (2004), *74th Annual Report*, Basle: BIS.

Bank for International Settlements (2006a), *76th Annual Report*, Basle: BIS.

Bank for International Settlements (2006b), 'The recent behaviour of financial market volatility', *BIS Papers*, **29**, (August), Basle: BIS.

Bank for International Settlements (2007), *Triennial Central Bank Survey of Foreign Exchange and Derivatives Market Activity in April 2007*, September, Basle: BIS.

Bank for International Settlements (various dates), *Quarterly Review*, Basle: BIS.

Blanchard, O., F. Giavazzi and F. Sa (2005), 'The US current account and the dollar', NBER working paper, no. 11137, Cambridge, MA: National Bureau of Economic Research.

Blinder, A.S. (1998), *Central Banking in Theory and Practice*, Cambridge, MA: MIT Press.

Blinder, A.S. (1999), 'Eight steps to a new financial order', *Foreign Affairs*, **78** (5) (September/October), 50–63.

Blinder, A., C. Goodhart, P. Hildebrand, D. Lipton and C. Wyplosz (2001), 'How do central banks talk?', in *Geneva Reports on the World Economy*, **3**, Geneva/London: ICBM/CEPR.

Bordo, M., B. Eichengreen, D. Klingebiel and M.S. Martinez-Peria (2001), 'Is the crisis problem growing more severe?', *Economic Policy*, **32** (April), 53–82.

Borio, C.E.V. (1997), 'The implementation of monetary policy in industrial countries: a survey', *BIS Economic Papers*, **47**, July, Basle: Bank for International Settlements.

Borio, C.E.V. (2002), 'Towards a macro-prudential framework for financial supervision and regulation?', lecture for the CESifo Summer Institute on Banking Regulation and Financial Stability, 17-18 July, Venice.

Borio, C.E.V. (2004), 'Market distress and vanishing liquidity: anatomy and policy options', *BIS Working Papers*, **158**, July, Basle: Bank for International Settlements.

Borio, C.E.V. and P. Lowe (2002), 'Asset prices, financial and monetary stability: exploring the nexus', *BIS Working Papers*, **114**, July, Basle: Bank for International Settlements.

Borio, C.E.V. and W. White (2004), 'Whiter monetary and financial stability? The implications of evolving policy regimes', *BIS Working Papers*, 147, February, Basle: Bank for International Settlements.

Borio, C.E.V., B. English and A.Filardo (2003), 'A tale of two perspectives: old or new challenges for monetary policy?', BIS working paper 127, February, Basle: Bank for International Settlements.

Briody, D. (2003), *The Iron Triangle. Inside the Secret World of the Carlyle Group*, New York: J. Wiley and Sons.

Brittan, S. (2005), 'China's currency is its own business', *Financial Times*, 24 June, p. 19.

Buiter, W.H., G.M. Corsetti and P.A. Pesenti (1998), 'Interpreting the ERM crisis: country-specific and systemic issues', *Princeton Studies in International Finance*, **84**, March, Princeton, NJ: Department of Economics, Princeton University Press.

Caballero, R.J., E. Farhi and P.O. Gourinchas (2006), 'An equilibrium model of "global imbalances" and low interest rates', NBER working paper no. 11996, Cambridge, MA.

Calverley, J.P. (2004), *Bubbles and How to Survive Them*, London and Boston, MA: Nicholas Brealey Publishing.

Calvo, G.A. and C.M. Reinhart (2002), 'Fear of floating', *Quarterly Journal of Economics*, **117** (2) (May), 379–408.

Carli, G. (1993), *Cinquant'anni di vita italiana*, Bari: Editori Laterza.

Caruana, J. (2005), 'Overview of Basel II and its reflections on financial stability', speech at the International Conference of Financial Stability and Implications of Basel II, Central Bank of the Republic of Turkey, 16 May, Istanbul, *BIS Review*, **34**, accessed at www.bis.org.

Cassese, S. (2006), *Oltre lo Stato*, Bari: Laterza.

Catte, P., G. Galli and S. Rebecchini (1994), 'Concerted interventions and the dollar: an analysis of daily data', in P.B. Kenen, F. Papadia and

F. Saccomanni (eds), *The International Monetary System*, Cambridge: Cambridge University Press, pp. 201–39.

Cecchetti, S.G., H. Genberg, J. Lipsky and S. Wadhwani (2000), *Asset Prices and Central Bank Policy*, London: Centre for Economic Policy Research.

Celati, L. (2004), *The Dark Side of Risk Management. How People Frame Decisions in Financial Markets*, London: FT Prentice Hall.

Centre for the Study of Financial Innovation (2006), *Banking Banana Skins*, London and New York: Centre for the Study of Financial Innovation.

Ciocca, P. (ed.) (1987), *Money and the Economy: Central Bankers' Views*, Basingstoke: Macmillan.

Ciocca, P. and G. Nardozzi (1996), *The High Price of Money. An Interpretation of World Interest Rates*, Oxford: Clarendon Press.

Clarida, R.H. (2000), 'G-3 exchange-rate relationships: a review of the record and of proposals for change', *Essays in International Economics*, **219**, September, Princeton, NJ: Department of Economics, Princeton University Press.

Coeuré, B. and J. Pisani-Ferry (2000), 'The euro, yen and dollar: making the case against benign neglect', in P.B. Kenen and A.K. Swoboda (eds), *Reforming the International Monetary and Financial System*, Washington, DC: International Monetary Fund, pp. 19–46.

Collignon, S., S. Bofinger, C. Johnson and B. De Maigret (1994), *Europe's Monetary Future*, London: Pinter Publishers.

Committee on the Global Financial System (2007), *Report on Institutional Investors and Asset Allocation*, Basle: Bank for International Settlements, accessed at www.bis.org.

Conseil d'Analyse Economique (1999), *Architecture Financière Internationale*, Paris: La Documentation Française.

Cooper, R. (1984), 'A monetary system for the future', *Foreign Affairs*, **63** (1), 166–84.

Corden, W.M. (2002), *Too Sensational: On the Choice of Exchange Rate Regimes*, Cambridge, MA and London: MIT Press.

Cottarelli, C. and C. Giannini (1997), 'Credibility without rules? Monetary frameworks in the post-Bretton Woods era', International Monetary Fund occasional paper no. 154, December, Washington, DC.

Counterparty Risk Management Policy Group II (2005), *Toward Greater Financial Stability. A Private Sector Perspective*, 27 July, accessed at www.crmpolicygroup.org.

Crockett, A. (1997), 'The theory and practice of financial stability', *Essays in International Finance*, **203**, April, Princeton, NJ: Department of Economics, Princeton University Press.

Crockett, A. (2000), 'In search of anchors for financial and monetary stability', paper presented at 22nd SUERF Colloquium, 27-29 April, Vienna.

Dale, R. (2004), *The First Crash. Lessons from the South Sea Bubble*, Princeton, NJ: Princeton University Press.

de Brouwer, G. (2001), *Hedge Funds in Emerging Markets*, Cambridge: Cambridge University Press.

de Cecco, M. (1974), *Money and Empire: The International Gold Standard*, London: Blackwell.

de Gaulle, C. (1970), *Mémoires d'espoir. Le Renouveau 1958–1962*, Paris: Plon.

De Grauwe, P. and I. Vansteenkiste (2001), 'Exchange rates and fundamentals. A non-linear relationship?', paper presented at the Conference on Understanding Exchange Rates, September, Amsterdam.

de Rato, R. (2005), *The Managing Director's Report on the Fund's Medium-Term Strategy*, 15 September, Washington, DC: International Monetary Fund, accessed at www.imf.org.

Desai, P. (2003), *Financial Crisis, Contagion and Containment*, Princeton, NJ: Princeton University Press.

Detken, C. and F. Smets (2004), 'Asset price booms and monetary policy', European Central Bank working paper no. 364, May, Frankfurt.

Dobson, W. (1991), *Economic Policy Coordination: Requiem or Prologue?*, Washington, DC: Institute for International Economics.

Dominguez, K.M. (2003), 'Foreign exchange intervention: Did it work in the 1990s?', in C.F. Bergsten and J. Williamson (eds), *Dollar Overvaluation and the World Economy*, Institute for International Economics special report 16, February, Washington, DC: IIE, pp. 217–46.

Dominguez, K.M. and J.A. Frankel (1993), *Does Foreign Exchange Intervention Work?*, Washington, DC: Institute for International Economics.

Dooley, M.P. and P. Garber (2005), 'Is It 1958 or 1968? Three notes on the longevity of the revived Bretton Woods system', *Brookings Papers on Economic Activity*, **1**, Washington: Brookings Institution.

Dooley, M.P., D. Folkerts-Landau and P. Garber (2003), 'An essay on the revived Bretton Woods system', National Bureau of Economic Research working paper no. 9971, September, Cambridge, MA, accessed at www.nber.org/papers/w9971.

Dooley, M.P., D. Folkerts-Landau and P. Garber (2004), 'The revived Bretton Woods system: the effects of periphery intervention and reserve management on interest rates and exchange rates in center countries', National Bureau of Economic Research working paper no. 10332, March, Cambridge, MA, accessed at www.nber.org/papers/w10332.

Dornbusch, R. (1980), *Open Economy Macroeconomics*, New York: Basic Books.

Dornbusch, R. (2001), 'Exchange rates and the choice of monetary-policy regimes. Fewer monies, better monies', *American Economic Review*, **91** (2) (May), 238–42.

Draghi, M. (2007), remarks of the Chairman of the FSF to the International Monetary and Financial Committee at the International Monetary Fund Spring Meeting, 14 April, Washington, DC, accessed at www.imf.org.

Eatwell, J. and L. Taylor (2000), *Global Finance at Risk. The Case for International Regulation*, New York: New Press.

The Economist (2000), 'Intervention: divine or comic?', 23 September, pp. 105–6.

The Economist (2005a), 'Who rates the raters', special report, 26 March, pp. 65–7.

The Economist (2005b), 'The global housing boom', special report, 18 June, pp. 62–4.

The Economist (2005c), 'Locust, pocus', 7 May, pp. 65–7.

The Economist (2005d), 'A great big banking gamble. Special report on China's banking industry', 29 October, pp. 77–9.

The Economist (2007), 'The uneasy crown', 10 February, pp. 73–5.

Ehrmann, M. and M. Fratzscher (2005a), 'How should central banks communicate?', European Central Bank working paper no. 557, November, Frankfurt.

Ehrmann, M. and M. Fratzscher (2005b), 'The timing of central bank communication', European Central Bank working paper no. 565, December, Frankfurt.

Eichengreen, B. (ed.) (1985), *The Gold Standard in Theory and History*, London: Methuen.

Eichengreen, B. (1994), *International Monetary Arrangements for the 21st Century*, Washington, DC: Brookings Institution.

Eichengreen, B. (1999a), *Toward a New International Financial Architecture. A Practical Post-Asia Agenda*, Washington, DC: Institute for International Economics.

Eichengreen, B. (1999b), 'Half-built dreams', *BASC News,* **2** (2) (Fall).

Eichengreen, B. (2000), 'The EMS crisis in retrospect', National Bureau of Economic Research working paper no. 8035, December, Cambridge, MA.

Eichengreen, B. (2002), *Financial Crises. And What to Do about Them*, Oxford: Oxford University Press.

Eichengreen, B. (2004), 'Financial instability', in B. Lomborg (ed.), *Global Crises, Global Solutions*, Cambridge: Cambridge University Press, pp. 251–8.

Eichengreen, B. and J.A. Frankel (1996), 'The SDR, reserve currencies, and the future of the international monetary system', in M. Mussa, J.M. Boughton and P. Isard (eds), *The Future of the SDR in Light of Changes in the International Financial System*, Washington, DC: International Monetary Fund, pp. 378–85.

Eichengreen, B. and A. Mody (1998), 'Interest rates in the north and capital flows to the south: is there a missing link?', *International Finance*, **1** (1) (October), 35–57.

Eichengreen, B. and C. Wyplosz (1993), 'The unstable EMS', Centre for Economic Policy Research discussion paper series 817, May, London.

Eichengreen, B., M. Mussa, E. Detragiache, G.M. Milesi-Ferretti, G. Dell'ariccia and A. Tweedie (1998), 'Capital account liberalization: theoretical and practical aspects', International Monetary Fund occasional paper no. 172, Washington, DC.

Eijffinger, S.C.W. and J. De Haan (1996), 'The political economy of central-bank independence', Department of Economics, Princeton University special papers in international economics **19**, May, Princeton, NJ.

Elias, D. (1999), *Dow 40 000: Strategies for Profiting from the Greatest Bull Market in History*, New York: McGraw-Hill.

European Central Bank (ECB) (2000), *Monthly Bulletin*, September, Frankfurt: ECB.

European Central Bank (2005a), *Review of the International Role of the Euro*, January, Frankfurt: ECB.

European Central Bank (2005b), 'Managing financial crises in emerging market economies – experience with the involvement of private sector creditors', a report by an International Relations Committee Task Force, European Central Bank occasional paper **32**, July Frankfurt.

European Central Bank (2005c), *Large EU Banks' Exposures to Hedge Funds*, November, accessed at www.ecb.int.

European Central Bank (2006a), *Financial Stability Review*, June.

European Central Bank (2006b), *Financial Stability Review*, December.

Evans, M.D.D. and R.K. Lyons (2004), 'A new micro model of exchange rate dynamics', National Bureau of Economic Research working papers series 10379, Cambridge, MA.

Evans, M.D.D. and R.K. Lyons (2007), 'Exchange rate fundamentals and order flow', National Bureau of Economic Research working papers series 13151, Cambridge, MA.

Feldstein, M. (1987), 'Correcting the trade deficit', *Foreign Affairs*, **65** (4), 795–806.

Feldstein, M. (1988), 'Feldstein on the dollar. Let the market decide', *The Economist*, 3 December, pp. 21–4.

Ferguson, N. (1998), *The World's Banker. The History of the House of Rothschild*, London: Weidenfeld & Nicolson.

Ferguson, N. (2001), *The Cash Nexus. Money and Power in the Modern World, 1700–2000*, Harmondsworth: Allen Lane/Penguin Press.

Ferguson, N. (2004a), *Empire. How Britain Made the Modern World*, London: Penguin Books.

Ferguson, N. (2004b), *Colossus. The Rise and Fall of the American Empire*, London: Penguin Books.

Ferguson, R., P. Hartmann, F. Panetta and R. Portes (2007), 'International financial stability', *Geneva Reports on the World Economy*, **9**, Geneva/London: ICBM/CEPR.

Financial Services Authority (FSA) (2005a), 'Hedge funds: a discussion of risk and regulatory engagement', FSA discussion paper 4, June, accessed at www.fsa.gov.uk.

Financial Services Authority (2005b), press release, 28 June, accessed at www.fsa.gov.uk.

Financial Stability Forum (FSF) (2000), 'Report of the Working Group on Highly Leveraged Institutions', 5 April, accessed at www.fsforum.org.

Financial Stability Forum (2006), press release, 17 March, accessed at www.fsforum.org.

Financial Stability Forum (2007), press release, 29 March, accessed at www.fsforum.org.

Financial Times (2004), 'Where money talks very loudly', 27 May, p. 1.

Financial Times (2007), 'Funds eclipse big banks in trading of US treasuries', 9 March, p. 1.

Fischer, S. (2000), 'On the need for an international lender of last resort', *Essays in International Finance*', **220** (November), Princeton, NJ: Department of Economics, Princeton University Press.

Fischer, S. (2001), 'Exchange rate regimes: Is the bipolar view correct?', *Journal of Economic Perspectives*, **15** (2) (Spring), 3–24.

Fischer, S. (2004), *IMF Essays from a Time of Crisis*, Cambridge, MA and London: MIT Press.

Frankel, J.A. (1999), 'No single currency regime is right for all countries or at all times', *Essays in International Finance*, **215** (August), Princeton, NJ: Department of Economics, Princeton University Press.

Frankel, J.A. and A. Rose (2002), 'An estimate of the effect of common currencies on trade and income', *Quarterly Journal of Economics*, **117**, May 437–66.

Fratzscher, M. (2004a), 'Communication and exchange rate policy', European Central Bank working paper series 363, May, Frankfurt.

Fratzscher, M. (2004b), 'Exchange rate policy strategies and foreign exchange interventions in the group of three economies, in C.F. Bergsten and J. Williamson (eds), *Dollar Adjustment: How Far? Against What?*, special report 17, November, Washington, DC: Institute for International Economics.

Fratzscher, M. (2005), 'How successful are exchange rate communication and interventions? Evidence from time-series and event-study approaches', European Central Bank working paper series 528, September, Frankfurt.

Frieden, J.A. (2006), *Global Capitalism. Its Fall and Rise in the Twentieth Century*, New York and London: W.W. Norton.

Friedman, B.M. (1999), 'The future of monetary policy: the central bank as an army with only a signal corps?', *International Finance*, **2** (3), November, 321–38.

Friedman, M. (1953), 'The case for flexible exchange rates', *Essays in Positive Economics*, Chicago: University of Chicago Press, pp. 157–203.

Funabashi, Y. (1988), *From the Plaza to the Louvre*, Washington, DC: Institute for International Economics.

Fukuyama, F. (2006), *America at the Crossroads. Democracy, Power, and the Neoconservative Legacy*, New Haven, CT and London: Yale University Press.

Galati, G. and M. Melvin (2004), 'Why has foreign trading surged? Explaining the 2004 triennial survey', *BIS Quarterly Review*, December, Basle: Bank for International Settlements, pp. 67–74.

Galati, G. and K. Tsatsaronis (2001), 'The impact of the euro on Europe's financial markets', Bank for International Settlements working papers 100, July, Basle.

Galbraith, J.K. (1993), *A Short History of Financial Euphoria*, New York: Viking.

Gandolfo, G. (2001), *International Finance and Open-Economy Macro-Economics*, Berlin: Springer.

Gapper, J. (2005), 'The market's true manipulators', *Financial Times*, 10 February, p. 17.

Garbaravicius, T. and F. Dierick (2005), 'Hedge funds and their implications for financial stability', European Central Bank occasional paper series 34, August, Frankfurt, accessed at www.ecb.int.

García Herrero, A., V. Gaspar, L. Hoogduin, J. Morgan and B. Winkler (eds) (2001), *Why Price Stability?*, Frankfurt: European Central Bank.

Giannini, C. (1999), 'Enemy of none but a common friend of all? An international perspective on the lender-of-last resort function', *Essays in International Finance*, **214** (June), Princeton, NJ: Department of Economics, Princeton University Press.

Giovanoli, M. (2000), 'A new architecture for the global financial market: legal aspects of international financial standard setting', in M. Giovanoli (ed.), *International Monetary Law. Issues for the New Millennium*, Oxford: Oxford University Press, pp. 3–59.

Gobat, J. (2001), 'Hong Kong SAR's strong fundamentals, policies generate quick recovery from Asian crisis', *IMF Survey*, **30** (12) 18 June.

Goldman Sachs (2000a), *The Weekly Analyst*, **32**, 12 September, New York: Goldman Sachs & Co.

Goldman Sachs (2000b), *The Weekly Analyst*, **34**, 26 September, New York: Goldman Sachs & Co.

Goldstein, M. (1994), 'Improving economic policy coordination: evaluating some new and some not-so-new proposals', in P.B. Kenen, F. Papadia and F. Saccomanni (eds), *The International Monetary System*, Cambridge: Cambridge University Press, pp. 298–324.

Goldstein, M. (1995), 'Exchange rate system and the IMF: a modest agenda', *Policy Analyses in International Economics*, **39**, June, Washington, DC: Institute for International Economics.

Goldstein, M. (ed.) (1999), *Safeguarding Prosperity in a Global Financial System. The Future International Financial Architecture* (Goldstein Report), Washington, DC: Institute for International Economics.

Goldstein, M. (2002), *Managed Floating Pens*, Washington, DC: Institute for International Economics.

Goldstein, M. (2004), 'China and the renminbi exchange rate', in C.F. Bergsten and J. Williamson (eds), 'Dollar adjustment: how far? Against what?', Institute for International Economics special report 17 November, Washington, DC.

Goldstein, M. (2005), 'The international financial architecture', in C.F. Bergsten (ed.), *The United States and the World Economy: Foreign Economic Policy for the Next Decade*, Washington, DC: Institute for International Economics, pp. 373–408.

Goldstein, M. (2006), 'Currency manipulation and enforcing the rules of the international monetary system', in E.M. Truman (ed.), *Reforming the IMF for the 21st Century*, special report 19, April, Washington, DC: Institute for International Economics, pp. 141–55.

Goldstein, M. and P. Turner (2004), *Controlling Currency Mismatches in Emerging Markets*, Washington, DC: Institute for International Economics.

Goldstein, M. and N. Lardy (2005), 'China's revaluation shows size really matters', *Financial Times*, 22 July, p. 19.

Goodhart, C.A.E. (1988), *The Evolution of the Central Banks*, Cambridge, MA: MIT Press.

Goodhart, C.A.E. (2000), 'Can central banking survive the IT revolution?', *International Finance*, **3** (2) (July), 189–203.

Goodhart, C.A.E. and L. Dai (2003), *Intervention to Save Hong Kong. The Authorities' Counter-Speculation in Financial Markets*, Oxford: Oxford University Press.

Goodhart, C.A.E. and L. Figliuoli (1991), 'Every minute counts in financial markets', *Journal of International Money and Finance*, **10**, 238–71.

Goodhart, C.A.E. and G. Illing (eds) (2002), *Financial Crises, Contagion and the Lender of Last Resort. A Reader*, Oxford: Oxford University Press.

Greenspan, A. (1996), 'The challenge of central banking in a democratic society', speech at the American Enterprise Institute for Public Policy Research, 5 December, Washington, DC, accessed at www.ny.frb.org.

Greenspan, A. (2002), *Economic Volatility*, remarks at a symposium of the Federal Reserve Bank of Kansas City, Jackson Hole, WY, 30 August Kansas City, MO: Federal Reserve Bank of Kansas City, 30 August, accessed at www.federalreserve.gov.

Greenspan, A. (2004), 'Current account', remarks before the Economic Club of New York, 2 March, New York, reported in *BIS Review*, **14**, accessed at www.ny.frb.org.

Greenspan, A. (2005a), 'Federal Reserve Board's Semiannual Monetary Policy Report to the Congress', testimony before the Committee on Banking, Housing and Urban Affairs, US Senate, 16 February, accessed at www.federalreserve.gov.

Greenspan, A. (2005b), 'China', testimony of Chairman of the Federal Reserve before the Committee of Finance, US Senate, 23 June, accessed at www.federalreserve.gov.

Grilli, V., D. Masciandaro and G. Tabellini (1991), 'Political and monetary institutions and public financial policies in the industrial countries', *Economic Policy*, **6** (13), 341–92.

Group of Seven (G7) Finance Ministers (1999), *Strengthening the International Financial Architecture*, report to the Cologne Economic Summit, 18-20 June, Cologne, accessed at www.us.treas.gov.

Group of Ten (G10) Deputies (1985), *The Functioning of the International Monetary System*, report to the G-10 Ministers and Governors, Washington, DC: International Monetary Fund.

Group of Ten Deputies (1989), *The Role of the IMF and the World Bank in the Context of the Debt Strategy*, report to the G-10 Ministers and Governors, Washington, DC: International Monetary Fund.

Group of Ten Deputies (1993), *International Capital Movements and Foreign Exchange Markets*, report to the G-10 Ministers and Governors, Washington, DC: International Monetary Fund.

Group of Ten Deputies (2001), *Consolidation in the Financial Sector*, report to the G-10 Ministers and Governors, Washington, DC: International Monetary Fund.

Gyohten, T. (2004), *Asset Price Bubbles – What Have We Learned?*, accessed at www.glocom.org/opinions/essays/20040921.

Haldane, A. and M. Kruger (2001), 'The resolution of international financial crises: private finance and public funds', Bank of Canada working paper 20, November, Ottawa.

Hawtrey, R.G. (1932), *The Art of the Central Banking*, second edn 1962, reprinted in 1970, London: Frank Cass & Co.

Himino, R. (2004), 'Basel II – towards a new common language', *BIS Quarterly Review*, September, Basle: Bank of International Settlements, pp. 41–9.

Hull, J. (2006), *Risk Management and Financial Institutions*, London: FT Prentice Hall.

Huntington, S. (1999), 'The lonely superpower', *Foreign Affairs*, **78** (2) March/April.

International Institute of Finance (IIF) (2004), *Principles for Stable Capital Flows and Fair Debt Restructuring in Emerging Markets*, accessed at www.iif.com.

International Monetary Fund (IMF) (1982), *IMF Survey*, **12** (11) (21 June), Washington, DC: IMF.

International Monetary Fund (1985), *IMF Survey*, **14** (19) (7 October), Washington, DC: IMF.

International Monetary Fund (1987), *IMF Survey*, **16** (5) (9 March), Washington, DC: IMF.

International Monetary Fund (1988), *IMF Survey*, **17** (1), 11 January, Washington, DC: IMF.

International Monetary Fund (1995a), *IMF Survey*, **24** (9), 8 May, Washington, DC: IMF.

International Monetary Fund (1995b), *World Economic Outlook*, May, Washington, DC: IMF.

International Monetary Fund (1995c), *International Capitals Markets*, August, Washington, DC: IMF.

International Monetary Fund (1997), *World Economic Outlook*, May, Washington, DC: IMF.

International Monetary Fund (1998a), *World Economic Outlook*, May, Washington, DC: IMF.

International Monetary Fund (1998b), *IMF Survey*, **27** (19), 19 October, Washington, DC: IMF.

International Monetary Fund (1999a), *World Economic Outlook*, May, Washington, DC: IMF.

International Monetary Fund (1999b), *International Capital Markets*, September, Washington, DC: IMF.

International Monetary Fund (2000a), *World Economic Outlook*, October, Washington, DC: IMF.

International Monetary Fund (2000b), *IMF Survey*, **29** (19), 9 October, Washington, DC: IMF.

International Monetary Fund (2001a), *Emerging Market Financing*, **2** (1), 13 February, Washington, DC: IMF.

International Monetary Fund (2001b), *World Economic Outlook*, May, Washington, DC: IMF.

International Monetary Fund (2001c), *World Economic Outlook*, October, Washington, DC: IMF.

International Monetary Fund (2002), *World Economic Outlook*, September, Washington, DC: IMF.

International Monetary Fund (2003a), *World Economic Outlook*, April, Washington, DC: IMF.

International Monetary Fund (2003b), *Global Financial Stability Report*, September, Washington, DC: IMF.

International Monetary Fund (2003c), 'The IMF and recent capital account crises', evaluation report produced by IMF Independent Evaluation Office, Washington, DC: IMF.

International Monetary Fund (2003d), public information notice PIN 03/138, 24 November, accessed at www.imf.org.

International Monetary Fund (2004a), *Global Financial Stability Report*, September, Washington, DC: IMF.

International Monetary Fund (2004b), *World Economic Outlook*, September, Washington, DC: IMF.

International Monetary Fund (2004c), *IMF Survey*, **33** (18), 11 October, Washington, DC: IMF.

International Monetary Fund (2005a), *Report on the Evaluation of the IMF's Approach to Capital Account Liberalization*, 2 April, Washington, DC: IMF, accessed at www.imf.org/external/np/ieo.

International Monetary Fund (2005b), *World Economic Outlook*, April, Washington, DC: IMF.

International Monetary Fund (2005c), *World Economic Outlook*, September, Washington, DC: IMF.

International Monetary Fund (2005d), *Progress Report on Crisis Resolution*, 21 September 2005, accessed at www.imf.org.

International Monetary Fund (2005e), *The Managing Director Report on the Fund's Medium Term Strategy to the International Monetary and Financial Committee*, 23 September, accessed at www.imf.org.

International Monetary Fund (2005f), press release, 05/135, 6 June, accessed at www.imf.org.

International Monetary Fund (2005g), public information notice PIN 05/106, 8 August, accessed at www.imf.org.

International Monetary Fund (2006a), *Offshore Financial Centres. The Assessment Program: A Progress Report*, Appendix II, 8 February, p. 12, accessed at www.imf.org.

International Monetary Fund (2006b), *World Economic Outlook*, April, Washington, DC: IMF.

International Monetary Fund (2006c), *IMF Survey*, **35** (8), 1 May, Washington, DC: IMF.

International Monetary Fund (2006d), *World Economic Outlook*, September, Washington, DC: IMF.

International Monetary Fund (2006e), 'Methodology for CGER exchange rate assessments', paper prepared by the IMF Research Department, 8 November, accessed at www.imf.org.

International Monetary Fund (2006f), press release 06/21, 1 February, accessed at www.imf.org.

International Monetary Fund (2007a), 'Recent trends in the hedge fund industry: growth, relevance and institutionalization', mimeo 22 February, Washington, DC: IMF.

International Monetary Fund (2007b), *Global Financial Stability Report*, April, Washington, DC: IMF.

International Monetary Fund (2007c), *World Economic Outlook*, April, Washington DC: IMF.

International Monetary Fund (2007d), 'Bilateral surveillance over members' policies', Executive Board decision adopted on 15 June, accessed at www.imf.org.

International Monetary Fund (2007e), press release 07/71, 14 April, accessed at www.imf.org.

International Monetary Fund (2007f), press release 07/72, 14 April, accessed at www.imf.org.

International Monetary Fund – Independent Evaluation Office (IMF–IEO) (2003), *The IMF and Recent Capital Account Crises. Indonesia, Korea, Brazil*, Washington DC: IMF.

International Monetary Fund and World Bank (2005), *The Standards and Codes Initiative: Is it Effective? And How Can it Be Improved?*, accessed at www.imf.org/external/standards/index.htm.

Isard, P. (1995), *Exchange Rate Economics*, Cambridge, MA: Cambridge University Press.

Issing, O. (2004), 'Asset prices and monetary policy', speech at the European Central Bank-CFS Symposium on capital markets and financial integration in Europe, 10 May, Frankfurt.

Issing, O., V. Gaspar, I. Angeloni and O. Tristani (2001), *Monetary Policy in the Euro Area. Strategy and Decision-Making at the European Central Bank*, Cambridge: Cambridge University Press.

James, H. (1996), *International Monetary Cooperation since Bretton Woods*, Washington, DC: International Monetary Fund.

James, H. (1997), *Rambouillet, 15 November 1975. Die Globalisierung der Wirtschafter*, Munich: Deutscher Taschenbuch Verlag.

James, H. (2001), *The End of Globalization. Lessons from the Great Depression*, Cambridge, MA: Harvard University Press.

Johnson, H. (1972), 'Political economy aspects of international monetary reform', *Journal of International Economics*, **2** (4) (September), 401–23.

Joint Economic Committee (1975), 'Report of the Subcommittee on International Economics of the Joint Economic Committee Congress of the United States', 94th Congress, 17 December, Washington, DC: US Government Printing Office.

JPMorgan (2000), *World Financial Markets*, IV, 6 October, New York: Morgan Guaranty Trust Company.

Jurgensen, P. (ed.) (1983), 'Rapport du groupe de travail sur les interventions sur les marchés des changes (Jurgensen Rapport)', in *Collection des rapports officiels*, Paris: La Documentation Française; English version: 'Report of the Working Group on Exchange Market Intervention (*Jurgensen Report*)', Washington, DC: Treasury Department.

Kay, J. (2004), *The Truth about Markets*, London: Penguin Books.

Kenen, P.B. (1988), *Managing Exchange Rates*, London: The Royal Institute of International Affairs/Routledge.

Kenen, P.B. (1996), 'From Halifax to Lyons: what has been done about crisis management?', *Essays in International Finance* 200, October, Princeton, NJ: Department of Economics, Princeton University Press.

Kenen, P.B. (2001), *The International Financial Architecture. What's New? What's Missing?*, November, Washington, DC: Institute for International Economics.

Kenen, P.B., F. Papadia and F. Saccomanni (eds) (1994), *The International Monetary System*, Cambridge: Cambridge University Press.

Kenen, P.B., J.R. Shafer, N.L. Wicks and C. Wyplosz (2004), 'International economic and financial cooperation: new issues, new actors, new responses', *Geneva Reports on the World Economy*, **6**, Geneva/London: ICBM/CEPR.

Keohane, R.O. (2005), *After Hegemony. Cooperation and Discord in the World Political Economy*, Princeton, NJ: Princeton University Press.

Keynes, J.M. ([1919] 1971), *The Economic Consequences of the Peace*, London: Macmillian, St. Martin's for the Royal Economic Society.

Keynes, J.M. (1936), *The General Theory of Employment, Interest, and Money*, London: Macmillan.

Kindleberger, C.P. (1978), *Manias, Panics, and Crashes. A History of Financial Crises*, New York: Basic Books. 4th edn (2000) published in New York: John Wiley.

Kindleberger, C.P. (1984), *A Financial History of Western Europe*, London: George Allen & Unwin.

Kindleberger, C.P. (1988), *The International Economic Order. Essays on Financial Crisis and International Public Goods*, Cambridge, MA: MIT Press.

Kindleberger, C.P. (2000), *Manias, Panics, and Crashes. A History of Financial Crises*, expanded and revised 4th edn, New York: John Wiley.

King, M.A. (1999), 'Challenges for monetary policy: new and old', *Bank of England Quarterly Bulletin*, **39** (4) (November), 397–411.

King, M.A. (2005), 'Monetary policy-practice ahead of theory', speech for the Mais Lecture 2005, Cass Business School, City University, 17 May, London, *BIS Review*, **36**, accessed at www.bis.org.

Kissinger, H. (1979), *White House Years*, Boston: Little, Brown and Co.

Kissinger, H. (1994), *Diplomacy*, New York: Simon & Schuster.

Kissinger, H. (2001), *Does America Need a Foreign Policy? Toward a Diplomacy for the 21st Century*, New York: Simon & Schuster.

Krueger, A. (2001), 'International financial architecture for 2002: a new approach to sovereign debt restructuring', speech at the National Economists' Club Annual Members' Dinner, American Enterprise Institute, 26 November, Washington, DC.

Krugman, P. (1989), *Exchange-Rate Instability*, Cambridge, MA: MIT Press.

Krugman, P. (1991), 'Has the adjustment process worked?', in *Policy Analyses in International Economics* 34, October, Washington, DC: Institute for International Economics.

Krugman, P. (1995), 'Monetary virtue leads two-peso tussle', *Financial Times*, 13 June, p. 21.

Krugman, P. (2000), 'The US would benefit from rescuing the euro', *New York Times*, 21 September.

Krugman, P. (2003), *The Great Unravelling: From Boom to Bust in Three Scandalous Years*, London: Allen Lane.

Kubelec, C. (2004), 'Intervention when exchange rate misalignments are large', in C.F. Bergsten and J. Williamson (eds), *Dollar Adjustment: How Far? Against What?*, Institute for International Economics special report 17, pp. 241–58, November, Washington, DC: IIE.

Kuroda, H. (2005), 'Thinking beyond borders: trends, challenges and opportunities in Asian economic integration', speech at J.B. Fernandez Memorial Lecture, 26 October, Manila.

Kusukawa, T. (1999), *Asian Currency Reform: The Option of a Common Basket Peg*, Tokyo: Fuji Research Institute Corporation.

Lamfalussy, A. (2000), *Financial Crises in Emerging Markets. An Essay on Financial Globalization and Fragility*, New Haven, CT and London: Yale University Press.

Lee, S. (1998), 'Managed or mismanaged trade? US–Japan relations during the Clinton presidency', in I.G. Cook, M.A. Doel, R.Y.F. Li and Y. Wang (eds), *Dynamic Asia: Business, Trade and Economic Development in Pacific Asia*, Aldershot: Ashgate, pp. 209–33.

Lehman Brothers (2000a), *Global Weekly Economic Monitor*, 8 September, New York: Lehman Brothers.

Lehman Brothers (2000b), *Global Weekly Economic Monitor*, 20 October, New York: Lehman Brothers.

Levy, A. and M. Pericoli (1999), 'Episodes of concerted intervention in 1993–1998: some stylised facts', mimeo, Servizio Studi, Banca d'Italia, Rome.

Lincoln, E.J. (1999), *Troubles Times. US–Japan Trade Relations in the 1990s*, Washington, DC: Brookings Institution Press.

Lowenstein, R. (2001), *When Genius Failed*, London: Fourth Estate.

Lynch, K. (1999), 'The temptation to intervene: problems created by the government intervention in the Hong Kong stock market', in J.J. Norton (ed.), *Yearbook of International Financial and Economic Law 1998*, London: Kluwer Law International, pp. 563–94.

Maeso-Fernandez, F., C. Osbat and B. Schnatz (2001), 'Determinants of the euro real effective exchange rate: a BEER/PEER approach', European Central Bank working paper, 85, November, Frankfurt.

Mandelbrot, B.B. and R.L. Hudson (2004), *The (Mis)Behaviour of Markets. A Fractal View of Risk, Ruin and Reward*, London: Profile Books.

McCarthy, C. (2007), 'Financial regulation: myth and reality', speech delivered at the British American Business London Insight Series and Financial Services Forum, 13 February, accessed at www.fsa.gov.uk.

McCauley, R.N. (1997), 'The euro and the dollar', *Essays in International Finance*, **205**, November, Princeton, NJ: Department of Economics, Princeton University Press.

McGregor (2006), 'China's bad loans outstrip reserves', *Financial Times*, 3 May, p. 1.

McKinnon, R.I. (1996), *The Rules of the Game: International Money and Exchange Rates*, Cambridge, MA: MIT Press.

McKinnon, R. (1999), 'Wading in the yen trap', *The Economist*, 24 July, pp. 77–9.

McKinnon, R.I. and K. Ohno (1997), *Dollar and Yen: Resolving Economic Conflict between the United States and Japan*, Cambridge, MA: MIT Press.

Meltzer, A. (2000), *Report of the International Financial Institutions Advisory Commission (Meltzer Commission Report)*, Washington, DC: International Monetary Fund.

Meredith, G. (2001), 'Why has the euro been so weak?', International Monetary Fund working paper, Washington, DC.

Merrill Lynch (2000), *Global Economic Trends*, September, New York: Merrill Lynch Pierce, Fenners & Smith Incorporated.

Micossi, S. and F. Saccomanni (1981), 'The substitution account: the problem, the techniques and the politics', *Quarterly Review*, **137**, Rome: Banca Nazionale del Lavoro.

Minsky, H.P. (1972), 'Financial stability revisited: the economics of disaster', in Board of Governors of the Federal Reserve System (ed.), *Reappraisal of the Federal Reserve Discount Mechanism*, **3** June, Washington, DC: Federal Reserve System.

Mishkin, F.S. (1997), 'The causes and propagation of financial instability: lessons for policymakers', in Federal Reserve Bank of Kansas City (ed.), *Symposium on Maintaining Financial Stability in a Global Economy*, Jackson Hole, WY, 28-30 August, Kansas City, MD: Federal Reserve Bank of Kansas City.

Mishkin, F.S. (2006), *The Next Great Globalization*, Princeton, NJ: Princeton University Press.

Mortimer (2006), *The Perfect King, the Life of Edward III, Father of the English Nation*, London: Jonathan Cape.

Mundell, R.A. (1968), *International Economics*, New York: Macmillan.

Mundell, R.A. (2000), 'A reconsideration of the twentieth century', *American Economic Review*, **90** (3), June 327–40.

Mussa, M., J.M. Boughton and P. Isard (eds) (1996), *The Future of the SDR in Light of Changes in the International Financial System*, Washington, DC: International Monetary Fund.

Mussa, M., P. Masson, A. Swoboda, E. Jadresic, P. Mauro and A. Berg (2000a), 'Exchange rate regimes in an increasingly integrated world economy', International Monetary Fund occasional paper 193, Washington, DC.

Mussa, M., A. Swoboda, J. Zettelmeyer and O. Jeanne (2000b), 'Moderating fluctuations in capital flows to emerging market economics' in P.B. Kenen and A.K. Swoboda (eds), *Reforming the International Monetary and Financial System*, Washington, DC: International Monetary Fund, pp. 75–142.

Noland, M. (1995), 'US–Japan trade friction and its dilemmas for US policy', *World Economy*, **18** (2), March 237–67.

Nye, J. (2002), *The Paradox of American Power: Why the World's Superpower Can't Go it Alone*, Oxford: Oxford University Press.

Obstfeld, M. and K. Rogoff (2000), 'Perspectives on OECD economic integration: implications for US current account adjustment', in Federal Reserve Bank of Kansas City (ed.), *Symposium on Global Economic Integration: Opportunities and Challenges*, Jackson Hole, WY, 24-26 August, Kansas City, MD: Federal Reserve Bank of Kansas City.

Obstfeld, M. and K. Rogoff (2005), 'Global current account imbalances and exchange rate adjustments', in *Brookings Papers on Economic Activity*, no. 1, Washington, DC: Brookings Institution Press.

Organisation for Economic Co-operation and Development (OECD) (2000), *EMU. One Year on*, February, Paris: OECD.

Organisation for Economic Co-operation and Development (2001), *OECD Economic Surveys. Euro Area*, May, Paris: OECD.

Organisation for Economic Co-operation and Development (2005), *Economic Outlook*, **78**, December, Paris: OECD.

Organisation for Economic Co-operation and Development (2006), *Economic Outlook*, **80**, November, Paris: OECD.

Ogawa, E. and T. Ito (2000), 'On the desirability of a regional basket currency arrangement', National Bureau of Economic Research working papers series 8002, Cambridge, MA.

Olson, M. (2000), *Power and Prosperity. Outgrowing Communist and Capitalist Dictatorships*, New York: Basic Books.

Padoa-Schioppa, T. (1985), 'Rules and institutions in the management of multi-country economies' in L. Tsoukalis (ed.) *The Political Economy of International Money. In Search of a New Order*, London: Sage Publications, pp. 261–81.

Padoa-Schioppa, T. (1994), *The Road to Monetary Union in Europe. The Emperor, the Kings, and the Genies*, Oxford: Clarendon Press.

Padoa-Schioppa, T. (2002), 'Central banks and financial stability: exploring an intermediate land', policy panel introductory paper at the Second ECB Central Banking Conference on The Transformation of the European Financial System, 24-25 October, Frankfurt: European Central Bank.

Padoa-Schioppa, T. (2004a), *Regulating Finance – Balancing Freedom and Risk*, Oxford: Oxford University Press.

Padoa-Schioppa, T. (2004b), *The Euro and its Central Bank. Getting United after the Union*, Cambridge, MA: MIT Press.

Padoa-Schioppa, T. (2005), 'Four lectures on international economic policy cooperation', lectures delivered at the European University Institute, 25-27 January, Firenze, unpublished.

Padoa-Schioppa, T. (2006), 'The IMF in perspective', in E.M. Truman (ed.), *Reforming the IMF for the 21st Century*, special report **19**, April, Washington, DC: Institute for International Economics.

Padoa-Schioppa, T. and F. Saccomanni (1994), 'Managing a market-led global financial system' in P.B. Kenen (ed.), *Managing the World Economy. Fifty Years After Bretton Woods*, Washington, DC: Institute for International Economics, pp. 235–68.

Padoa-Schioppa, T. and F. Saccomanni (1996), 'What role for the SDR in a market-led international monetary system?', in M. Mussa, J.M. Boughton and P. Isard (eds), *The Future of the SDR in Light of Changes in the International Financial System*, Washington, DC: International Monetary Fund, pp. 378–86.

Persaud, A. (2003), *Liquidity Black Holes: Understanding, Quantifying and Managing Financial Liquidity Risk*, London: Risk Books.

Persaud, A. (2004), 'Why risk managers can be dangerous', speech at a debate at the London School of Economics, 14 October 2004, accessed at London, www.gam.com.

Phillips, M. and G.T. Sims (2000), 'US insists dollar policy remains unchanged', *Wall Street Journal Europe*, 25 September, p. 1.

Prasad, E. (ed.) (2004), *China's Growth and Integration into the World Economy – Prospects and Challenges*, International Monetary Fund occasional paper 232, Washington, DC: IMF.

Putnam, R.D. and N. Bayne (1984), *Hanging Together. The Seven-Power Summits*, Cambridge, MA: Harvard University Press.

Rodrik, D. (1997), *Has Globalization Gone Too Far?*, Washington, DC: Institute for International Economics.

Rogoff, K.S. (1999), 'International institutions for reducing global financial instability', *Journal of Economic Perspectives*, **13** (4) (Spring), 21–42.

Rogoff, K.S., A.M. Husain, A. Mody, R. Blooks and N. Oomes (2004), 'Evolution and performance of exchange rate regimes', International Monetary Fund occasional paper 229, Washington, DC: IMF.

Rose, A.K. (2000), 'One money, one market: the effect of common currencies on trade', *Economic Policy – A European Forum*, **30** (April), 7–45.

Rubin, R.E. and J. Weisberg (2003), *In an Uncertain World*, New York: Thomson/Texere.

Saccomanni, F. (1988), 'On multilateral surveillance', in P. Guerrieri and P.C. Padoan (eds), *The Political Economy of International Co-operation*, London: Croom Helm, pp. 58–86.

Saccomanni, F. (2000), 'A new architecture or new system? A survey of international monetary reform in the 1990s', in P. Savona (ed.), *The New Architecture of the International Monetary System*, Boston, MA: Kluwer Academic Publishers, pp. 15–41.

Saccomanni, F. (2005), 'Managing monetary and financial instability in an international context', paper presented at ECB Colloquium in honour of Tommaso Padoa-Schioppa, Frankfurt, 27 April.

Sarno, L. and M.P. Taylor (2001a), 'Official intervention in the foreign exchange market: is it effective and, if so, how does it work?', *Journal of Economic Literature*, **39**, 839–68.

Sarno, L. and M.P. Taylor (2001b), 'The microstructure of the foreign-exchange market: a selective survey of the literature', *Princeton Studies in International Economics*, **89** (May), Princeton, NJ: Department of Economics, Princeton University Press.

Sarno, L. and M.P. Taylor (2002), *The Economics of Exchange Rates*, Cambridge: Cambridge University Press.

Shanmugaratnam, T. (2006), 'Asian monetary integration: will it ever happen?', Per Jacobsson Lecture, September, Singapore.

Shiller, R.J. (2005), *Irrational Exuberance*, Princeton, NJ: Princeton University Press.

Shiratsuka, S. (2005), 'The asset price bubble in Japan in the 1980s: lessons for financial and macroeconomic stability', *BIS Papers*, **21** (April), Basle: Bank for International Settlements.

Sims, G.T. (2004), 'ECB to end "code word" clues to its rate moves', *Wall Street Journal Europe*, 15 July, p. 1.

Solomon, R. (1982), *The International Monetary System, 1945–1981*, New York: Harper & Row.

Solomon, R. (1999), *Money on the Move. The Revolution in International Finance since 1980*, Princeton, NJ: Princeton University Press.

Solomon, S. (1995), *The Confidence Game. How Unelected Central Bankers are Governing the Changed Global Economy*, New York: Simon & Schuster.

Steil, B. and R.E. Litan (2006), *Financial Statecraft. The Role of Financial Markets in American Foreign Policy*, New Haven, CT and London: Yale University Press.

Stiglitz, J.E. (1994), 'The role of the state in financial markets', in M. Bruno and B. Pleskovic (eds), *Proceedings of the World Bank Annual Conference on Development Economics 1993*, special issue to *The World Bank Economic Review and The World Bank Research Observer*, Washington, DC: The World Bank, pp. 19–52.

Stiglitz, J.E. (2002), *Globalization and its Discontents*, London: Allen Lane/Penguin Press.

Stiglitz, J.E. (2003), *The Roaring Nineties. Seeds of Destruction*, London: Allen Lane/Penguin Press.

Stiglitz, J. (2005), 'America has little to teach China about a steady economy', *Financial Times*, 27 July, p. 17.

Stiglitz, J.E. (2006), *Making Globalization Work*, London: Allen Lane/Penguin Press.

Strange, S. (1986), *Casino Capitalism*, reprinted in 1997 by Oxford: Blackwell, Manchester: Manchester University Press.

Strange, S. (1998), *Mad Money. When Markets Outgrow Governments*, Michigan: University of Michigan Press.

Summers, L.H. (2000), 'International financial crises: causes, prevention, and cures', *American Economic Review – Papers and Proceedings*, **90** (2) (May), 1–16.

Summers, L.H. (2006), 'A lack of fear is cause for concern', *Financial Times*, 27 December, p. 13.

Taylor, J.B. (2007), *Global Financial Warriors*, New York: W.W. Norton.

Taylor, M.P. (1995), 'The economics of exchange rates', *Journal of Economic Literature*, **33** (1) (March), 13–47.

Tirole, J. (2002), *Financial Crises, Liquidity, and the International Monetary System*, Princeton, NJ and Oxford: Princeton University Press.

Tivegna, M. and G. Chiofi (2004), *News and Exchange Rate Dynamics News*, Aldershot: Ashgate.

Tobin, J. (1978), 'A proposal for international monetary reform', *Eastern Economic Journal*, **4** (July/October), 153–9.

Tobin, J. (1998), 'Financial globalization: can national currencies survive?', in *Annual Bank Conference on Development Economics*, 20-21 April, Washington, DC: World Bank.

Tolstoy, L. ([1864] 1982) *War and Peace*, translated by Rosemary Edmunds, London: Penguin.

Trichet, J.C. (2005), 'Asset price bubbles and monetary policy', speech at the Mas Lecture, 8 June, Singapore, published in *BIS Review*, **44**, 15 June.

Trichet, J.C. (2007), 'Some reflections on the development of credit derivatives', speech to the 22nd Annual General Meeting of the International Swaps and Derivatives Association, 18 April, Boston, MA.

Truman E. (2006), 'Overview on the IMF reform', in E.M. Truman (ed.), *Reforming the IMF for the 21st Century*, special report **19**, April, Washington, DC: Institute for International Economics, pp. 31–126.

Tsang, D. (1998), 'Speech at the Hong Kong Trade Development Council', Hong Kong Trade Development Council, 29 September, Frankfurt.

US Administration (2006), *Economic Report of the President*, transmitted to the Congress in February, Washington, DC: US Government Printing Office.

US Treasury (2005), *Report to Congress on International Economic and Exchange Rate Policies*, May, Washington, DC: Treasury Department.

US Treasury (2006), *Report to Congress on International Economic and Exchange Rate Policies*, May, Washington, DC: Treasury Department.

Van Duyn, A. and P. Munter (2004), 'How Citigroup shook Europe's bond markets with two minutes of trading', *Financial Times*, 10 September, p. 17.

Visco, I. (2001), 'Globalization', memorandum submitted to the Select Committee on Economic Affairs, House of Lords, 29 November, London.

Vitale, P. (2006), 'A Market microstructure analysis of foreign exchange intervention', European Central Bank working paper series 629, May, Frankfurt.

Volcker, P. (1995), 'The quest for exchange rate stability: realistic or quixotic?', presented in The Stamp 50th Anniversary Lecture, The Senate House, University of London, 29 November, London.

Volcker, P. and T. Gyohten (1992), *Changing Fortunes. The World's Money and the Threat to American Leadership*, New York: Times Books.

Wang, T. (2004), 'Exchange rate dynamics', in E. Prasad (ed.), *China's Growth and Integration into the World Economy – Prospects and Challenges*, IMF Occasional Paper 232, Washington, DC: International Monetary Fund, pp. 21–28.

White, W.R. (2006), 'Is price stability enough?', Bank for International Settlements working papers 205, April, Basle.

Wilhelmsen, B.R. and A. Zaghini (2005), 'Monetary policy predictability in the euro area: an international comparison', European Central Bank working paper series 504, July, Frankfurt.

Willett, T.D. (2000), 'International financial markets as sources of crises or discipline: the too much, too late hypothesis', *Essays in International Finance*, **218**, May, Princeton, NJ: Department of Economics, Princeton University Press.

Williamson, J. (1983), *The Exchange Rate System*, Washington, DC: Institute for International Economics.

Williamson, J. (1990), 'What Washington means by policy reform', in J. Williamson (ed.), *Latin American Adjustment: How Much Has Happened?*, Washington, DC: Institute for International Economics, pp. 7–20.

Williamson, J. (ed.) (1994), *Estimating Equilibrium Exchange Rates*, Washington, DC: Institute for International Economics.

Williamson, J. (2000), *Exchange Rate Regimes for Emerging Markets: Reviving the Intermediate Option*, Washington, DC: Institute for International Economics.

Williamson, J. (2005), *Curbing the Boom–Bust Cycle: Stabilizing Capital Flows to Emerging Markets*, Washington, DC: Institute for International Economics.

Williamson, J. and M. Mahar (1998), 'A survey of financial liberalization', *Essays in International Finance*, **211**, November, Princeton, NJ: Department of Economics, Princeton University Press.

Wolf, M. (2004), *Why Globalization Works. The Case of the Global Market Economy*, New Haven, CT and London: Yale University Press.

Woodall, P. (1999), 'The navigators', *The Economist*, special report, Survey of the World Economy, 25 September.

Woodford, M. (2000), 'Monetary policy in a world without money', *International Finance*, **3** (2), July, 229–60.

Woodward, B. (2000), *Maestro. Greenspan's Fed and the American Boom*, New York: Simon & Schuster.

World Bank (2001a), *Global Development Finance. Building Coalitions for Effective Development Finance*, Washington, DC: World Bank.

World Bank (2001b), *Finance for Growth. Policy Choices in a Volatile World*, Washington, DC: World Bank.

World Bank (2006), *Financial Structure and Economic Development Database*, accessed at www.worldbank.org.

Yam, J. (1999), 'Causes and solutions to the recent financial turmoil in the Asian region', speech at a Symposium in Commemoration of 50 Years of Central Banking in the Philippines, 5 January, Manila: Bangko Sentral ng Pilipinas.

Zilioli, C. (2003), 'Accountability and independence: irreconcilable values or complementary instruments for democracy? The specific case of the European Central Bank', in G. Vandersanden (ed.), *Mélanges en Hommage à Jean-Victor Louis*, Brussels: Université Libre de Bruxelles, pp. 395–422.

Zhou, X. (2006), 'Remarks on China's trade balance and exchange rate', speech presented at the China Development Forum, 20 March, reprinted in *BIS Review*, **54** (19) (June), accessed at www.bis.org.

Index